Anatomy & Physiology II
BIO 212 Laboratory Manual
Owens Community College | First Edition

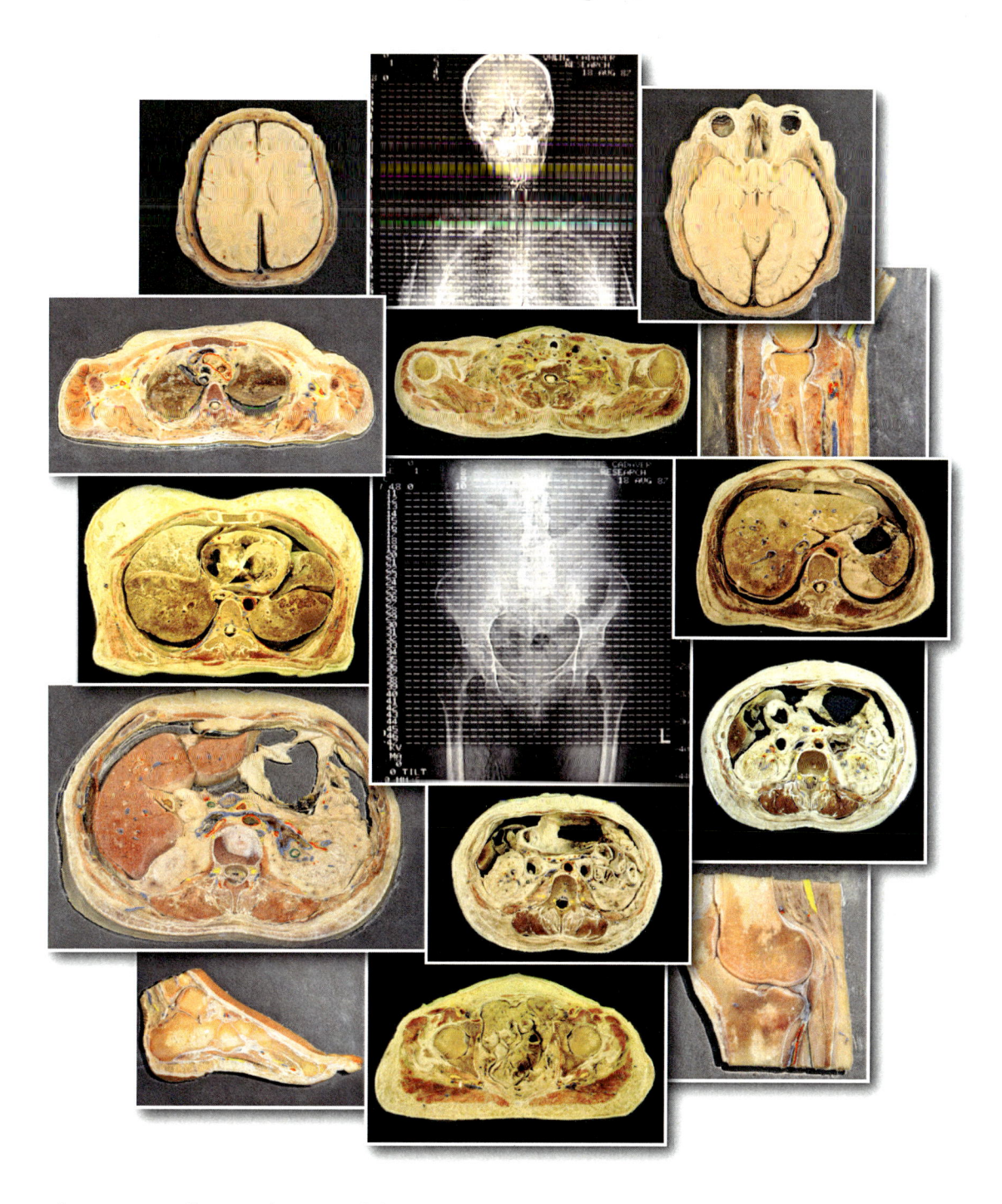

Thomas A. Mika • Robert J. Klein • Anne E. Bullerjahn
Robert L. Connour • Lesa M. Swimmer • Ruby E. White
Matthew W. Gosses • Tara E. Carter • April M. Andrews • Julie L. Maier

VAN-GRINER

Anatomy and Physiology II Laboratory Manual

BIO 212
Owens Community College
Thomas A. Mika, Robert J. Klein, Anne E. Bullerjahn, Robert L. Connour, Lesa M. Swimmer,
Ruby E. White, Matthew W. Gosses, Tara E. Carter, April M. Andrews, Julie L. Maier
First Edition

Copyright © by Biology Department, Owens Community College
Copyright © by Van-Griner, LLC

Photos and other illustrations are owned by Van-Griner, used under license, or licensed from authors.
All products used herein are for identification purposes only, and may be trademarks or registered trademarks of their respective owners.

All rights reserved. No part of this book may be reproduced or transmitted in any form or by any means, electronic or mechanical, including photocopying, recording or by any information storage and retrieval system, without written permission from the author and publisher.

The information and material contained in this manual are provided "as is," and without warranty of any kind, expressed or implied, including without limitation any warranty concerning accuracy, adequacy, or completeness of such information. Neither the authors, the publisher nor any copyright holder shall be responsible for any claims, attributable errors, omissions, or other inaccuracies contained in this manual. Nor shall they be liable for damages of any type, including but not limited to, direct, indirect, special, incidental, or consequential damages arising out of or relating to the use of such material or information.

These experiments are designed to be used in college or university level laboratory courses, and should not be conducted unless there is an appropriate level of supervision, safety training, personal protective equipment and other safety facilities available for users. The publisher and authors believe that the lab experiments described in this manual, when conducted in conformity with the safety precautions described herein and according to appropriate laboratory safety procedures, are reasonably safe for students for whom this manual is directed. Nonetheless, many of the experiments are accompanied by some degree of risk, including human error, the failure or misuse of laboratory or electrical equipment, mis-measurement, spills of chemicals, and exposure to sharp objects, heat, blood, body fluids or other liquids. The publisher and authors disclaim any liability arising from such risks in connection with any of the experiments in the manual. Any users of this manual assume responsibility and risk associated with conducting any of the experiments set forth herein. If students have questions or problems with materials, procedures, or instructions on any experiment, they should always ask their instructor for immediate help before proceeding.

Printed in the United States of America
10 9 8 7 6 5 4 3 2 1
ISBN: 978-1-61740-488-7

Van-Griner Publishing
Cincinnati, Ohio
www.van-griner.com

CEO: Mike Griner
President: Dreis Van Landuyt
Project Manager: Maria Walterbusch
Customer Care Lead: Julie Reichert

Gosses 212 488-7 F17
188766
Copyright © 2019

VAN-GRINER

TABLE OF CONTENTS

Rules for Safety in the Laboratory v

Part 1 **Muscles** 1
Muscle List and Descriptions 2
Human Musculature 20
Cat Musculature 34

Part 2 **Organs and Circulatory System** 49
Organs and Vessels List 50
Human Circulatory System Pathways 55
Cat Circulatory System Vessels 85

Part 3 **Nervous System** 91
Central Nervous System—The Brain 92
Central Nervous System—The Spinal Cord 105
Peripheral Nervous System—Autonomic Nervous System 107
Cat Nervous System Guide 111

Part 4 **Special Senses** 113
Ear 113
Eye 116
Integumentary System 120
Sensory Tests 122

Part 5 **Reproductive Division** 137
Mitosis and Meiosis 137
Male Reproductive System 142
Female Reproductive System 146
Embryology Development 152

Part 6 **Genetics** 165
Genetics Terminology 165
Genetics Problems 167
Human Karyotyping 175

RULES FOR SAFETY IN THE LABORATORY

1. No food or drinks are permitted in the laboratories. No smoking.

2. Learn the exact locations of fire extinguishers, fire alarms, fire blankets, first-aid kits, eye wash stations, chemical showers, fume hoods, and other safety features in the laboratory, as well as how to use this equipment.

3. No unauthorized persons shall be admitted to the laboratories.

4. Handle all chemicals carefully, keeping them away from face, skin, and clothing.

5. Read labels. Use chemicals only from clearly labeled containers. If not labeled, do not use.

6. Always replace caps, covers, and stoppers on chemical containers.

7. Mix chemicals according to instructions only.

8. Safety glasses should be worn when working with hazardous chemicals. It may be necessary to work under the fume hood with the glass door below eye level.

9. Do not take any chemicals or supplies from the laboratories unless you have permission from the instructor.

10. When heating chemicals in a test tube, keep the open end of the tube pointed away from yourself and others.

11. If a mercury thermometer breaks, immediately contact the instructor to assist in cleaning up the mercury in the correct manner. Avoid skin contact with mercury.

12. Wipe up spills with damp paper towels.

13. Throw waste materials into the proper containers. Broken glassware should be placed in the glass disposal box. Any materials with microorganism contamination should be placed into the proper autoclave bag.

14. Wash your hands at the end of each laboratory session.

15. Your work area should be clean. Equipment should be returned to its proper place at the end of the laboratory session.

16. Report any accidents, spills, or breakage immediately to the instructor.

PART 1
MUSCLES

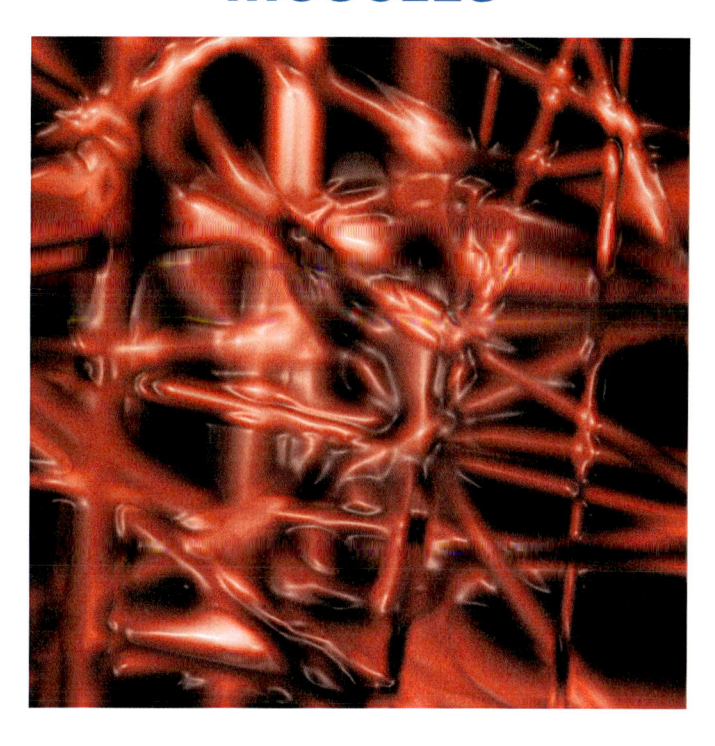

MUSCLE LIST AND DESCRIPTIONS

Table 1. Human Muscles and Cat Muscle Equivalents.

Human	Cat Equivalent
Pectoralis major	Same
Pectoralis minor	Same
Trapezius	General trapezius
Deltoid	General deltoid
Linea alba	Same
External oblique	Same
Internal oblique	Same
Rectus abdominis	Same
Transversus abdominis	Omit from cat
Latissimus dorsi	Same
Lumbodorsal fascia	Same
Triceps brachii (all three heads)	Same
Gracilis	Same
Sartorius	Same
Tensor fascia latae	Same
Gluteus maximus	Same
Gluteus medius	Same
Gluteus minimus	Omit from cat
Tibialis anterior	Same
Gastrocnemius	Same
Soleus	Same
Sacrospinalis/Erector spinae	Same
Temporalis	Same
Masseter	Same
Digastric	Same

Table 1. Human Muscles and Cat Muscle Equivalents (continued).

Human	Cat Equivalent
Sternohyoid	Same
Sternocleidomastoid	Omit from cat
Levator scapulae	Levator scapulae ventralis
Rhomboideus major	Rhomboideus
Rhomboideus minor	Rhomboideus
Splenius capitis	Splenius
Supraspinatus	Same
Infraspinatus	Same
Biceps brachii	Same
Brachialis	Same
Pectineus	Same
Adductor longus	Same
Adductor magnus	Adductor femoris
Adductor brevis	Adductor femoris
Vastus medialis*	Same
Vastus intermedius*	Omit from cat
Vastus lateralis*	Same
Rectus femoris*	Same
Biceps femoris**	Same
Semimembranosus**	Same
Semitendinosus**	Same

* QUADRICEPS FEMORIS GROUP
- Rectus femoris
- Vastus medialis
- Vastus intermedius
- Vastus lateralis

**HAMSTRING MUSCLE GROUP
- Biceps femoris
- Semimembranosus
- Semitendinosus

MUSCLE INSERTIONS, ORIGINS, AND ACTIONS

VENTRAL THORAX

PECTORALIS MAJOR

A superficial, broad, triangular-shaped muscle extending from the midline (at the *linea alba*) to the humerus at the upper thoracic area. The muscle lies in two parts. The cranial portion is overlapped by the *pectoantebrachialis*. The larger caudal portion continues to the superior margin of the *pectoralis minor*. Muscle fibers of the *pectoralis major* run at right angles to the longitudinal midline of the body.

- **Origin:** sternum, clavicle, ribs (2nd to 6th)
- **Insertion:** humerus
- **Action:** adducts, rotates, flexes arm medially

PECTORALIS MINOR

A superficial, very broad, triangular-shaped muscle extending posteriorly from the midline (at the *linea alba*) to the humerus at the mid-thoracic area. The *pectoralis minor* is covered by the *pectoralis major*. The muscle fibers of the *pectoralis minor* run obliquely to the midline of the body. The direction of these fibers helps to differentiate the *pectoralis minor* from the *pectoralis major*. The *pectoralis minor* is also larger and thicker than the *pectoralis major*.

- **Origin:** ribs (3rd to 5th)
- **Insertion:** coracoid process of scapula
- **Action:** protracts and depresses scapula

DORSAL SHOULDER

TRAPEZIUS

A large, diamond shape muscle that extends from the head through the thoracic vertebrae.

- **Origins:** external occiptial protuberance, spinous process of thoracic vertebrae
- **Insertions:** lateral clavicle, spine, and acromion process of scapula
- **Action:** elevates, rotates, retracts, and depresses the scapula; extends the head

GENERAL TRAPEZIUS (CAT)

Clavotrapezius

A large muscle on the cat (part of the *trapezius* on the human) anterior to the *acromiotrapezius* extending from the neck to the shoulder.

- **Origin (in cat):** occipital bone at lambdoidal suture
- **Insertion (in cat):** clavicle
- **Action (in cat):** adducts, rotates scapula superiorly

Acromiotrapezius

A thin, flat muscle on the cat (part of the *trapezius* on the human) extending from mid-back to shoulder.

- **Origin (in cat):** spinous processes of cervical vertebrae
- **Insertion (in cat):** spine of scapula
- **Action (in cat):** adducts, rotates scapula superiorly

Spinotrapezius

This triangular-shaped muscle on the cat (part of the *trapezius* on the human) is located posterior to the *acromiotrapezius* down from the mid-back.

- **Origin (in cat):** spinous processes of thoracic vertebrae
- **Insertion (in cat):** fascia at the scapula
- **Action (in cat):** adducts, rotates scapula superiorly

DELTOID

A triangular shaped muscle that is located on the rounded portion of the shoulder.

- **Origin:** acromion and spine of scapula
- **Insertion:** deltoid tuberosity of humerus
- **Action:** abducts, flexes, and extends arm

GENERAL *DELTOID* (CAT)

Clavodeltoid (or Clavobrachialis)

This triangular muscle on the cat (part of the *deltoid* on the human) is a continuation of the *clavotrapezius* onto the shoulder and arm.

- **Origin (in cat):** clavicle
- **Insertion (in cat):** ulna
- **Action (in cat):** flexes, extends forearm

Acromiodeltoid

This short muscle on the cat (part of the *deltoid* on the human) extends from the *levator scapulae ventralis* to the *clavobrachialis*.

- **Origin (in cat):** acromion process of scapula
- **Insertion (in cat):** lateral surface of *spinodeltoid* muscle
- **Action (in cat):** flexes and rotates upper arm

Spinodeltoid

This short muscle on the cat (part of the *deltoid* on the human) lies ventral to the *acromiotrapezius* and posterior to the *acromiodeltoid*.

- **Origin (in cat):** spinous process of scapula
- **Insertion (in cat):** deltoid tuberosity of the humerus
- **Action (in cat):** flexes and rotates upper arm

VENTRAL ABDOMEN

LINEA ALBA

The aponeuroses of the abdominal muscles meet at the midline of the abdomen forms this "white line;" a thin, tough and fibrous band which extends from the xiphoid process to the pubis symphysis. The aponeuroses of the abdominal muscles reflect, right and left, at the *linea alba*.

EXTERNAL ABDOMINAL OBLIQUE

Arising from aponeurosis at the *linea alba*, this wide, thin superficial muscle extends laterally over the entire abdomen and ventral thorax.

- **Origin:** ribs (8th to 12th)
- **Insertion:** crest of ilium and aponeurosis at *linea alba*
- **Action:** contraction and compression of abdomen, rotates vertebral column laterally.

INTERNAL ABDOMINAL OBLIQUE

Arising from aponeurosis at the *linea alba,* this wide, thin muscle is located deep to the *external abdominal oblique* and extends laterally over the abdomen.

- **Origin:** crest of ilium
- **Insertion:** ribs (3rd and 4th)
- **Action:** compresses contents of abdomen, rotates and laterally flexes vertebral column

RECTUS ABDOMINIS

A long, flat, wide muscle lying directly lateral to the *linea alba* and medial to the *external* and *internal abdominal oblique* muscles, extending the entire length of the abdominal wall.

- **Origin:** pubis symphysis
- **Insertion:** cartilage at ribs (5th, 6th, 7th), xiphoid process
- **Action:** vertebral column flexion, abdominal compression

TRANSVERSUS ABDOMINIS

This deepest of the abdominal muscles, it lies directly deep to the *internal abdominal oblique*. The fibers of this muscle reflect transversely across the abdomen from the *linea alba*.

- **Origin:** crest of ilium, cartilage of ribs (6th to 12th)
- **Insertion:** aponeurosis at *linea alba*
- **Action:** compression of abdomen

DORSAL BACK

LATISSIMUS DORSI

This large, flat triangular-shaped muscle extends from mid-back to the humerus.

- **Origin:** spinous processes of T-6 to L-5 vertebrae, crests of sacrum and ilium and vertebrae, ribs (10th, 11th, 12th).
- **Insertion:** humerus
- **Action:** extends, adducts, rotates arm medially

LUMBODORSAL FASCIA (IN CAT)

This is a thin fascia sheath extending from the medial edge of the *latissimus dorsi* to the superior edge of the *gluteus maximus* in the lumbar region on the back.

DORSAL ARM

TRICEPS BRACHII

The largest upper arm muscle is located on the posterior upper arm. The muscle consists of three heads; *triceps brachii,* long head; *triceps brachii,* medial head; *triceps brachii,* lateral head.

PART 1: MUSCLES

Triceps brachii—Lateral Head

This muscle head is located superficially on the posterior/lateral surface of the humerus.

- **Origin:** humerus
- **Insertion:** olecranon process of ulna
- **Action:** extends arm

Triceps brachii—Medial Head

This muscle head is located deep against the humerus, between the *triceps brachii,* lateral head and the *triceps brachii,* long head.

- **Origin:** humerus
- **Insertion:** olecranon process of ulna
- **Action:** extends arm

Triceps brachii—Long Head

This muscle head is located superficially on the posterior/medial surface of the humerus.

- **Origin:** scapula
- **Insertion:** olecranon process of ulna
- **Action:** extends arm

VENTRAL THIGH

GRACILIS

This long, narrow muscle lies superficially on the medial side of the thigh between the pelvis and the knee.

- **Origin:** pubis
- **Insertion:** tibia
- **Action:** flexes knee, adducts thigh at hip

SARTORIUS

This long, narrow muscle extends diagonally across the anterior thigh from the pelvis to the medial side of the knee.

- **Origin:** spine of ilium
- **Insertion:** tibia
- **Action:** laterally rotates, flexes, and abducts the thigh. Flexes the leg at the knee.

TENSOR FASCIAE LATAE

This thin, wide fan-shaped muscle and tendon sheath covers the *vastus lateralis* on the lateral surface of the thigh.

- **Origin:** iliac crest
- **Insertion:** tibia
- **Action:** flexes and abducts the thigh at hip, helps lock knee in extension

DORSAL BUTTOCK

GLUTEUS MAXIMUS

This is a large-bodied posterior muscle covering the ischial tuberosity in the buttock region.

- **Origin:** iliac crest, sacrum, coccyx
- **Insertion:** greater trochanter of femur
- **Action:** extends, abducts, and rotates thigh laterally

GLUTEUS MEDIUS

This is a thick, bulky muscle is deep to the *gluteus maximus* in the buttock region.

- **Origin:** crest of ilium
- **Insertion:** greater trochanter of femur
- **Action:** abducts femur, rotates thigh medially

GLUTEUS MINIMUS

This is a small, thin muscle lying deep to the *gluteus medius* in the buttock region.

- **Origin:** ilium
- **Insertion:** greater trochanter of femur
- **Action:** abducts femur, rotates thigh medially

VENTRAL LEG

TIBIALIS ANTERIOR

This elongated muscle is located superficially along the anterior/lateral edge of the tibia.

- **Origin:** lateral condyle of tibia
- **Insertion:** metatarsals
- **Action:** dorsiflexion of foot

DORSAL LEG

GASTROCNEMIUS

This large double-headed muscle is located on the posterior surface of the calf.

- **Origin:** lateral condyle of femur
- **Insertion:** calcaneus
- **Action:** flexes leg, plantar flexion of foot

SOLEUS

This flat, elongated muscle is located on the lateral side of the lower leg, deep to the *gastrocnemius*.

- **Origin:** tibia and fibula
- **Insertion:** calcaneus
- **Action:** plantar flexion of foot

PART 1: MUSCLES

DORSAL BACK

SACROSPINALIS (OR ERECTOR SPINAE)

The largest muscle mass of the back. These muscles are in three groups: *Spinalis dorsi, Longissimus dorsi, Iliocostalis.* They lie in a mid-dorsal line, parallel to the spine in the thoracic region of the back, extending from the sacrum upward along the back and neck to the base of the skull. There are three longitudinal divisions (columns):

- ***Spinalis dorsi* group:** medial column
- ***Longissimus dorsi* group:** intermediate column
- ***Iliocostalis* group:** lateral column

These muscles could be referred to by the collective names, *Sacrospinalis* or *Erector spinae.*

- **Origin of groups:** crests of sacrum and ilium, spinous processes of T-11 and T-12
- **Insertion:** ribs, transverse and spinous processes of vertebrae
- **Action:** extends head and vertebral column, maintains erect posture, and lateral flexion of spine

LATERAL HEAD

TEMPORALIS

This flat muscle lies on top of the skull, medial to the ear and posterior to the eye.

- **Origin:** parietal bone
- **Insertion:** coronoid process and ramus of the mandible
- **Action:** elevates and retracts the mandible, assists in lateral movements of the mandible

MASSETER

This short, thick muscle extends diagonally across the lateral lower jaw from the lateral, inferior edge of the orbit to the angle of the mandible.

- **Origin:** zygomatic arch, maxilla
- **Insertion:** ramus and coronoid process of mandible
- **Action:** closes lower jaw, mastication (chewing)

PART 1: MUSCLES

LATERAL NECK

DIGASTRIC

This double-bellied (anterior-posterior) muscle lies superficial to the *mylohyoid* at the bottom of the jaw in the curve of the mandible.

- **Origin:** mandible and mastoid process of temporal bone
- **Insertion:** hyoid
- **Action:** elevates hyoid, opens jaw

STERNOHYOID

This thin, ribbon-like muscle extends longitudinally from the hyoid to the sternum on the anterior surface of the neck superficial and medial to the thyroid cartilage of larynx.

- **Origin:** manubrium of sternum, medial end of clavicle
- **Insertion:** hyoid
- **Action:** depression of hyoid

STERNOCLEIDOMASTOID

This wide muscle extends from the mastoid process across the neck laterally to the sternum and clavicle. Contracting bilaterally (together), these muscles flex the vertebral column in the cervical area. Contracting unilaterally (singly), the muscle rotates the head and flexes the neck laterally. Two separate muscles, the *sternomastoid* and *cleidomastoid* in the cat.

- **Origin:** sternum and clavicle
- **Insertion:** mastoid process of temporal bone
- **Action:** extends head, flexes cervical vertebrae, and rotates head

DORSAL NECK AND SHOULDER

LEVATOR SCAPULAE (LEVATOR SCAPULAE VENTRALIS IN CAT)

This ribbon-shaped muscle extends at a right angle from the *spinodeltoid,* partially deep to the *clavotrapezius.*

- **Origin:** transverse processes of C-1 to C-4 vertebrae
- **Insertion:** ventral edge of scapula
- **Action:** elevates, rotates scapula

RHOMBOIDEUS (MAJOR AND MINOR IN HUMAN ONLY)

This fan-shaped muscle lies deep to the *acromiotrapeius* and *spinotrapezius* and connects the shoulder to the mid-dorsal back.

- **Origin:** spinous processes of T-2 to T-5 vertebrae (in major) spinous processes of C-7 and T-1 vertebrae (in minor)
- **Insertion:** ventral, medial edge of scapula
- **Action:** adducts, elevates and rotates scapula

SPLENIUS CAPITIS (SPLENIUS IN CAT)

This flat, wide muscle lies deep to the *clavotrapezius* and covers the dorsal side of the neck.

- **Origin:** spinous process of C-7 to T-4 vertebrae
- **Insertion:** mastoid process of temporal bone
- **Action:** extends and rotates head

SUPRASPINATUS

This muscle lies deep to the *acromiotrapezius* and superior to the spine of the scapula.

- **Origin:** supraspinous fossa of the scapula
- **Insertion:** greater tubercle of the humerus
- **Action:** abducts arm

INFRASPINATUS

This muscle lies deep to the *acromiotrapezius* and inferior to the spine of the scapula.

- **Origin:** infraspinous fossa of the scapula
- **Insertion:** greater tubercle of the humerus
- **Action:** rotates upper arm laterally

VENTRAL ARM

BICEPS BRACHII

This elongated muscle is located on the ventral/medial surface of the humerus.

- **Origin:** coracoid process of scapula
- **Insertion:** radial tuberosity
- **Action:** flexes forearm

BRACHIALIS

This muscle is located on the lateral surface of the humerus; anterior to the *triceps brachii lateral head*.

- **Origin:** humerus
- **Insertion:** coranoid process of ulna
- **Action:** flexes forearm

VENTRAL THIGH

PECTINEUS

This small muscle, lying deep to the *sartorius* and superior to the *adductor longus*, extends across the front of the groin diagonally from the pelvis to the proximal end of the femur.

- **Origin:** superior aspect of pubis
- **Insertion:** lesser trochanter of femur
- **Action:** medially rotates, flexes, and adducts thigh

ADDUCTOR LONGUS

This fan-shaped muscle, lying deep to the *sartorius* and inferior to the *pectineus*, extends diagonally from the pelvis to the posterior aspect at the shaft of the femur.

- **Origin:** anterior aspect of pubis
- **Insertion:** posterior aspect of femur
- **Action:** adducts thigh and flexes and medially rotates thigh

ADDUCTOR MAGNUS (ADDUCTOR FEMORIS IN CAT)

This larger fan-shaped muscle, lying deep to the *adductor longus* and inferior to the *adductor brevis*, extends diagonally from the pelvis to the posterior aspect of the shaft of the femur. It combines with the *adductor brevis* to form the *adductor femoris* in the cat.

- **Origin:** pubis and ischial tuberosity
- **Insertion:** posterior aspect of femur
- **Action:** adduction and medial rotation of thigh

ADDUCTOR BREVIS (ADDUCTOR FEMORIS IN CAT)

This fan-shaped muscle, lying deep to the *adductor longus* and superior to the *adductor magnus,* extends diagonally from the pelvis to the posterior aspect at the shaft of the femur. It combines with the *adductor magnus* to form *the adductor femoris* in the cat

- **Origin:** pubis
- **Insertion:** posterior aspect of proximal half of femur
- **Action:** adduct, flexion, and medial rotation of thigh

QUADRICEPS FEMORIS

This large muscle group in the lateral thigh of the leg is the prime mover of knee extension. As the name implies, the muscle has four heads

- *Vastus medialis*
- *Vastus intermedius*
- *Vastus lateralis*
- *Rectus femoris*

All four heads merge to form a single tendon to the patella and extends inferiorly over the patella as the patellar tendon to the tibial tuberosity.

Vastus medialis

This is the medial muscle of the *quadriceps femoris* group. It lies deep in the thigh, extending along the entire medial surface of the femur.

- **Origin:** femur
- **Insertion:** patella, by ligament to tuberosity and medial condyle of tibia
- **Action:** extending leg at knee

Vastus intermedius

This muscle of the *quadriceps femoris* group lies deep in the thigh between the *vastus medialis* and the *vastus lateralis* extending along the proximal half of the anterior surface of the femur.

- **Origin:** anterior surface of femur
- **Insertion:** patella to tuberosity of tibia
- **Action:** extends leg at knee

Vastus lateralis

This is the lateral muscle of the *quadriceps femoris* group. It lies deep in the thigh, extending along the entire lateral surface of the femur.

- **Origin:** greater trochanter of femur
- **Insertion:** patella, by ligament to tuberosity of tibia
- **Action:** extends leg at knee

Rectus femoris

This is the anterior muscle of the *quadriceps femoris* group. It lies deep in the thigh, extending along the entire anterior surface of the femur from the pelvis to the knee.

- **Origin:** ilium
- **Insertion:** patella, by ligament of tuberosity of tibia
- **Action:** flexes hip, extend leg at knee

DORSAL THIGH

HAMSTRING MUSCLES

This large muscle group located at the posterior, lower thigh is responsible (along with the *gluteus maximus*) for flexing the knee and extending the hip during walking and running.

The muscle group consists of three components:

- *Biceps femoris*
- *Semimembranosus*
- *Semitendinosus*

The pit at the rear of the knee is formed by the tendons of these muscles; *biceps femoris* tendon on the lateral side, *semimembranosus* and *semitendinosus* tendon on the medial side.

The muscles extend superiorly to the pelvis at the tuberosity of the ischium.

Biceps femoris

This large, bulky muscle, the medial member of the hamstring group, covers the lateral surface of upper leg (thigh).

- **Origin:** ischium and femur
- **Insertion:** lateral condyle of tibia and head of fibula
- **Action:** extends thigh, flexes the knee

Semimembranosus

This elongated muscle is the anterior, medial member of the hamstring group. It extends from the ischium to the knee on the posterior side of the thigh.

- **Origin:** ischial tuberosity
- **Insertion:** medial condyle of tibia
- **Action:** extends thigh, flexes the knee

Semitendinosus

This elongated muscle is the posterior member of the hamstring group. It extends from the ischium to the knee on the posterior side of the thigh.

- **Origin:** ischial tuberosity
- **Insertion:** proximal, medial surface of tibia
- **Action:** extends thigh, flexes the knee

PART 1: MUSCLES

HUMAN MUSCULATURE

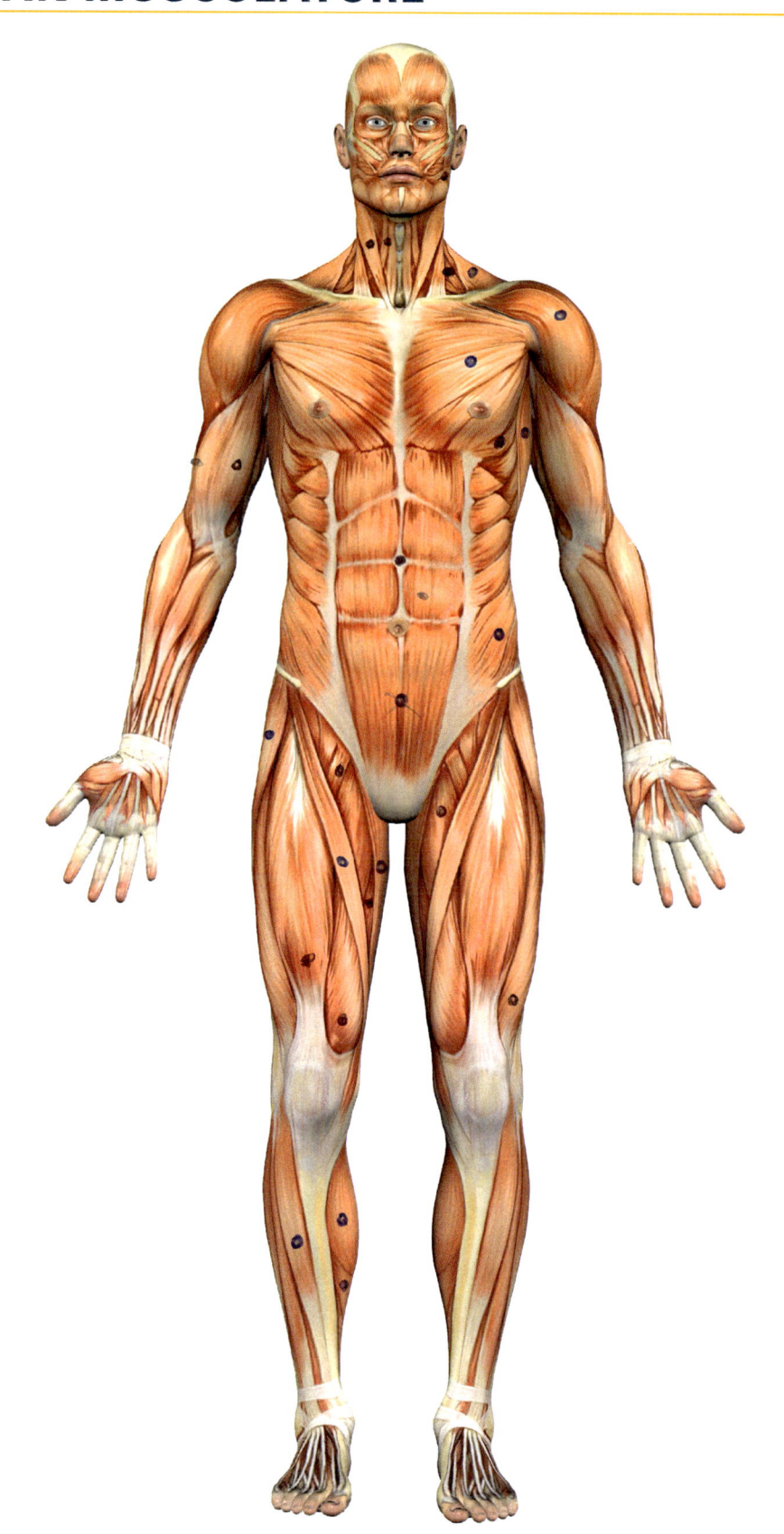

Figure 1. Ventral Aspect.

PART 1: MUSCLES

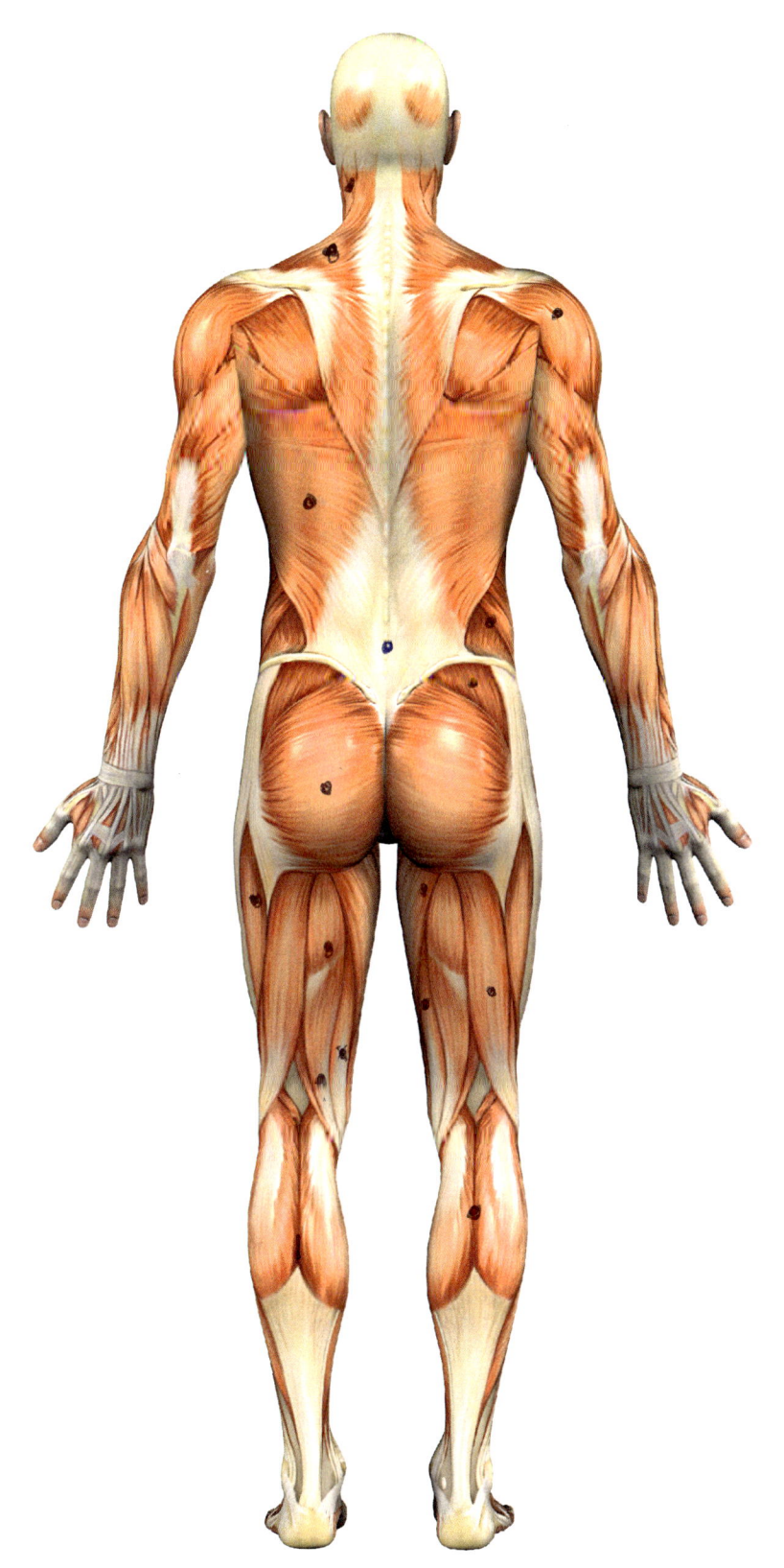

Figure 2. Dorsal Aspect.

21

PART 1: MUSCLES

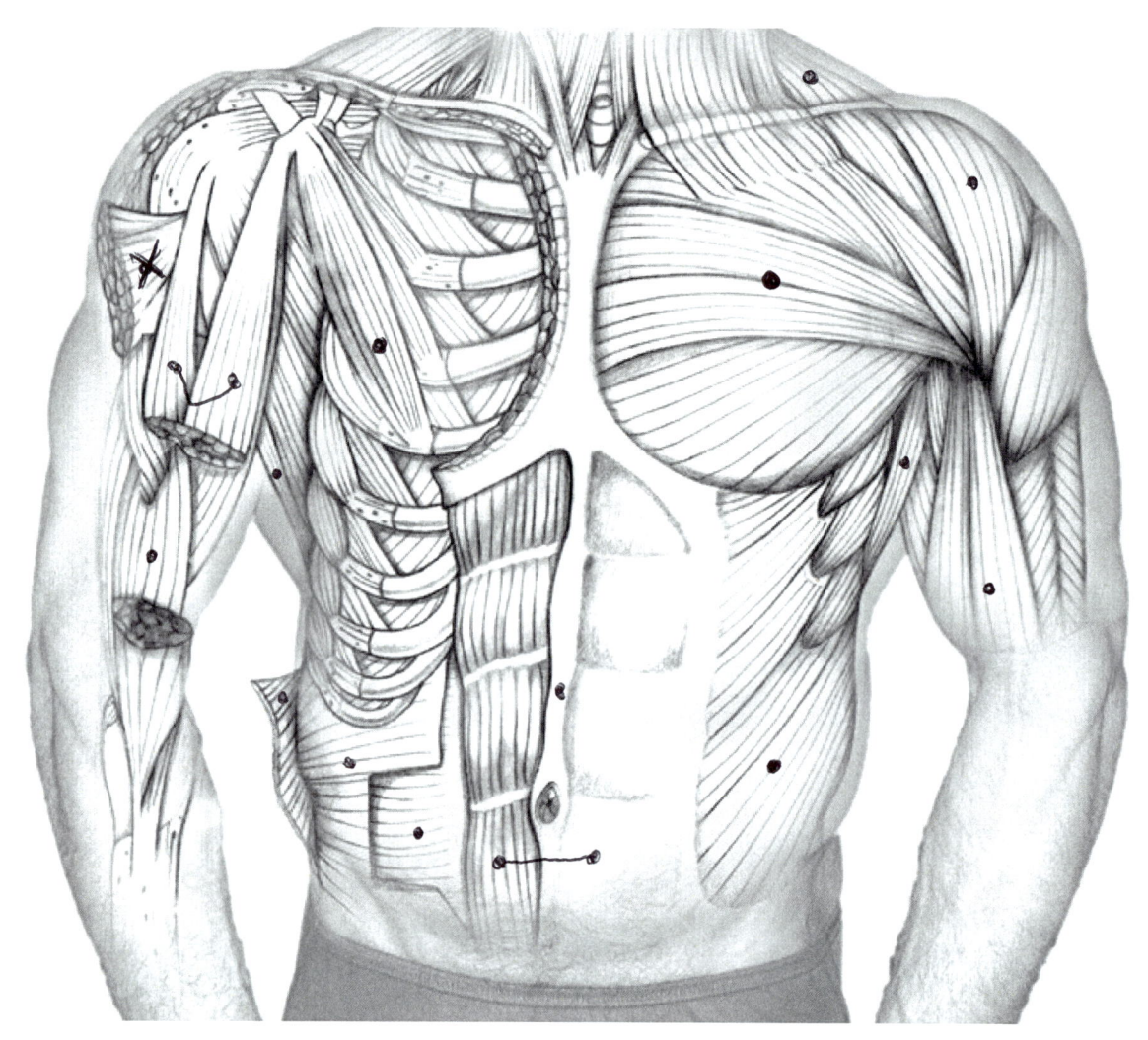

Figure 3. Ventral Thorax and Abdomen.

Locate the following structures:

- Biceps brachii
- Brachialis
- Deltoid
- External oblique
- Internal oblique
- Linea alba
- Pectoralis major
- Pectoralis minor
- Rectus abdominis
- Transversus abdominis

Additional structures:

- Coracobrachialis
- External intercostals
- Internal intercostals
- Platysma
- Serratus anterior
- Subclavius
- Subscapularis
- Teres major

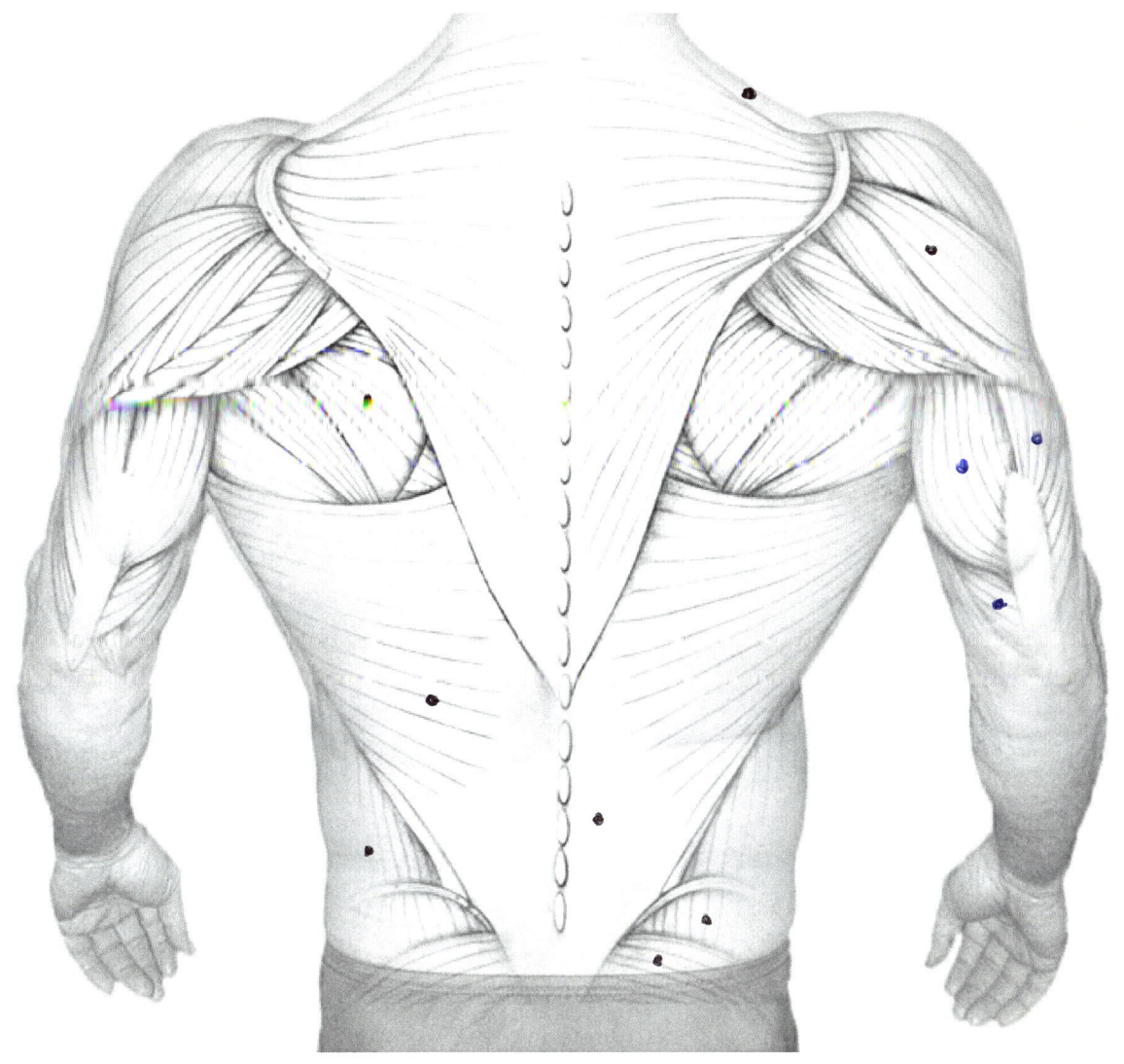

Figure 4. Superficial Dorsal Shoulders, Back, and Arms.

Locate the following structures:

- Deltoid
- External oblique
- Gluteus maximus
- Gluteus medius
- Infraspinatus
- Latissimus dorsi
- Lumbodorsal fascia
- Trapezius
- Triceps brachii (lateral head)
- Triceps brachii (long head)
- Triceps brachii (medial head)

Additional structures:

- Teres major
- Teres minor

PART 1: MUSCLES

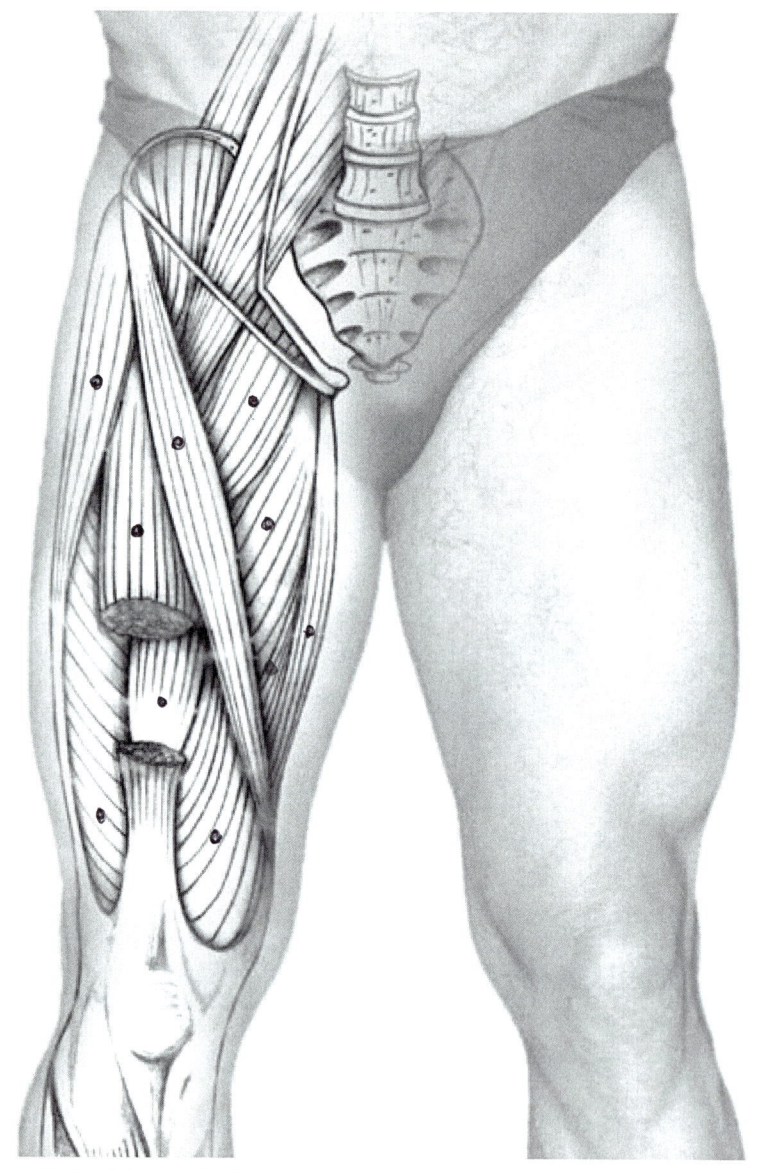

Figure 5. Superficial Ventral Thigh, Right.

Locate the following structures:

- Adductor longus
- Adductor magnus
- Gracilis
- Pectineus
- Rectus femoris (cut)
- Sartorius
- Tensor fasciae latae
- Vastus intermedius
- Vastus lateralis
- Vastus medialis

Additional structures:

- Iliacus
- Psoas major
- Psoas minor
- Quadratus lumborum

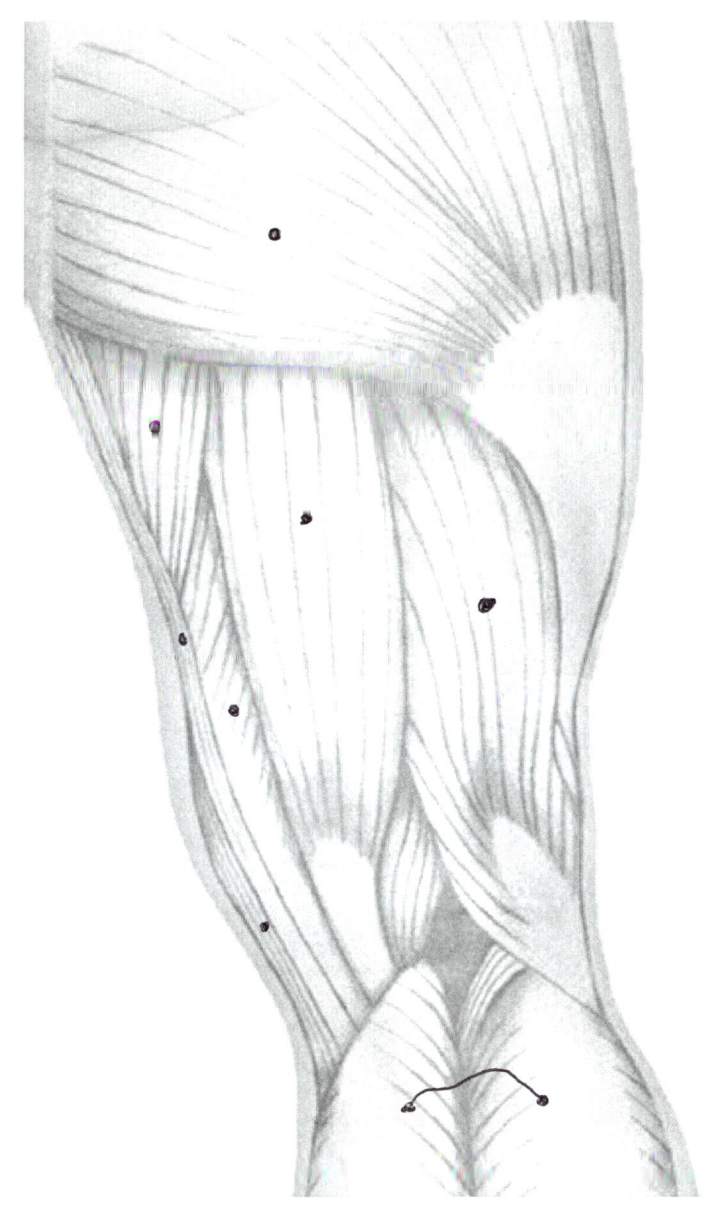

Figure 6. Superficial Dorsal Thigh, Right.

Locate the following structures:

- Adductor magnus
- Biceps femoris
- Gastrocnemius
- Gluteus maximus
- Gracilis
- Sartorius
- Semimembranosus
- Semitendinosus

Additional structures:

- Plantaris

Figure 7. Superficial Ventral Leg, Right.

Locate the following structures:
- Gastrocnemius
- Quadriceps femoris
- Soleus
- Tibialis anterior

Additional structures:
- Flexor digitorum longus
- Tendon of quadriceps femoris

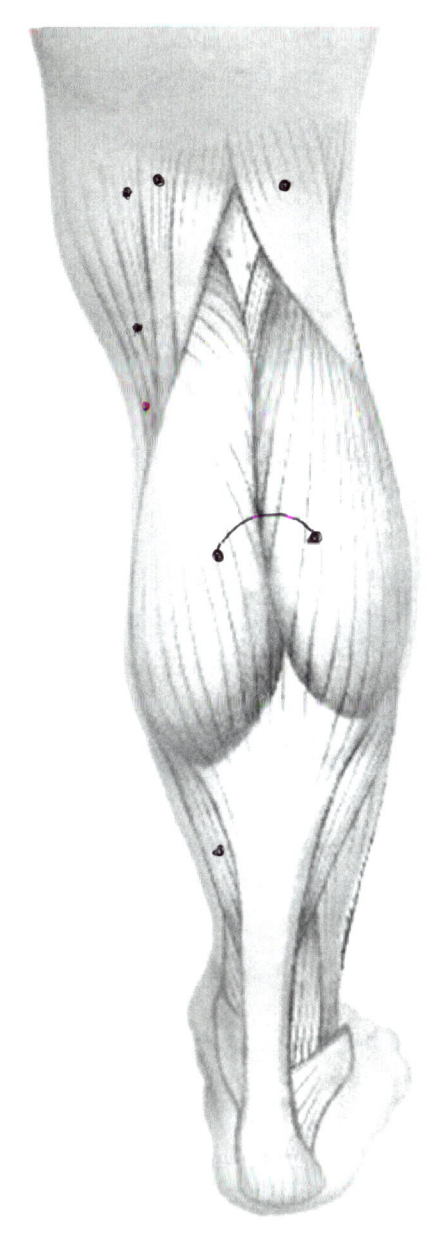

Figure 8. Superficial Dorsal Leg, Right.

Locate the following structures:

- Biceps femoris
- Gastrocnemius
- Gracilis
- Sartorius
- Semimembranosus
- Semitendinosus
- Soleus

Additional structures:

- Flexor digitorum longus
- Flexor hallucis longus
- Peroneus longus
- Plantaris

PART 1: MUSCLES

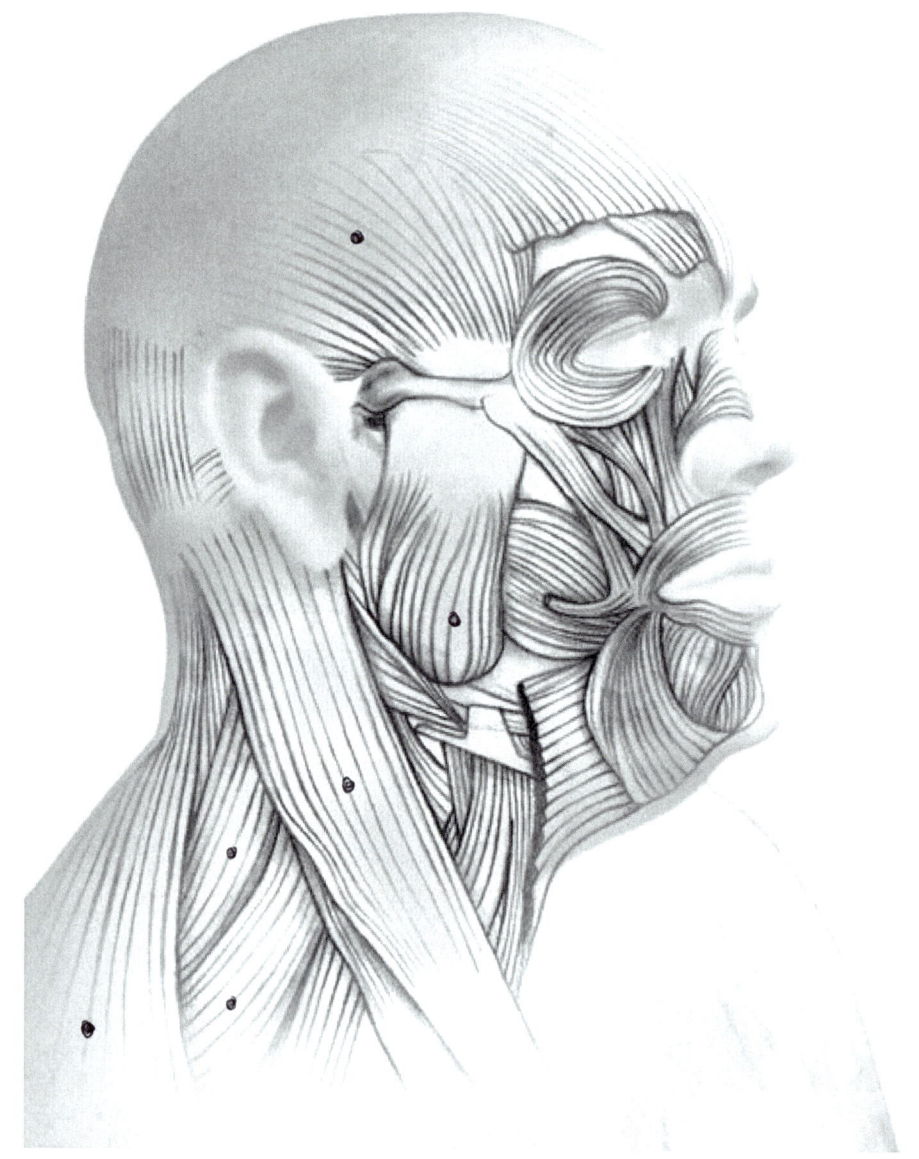

Figure 9. Deep Lateral Head and Neck, Right.

Locate the following structures:

- Levator scapulae
- Masseter
- Splenius capitis
- Sternocleidomastoid
- Temporalis
- Trapezius

Additional structures:

- Buccinator
- Depressor anguli oris
- Depressor labii inferioris
- Frontalis
- Mentalis
- Nasalis
- Occipitalis
- Orbicularis oculi
- Platysma
- Zygomaticus major
- Zygomaticus minor

PART 1: MUSCLES

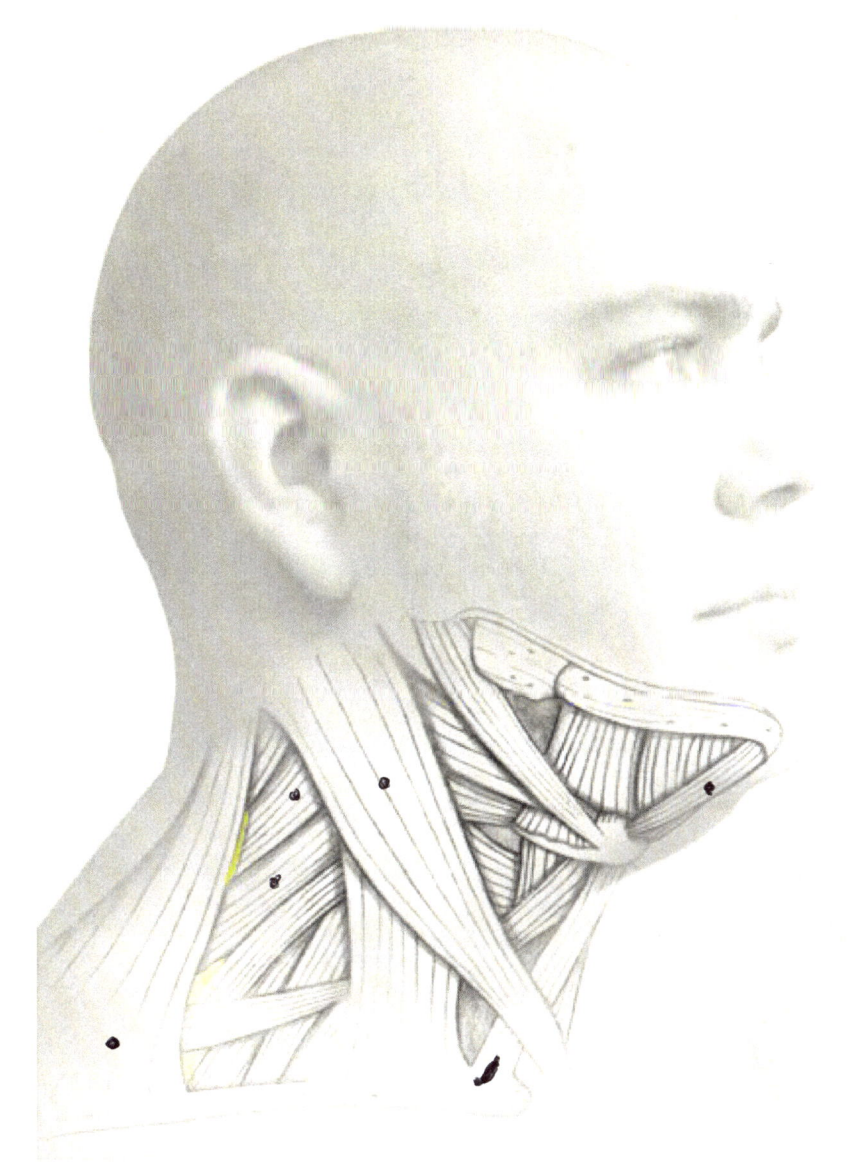

Figure 10. Deep Lateral Neck, Right.

Locate the following structures:

- Digastric (anterior belly)
- Digastric (posterior belly)
- Levator scapulae
- Splenius capitis
- Sternocleidomastoid
- Sternohyoid
- Trapezius

Additional structures:

- Anterior scalene
- Hyoglossus
- Middle scalene
- Mylohyoid
- Omohyoid (inferior belly)
- Omohyoid (superior belly)
- Posterior scalene
- Semispinalis capitis
- Stylohyoid
- Thyrohyoid

29

PART 1: MUSCLES

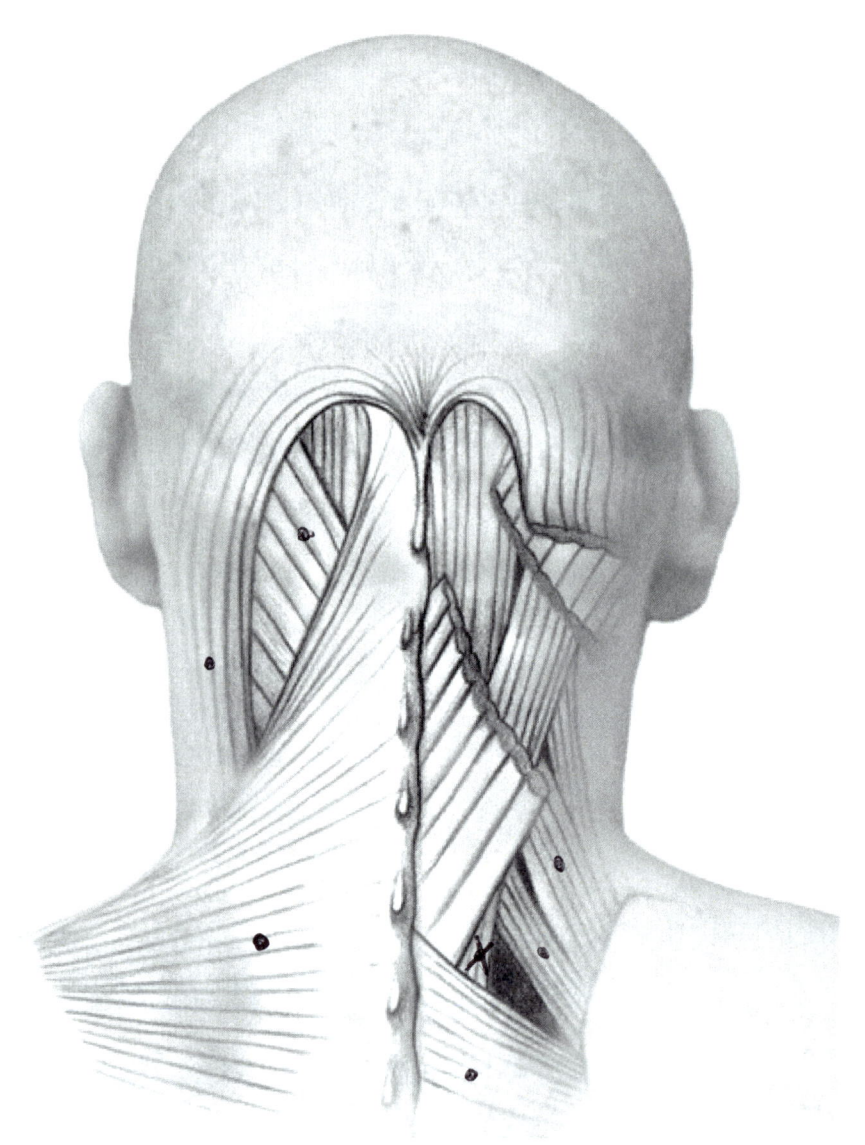

Figure 11. Dorsal Neck and Shoulders.

Locate the following structures:
- Levator scapulae
- Rhomboideus major
- Rhomboideus minor
- Splenius capitis
- Sternocleidomastoid
- Trapezius

Additional structures:
- Longissimus capitis
- Semispinalis capitis
- Splenius cervicis

30

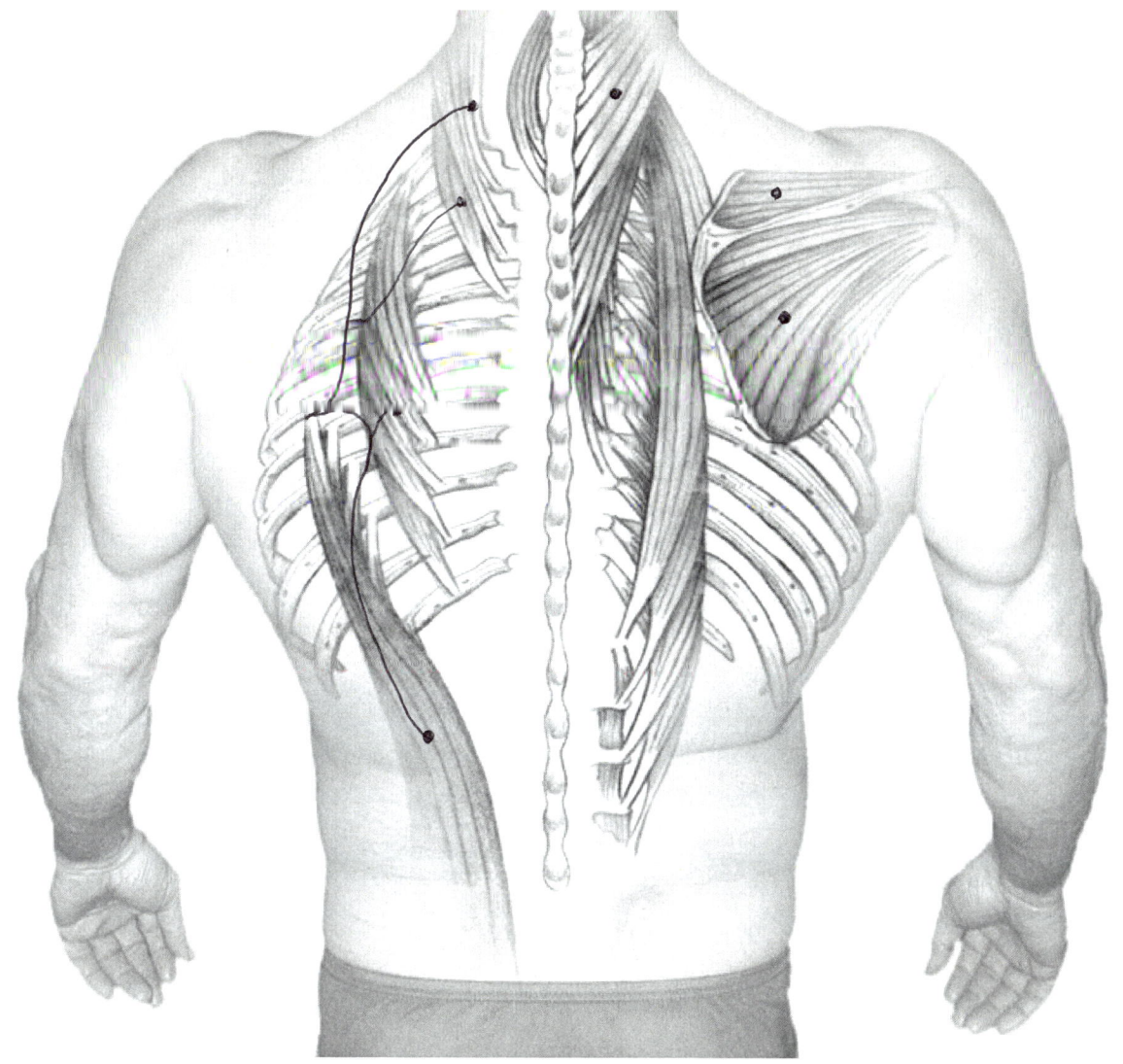

Figure 12. Deep Dorsal Shoulder and Back.

Locate the following structures:

Supraspinatus

Infraspinatus

Sacrospinalis
- Iliocostalis lumborum
- Iliocostalis thoracis
- Longissimus capitis
- Longissimus cervicis
- Longissimus thoracis
- Spinalis cervicis

Additional structures:
- Intertransversarii
- Semispinalis thoracis
- Splenius capitis
- Splenius cervicis

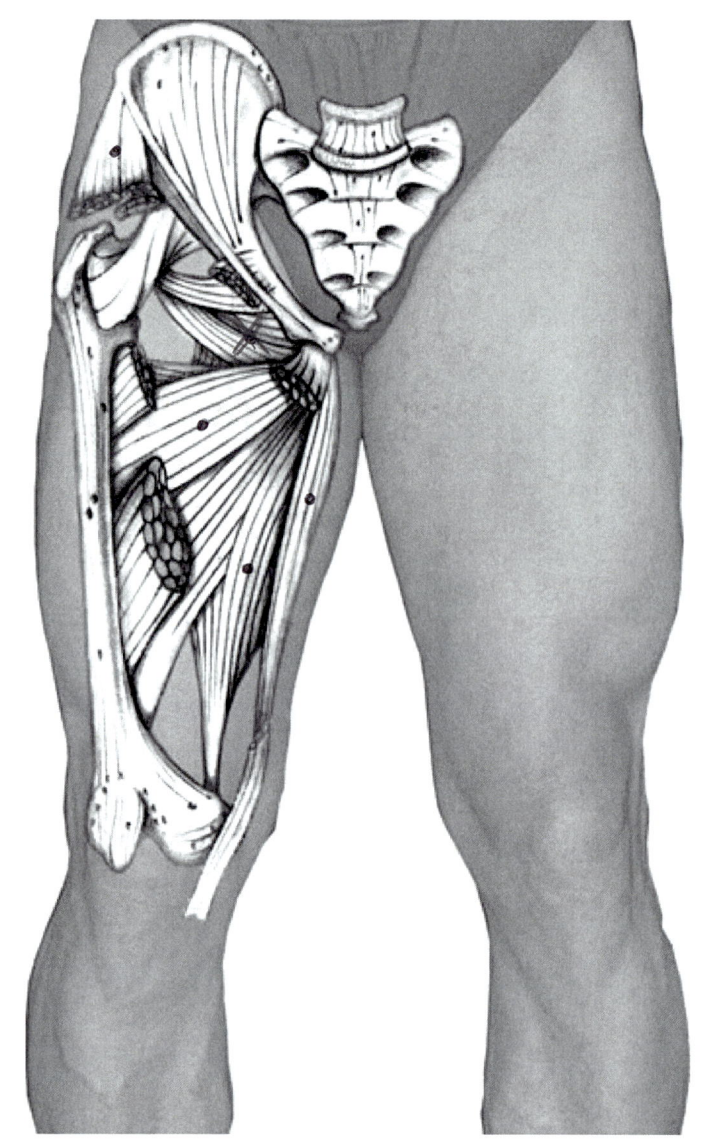

Figure 13. Deep Ventral Thigh, Right.

Locate the following structures:

- Adductor brevis
- Adductor longus
- Adductor magnus
- Gracilis
- Pectineus
- Rectus femoris
- Sartorius
- Tensor fasciae latae

Additional structures:

- Adductor minimus
- Femur
- Hip joint capsule
- Obturator externus
- Patella

PART 1: MUSCLES

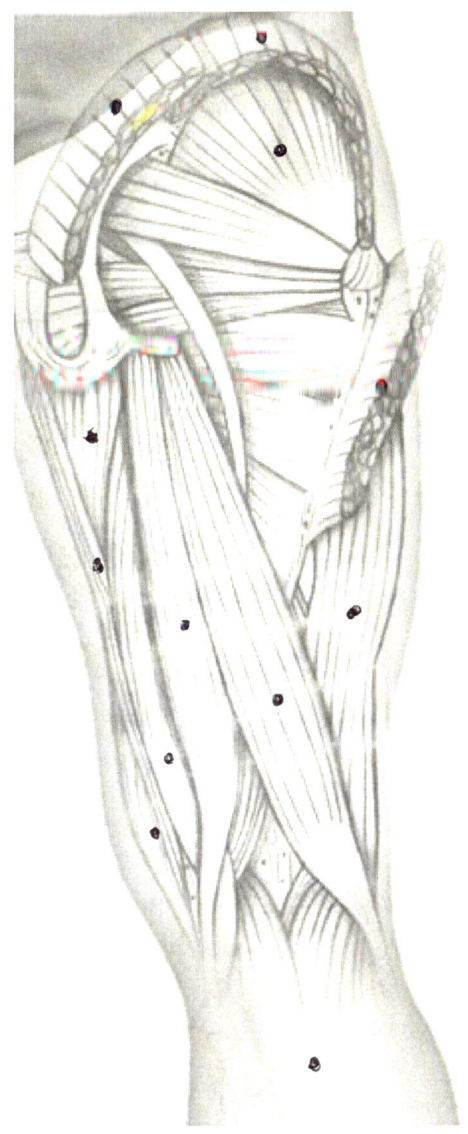

Figure 14. Deep Dorsal Thigh, Right.

Locate the following structures:

- Adductor magnus
- Biceps femoris
- Gastrocnemius
- Gluteus maximus (cut)
- Gluteus medius (cut)
- Gluteus minimus
- Gracilis
- Sartorius
- Semimembranosus
- Semitendinosus
- Vastus lateralis

Additional structures:

- Inferior gemellus
- Obturator internus
- Piriformis
- Plantaris
- Quadriceps femoris
- Superior gemellus

33

PART 1: MUSCLES

CAT MUSCULATURE

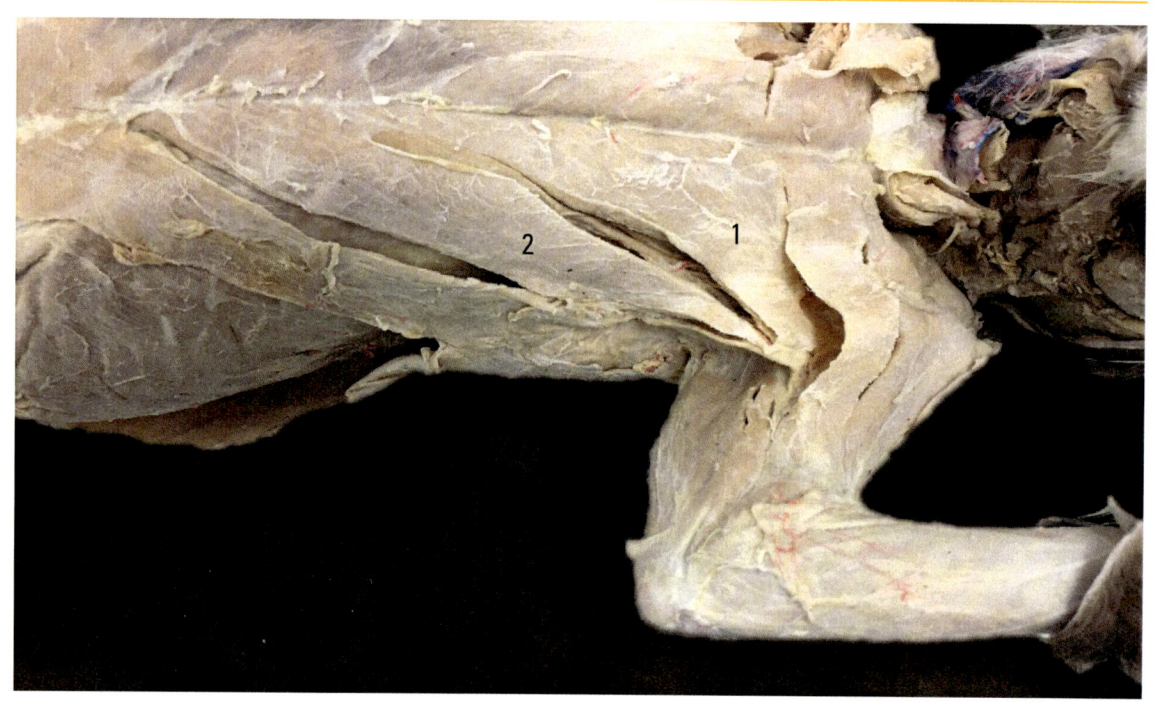

Figure 15. Ventral Thorax.

1. Pectoralis major
2. Pectoralis minor

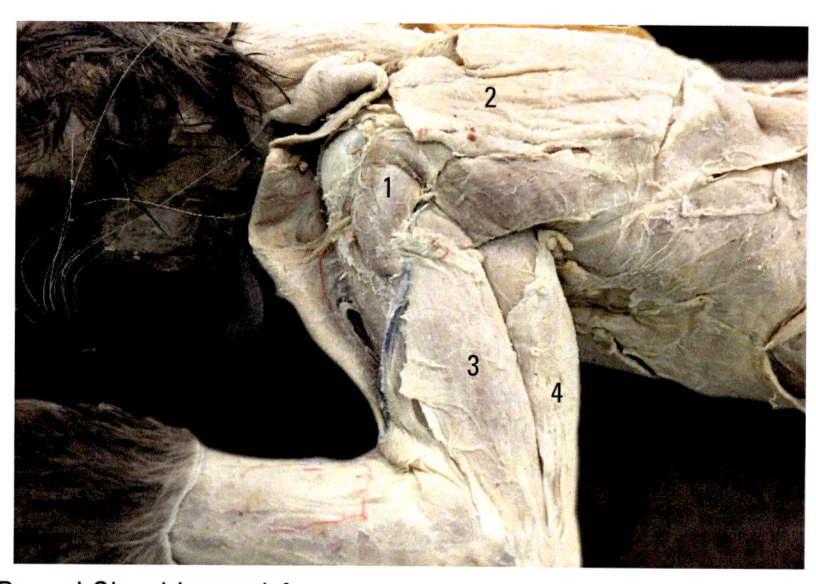

Figure 16. Dorsal Shoulder and Arm.

1. General deltoid
2. General trapezius
3. Triceps brachii lateral head
4. Triceps brachii long head

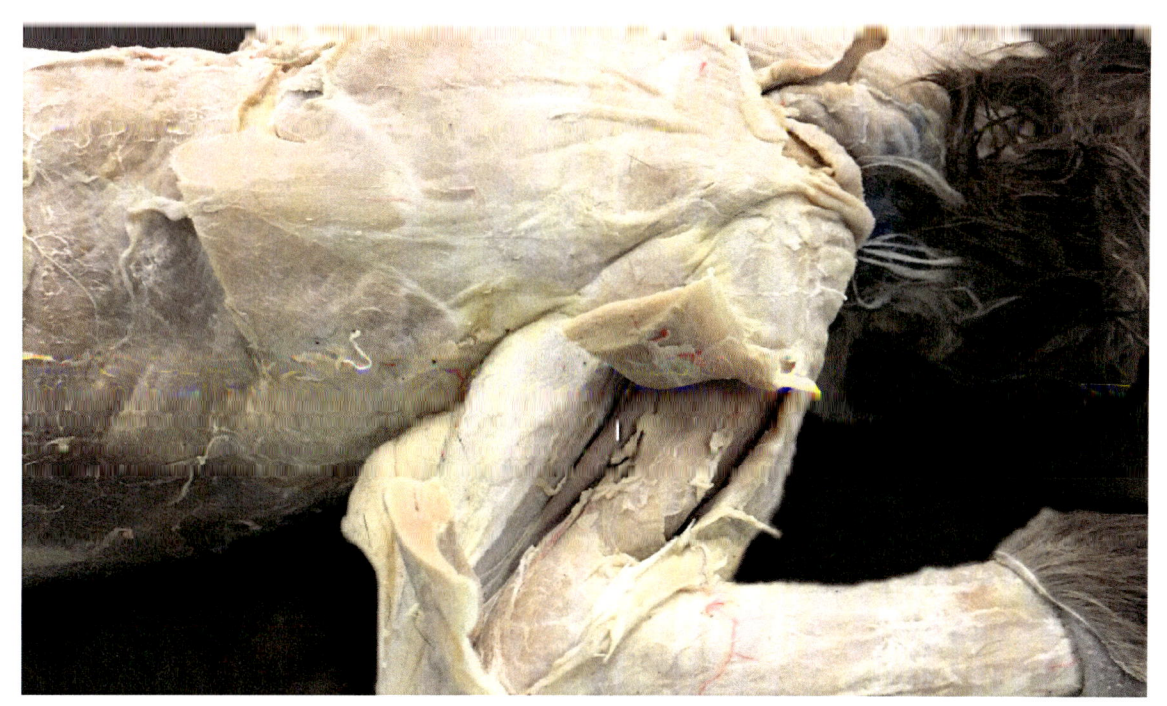

Figure 17. Dorsal Arm.

1. Triceps brachii medial head

PART 1: MUSCLES

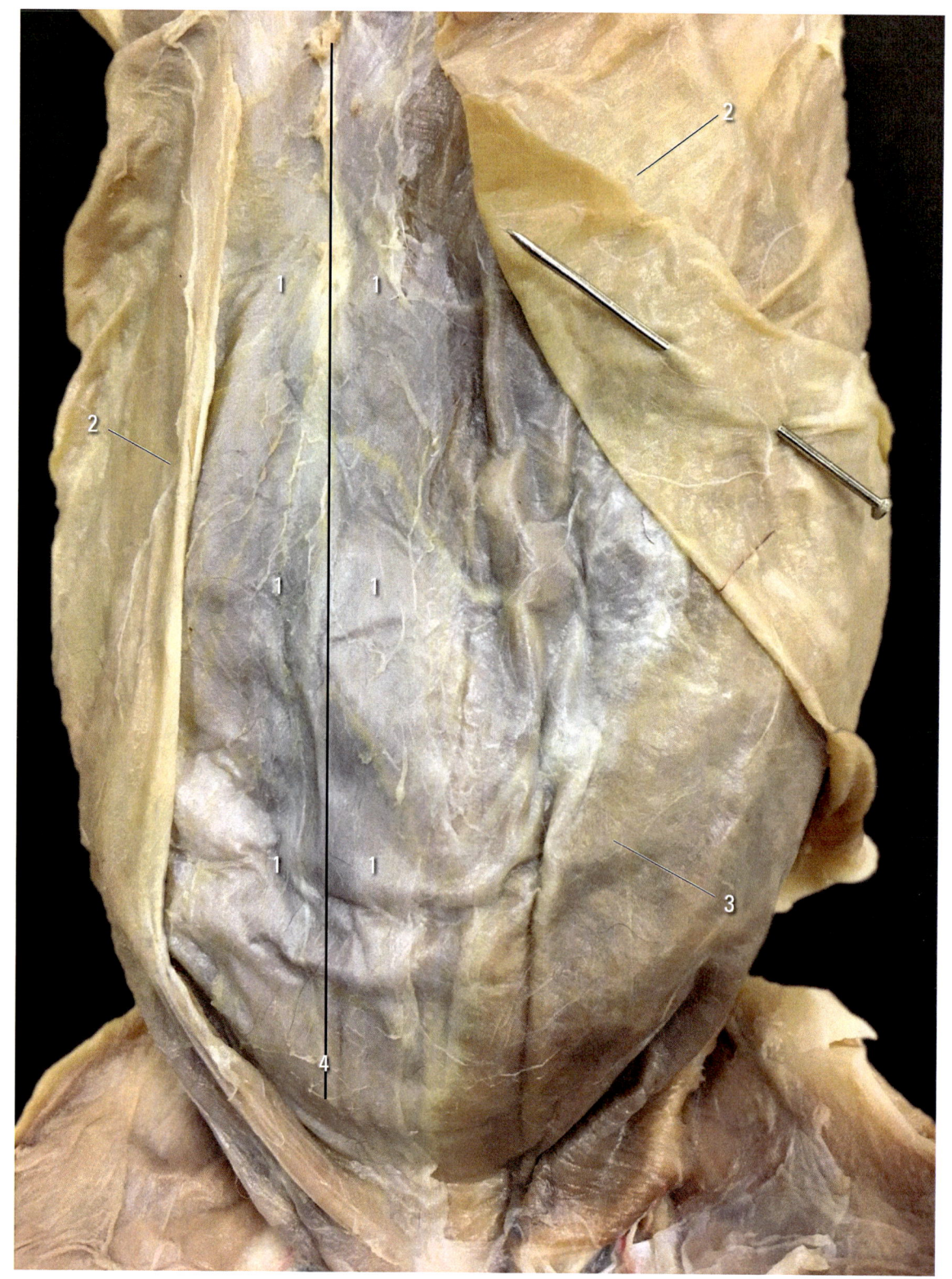

Figure 18. Abdominal Muscles.

1. Rectus abdominus
2. External oblique
3. Internal oblique
4. Linea alba

Figure 19. Dorsal Back.

1. Latissimus dorsi
2. Lumbodorsal fascia

PART 1: MUSCLES

Figure 20. Dorsal Back.

1. Sacrospinalis

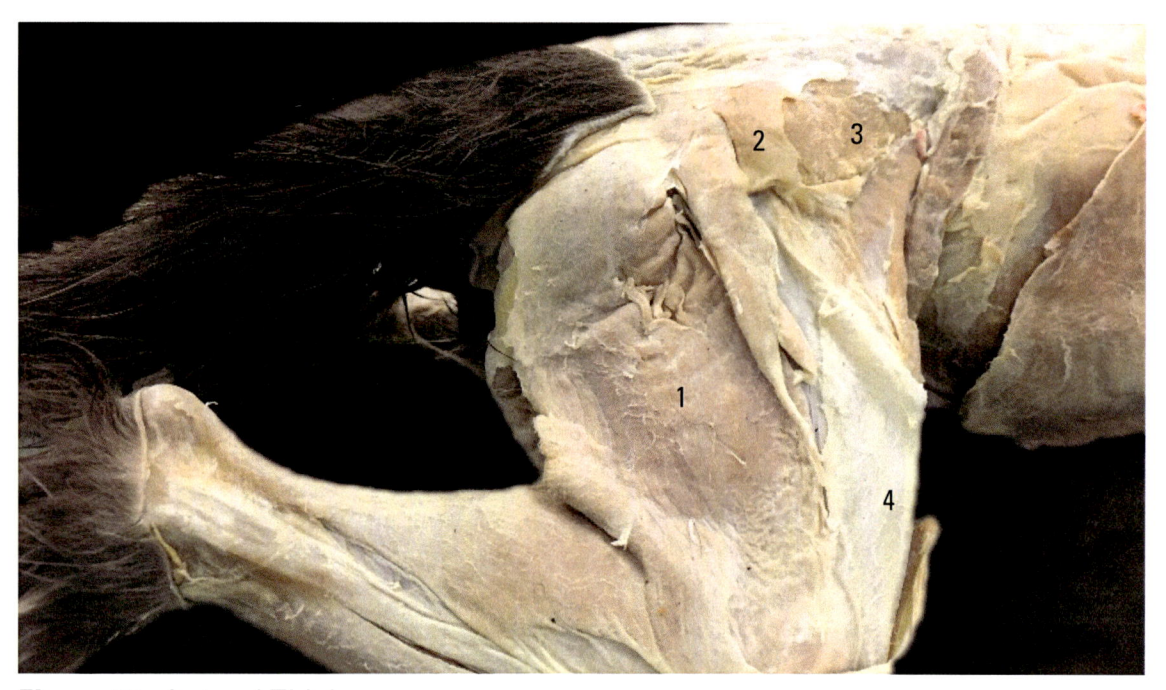

Figure 21. Lateral Thigh.

1. Biceps femoris
2. Gluteus maximus
3. Gluteus medius
4. Tensor fasciae latae

PART 1: MUSCLES

Figure 22. Dorsal Back (deep).

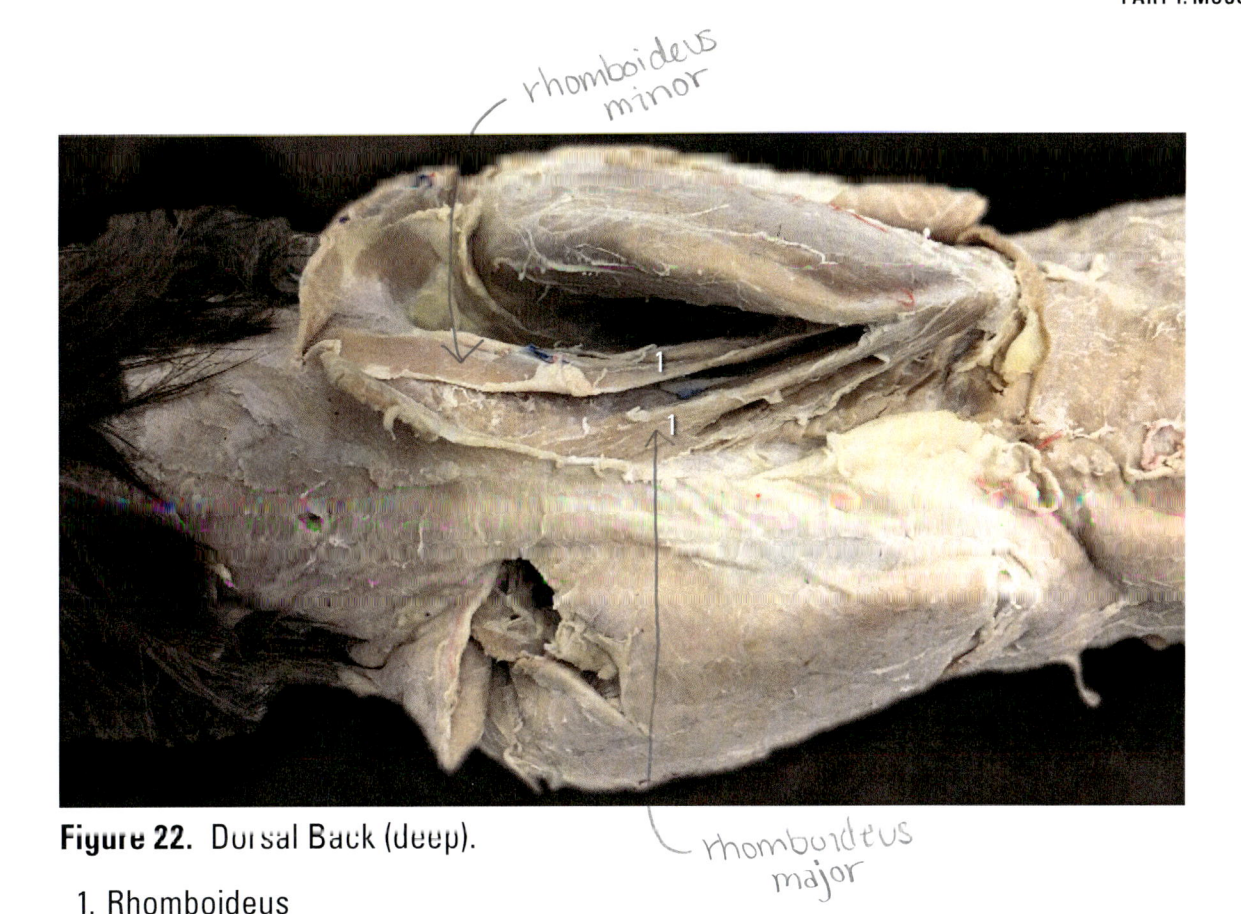

1. Rhomboideus *(rhomboideus minor, rhomboideus major)*

Figure 23. Dorsal Back (deep).

1. Infraspinatus   2. Supraspinatus

39

PART 1: MUSCLES

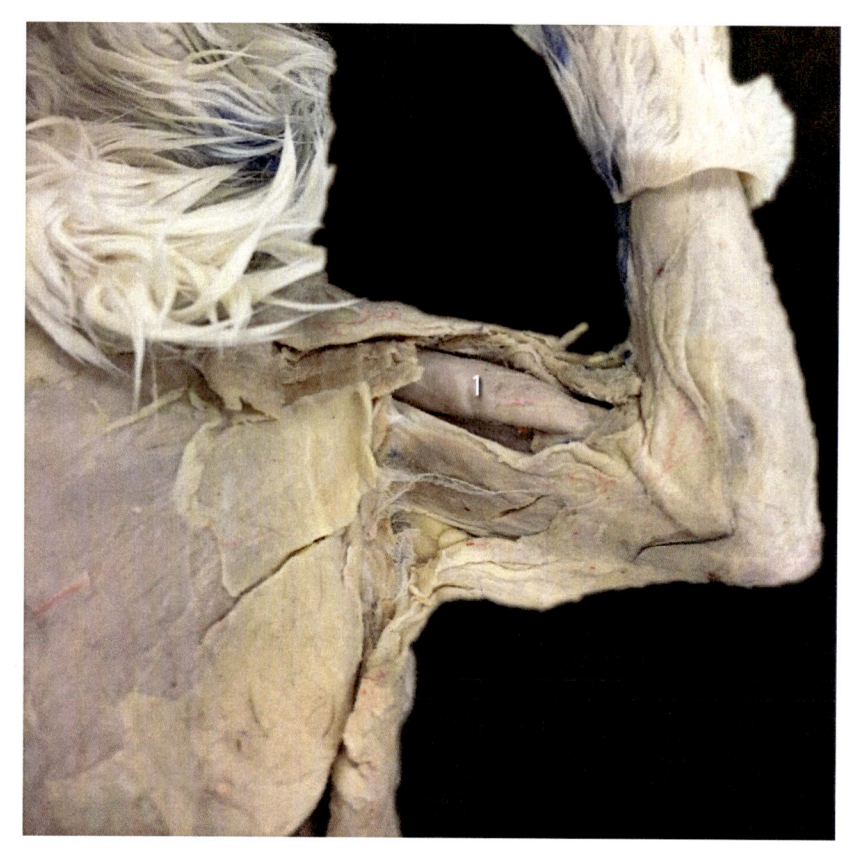

Figure 24. Ventral Arm.

1. Biceps brachii

Figure 25. Dorsal Arm.

40 1. Brachialis

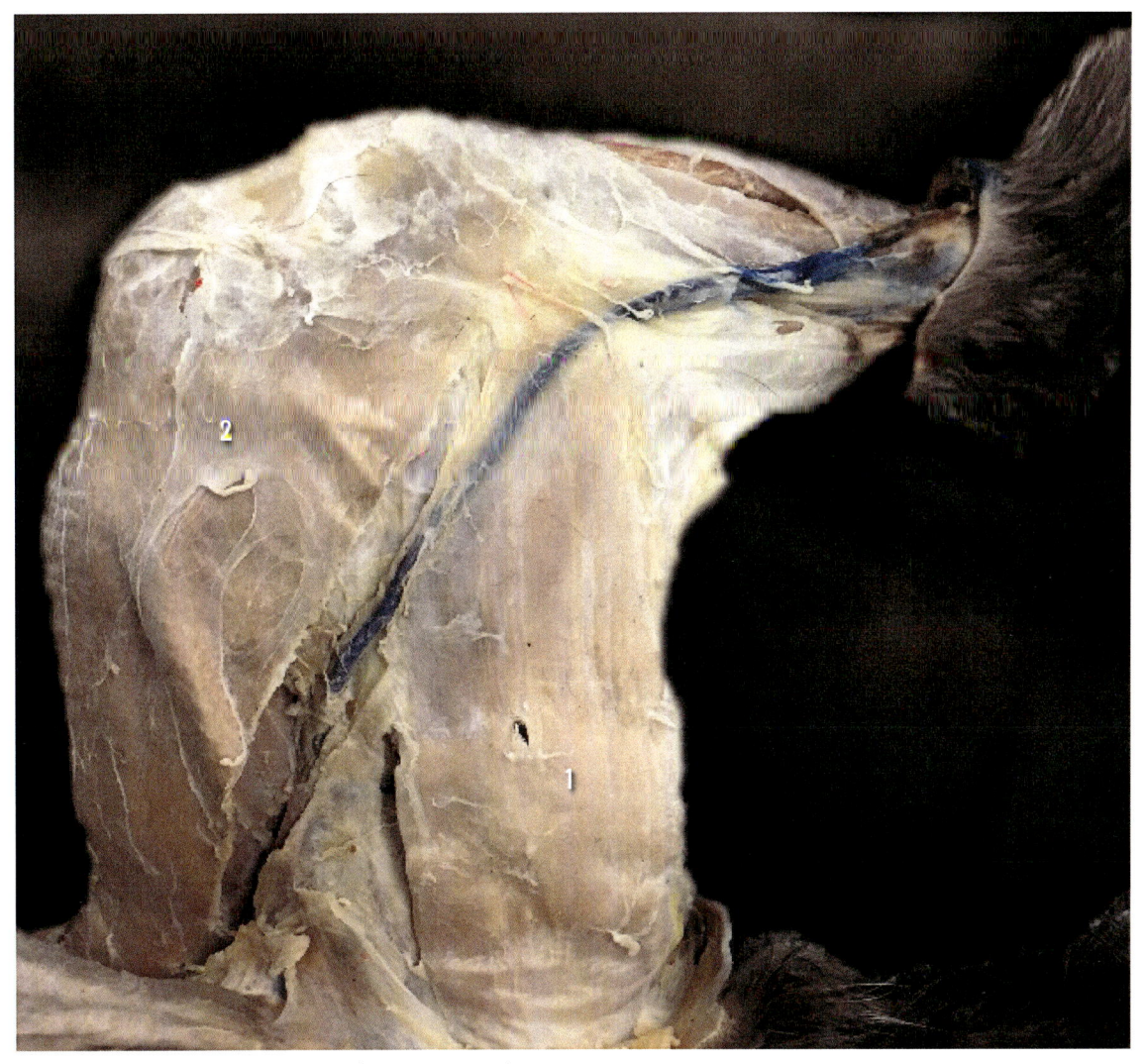

Figure 26. Ventral Thigh (superficial).

1. Gracilis
2. Sartorius

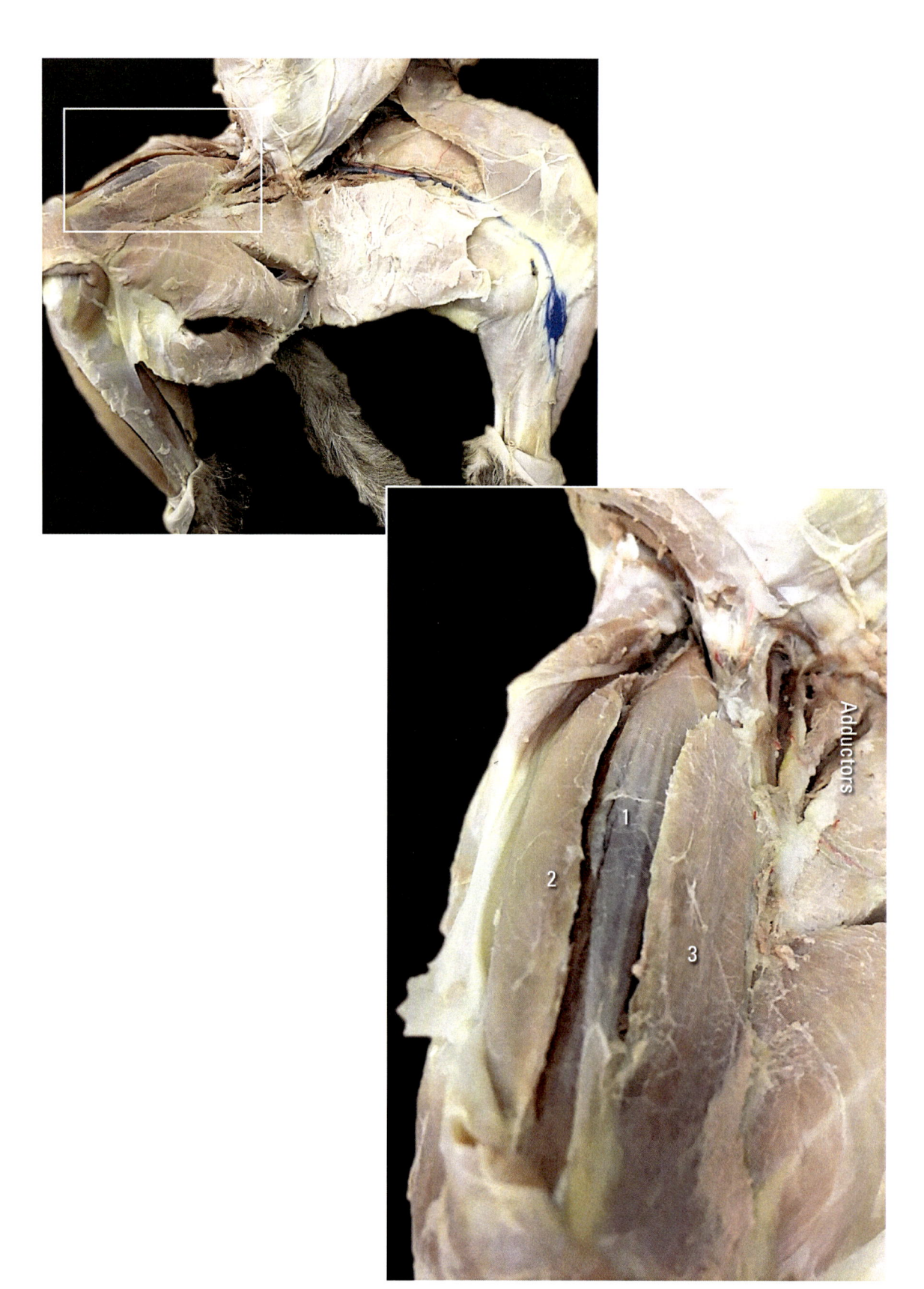

Figure 27. Ventral Thigh—Quadriceps.

1. Rectus femoris
2. Vastus lateralis
3. Vastus medialis

PART 1: MUSCLES

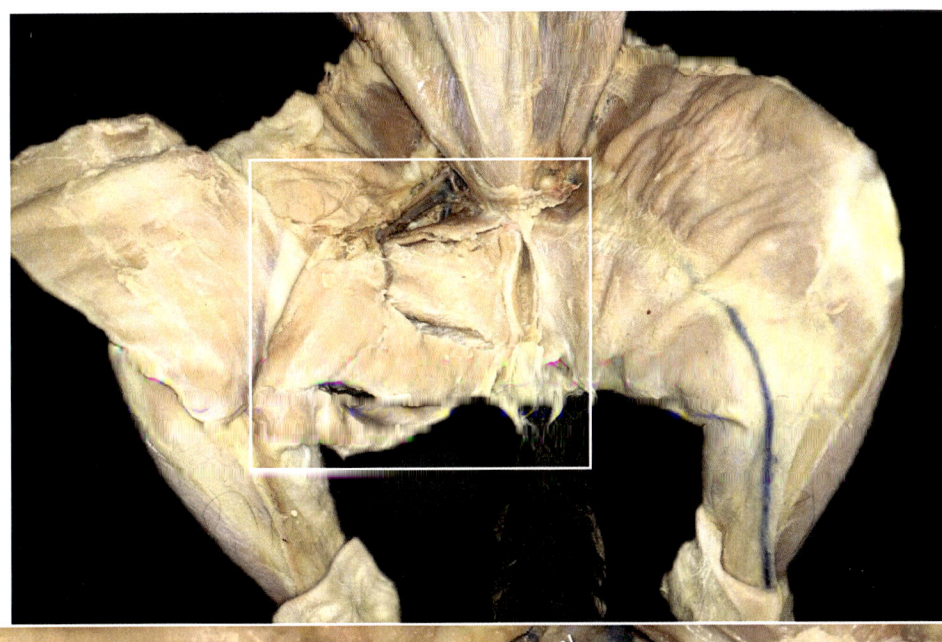

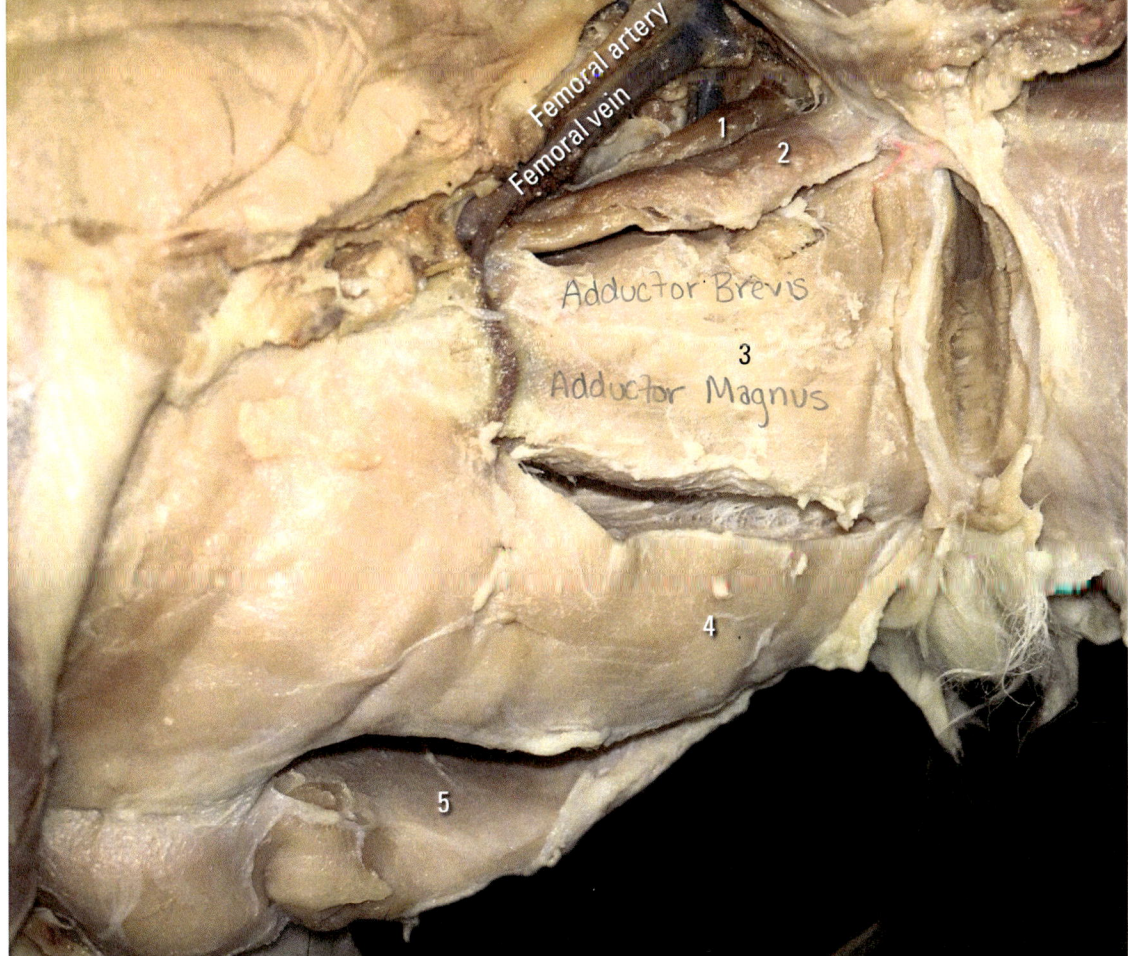

Figure 28. Ventral Thigh.

1. Pectineus
2. Adductor longus
3. Adductor femoris
4. Semimembranosus
5. Semitendinosus

43

PART 1: MUSCLES

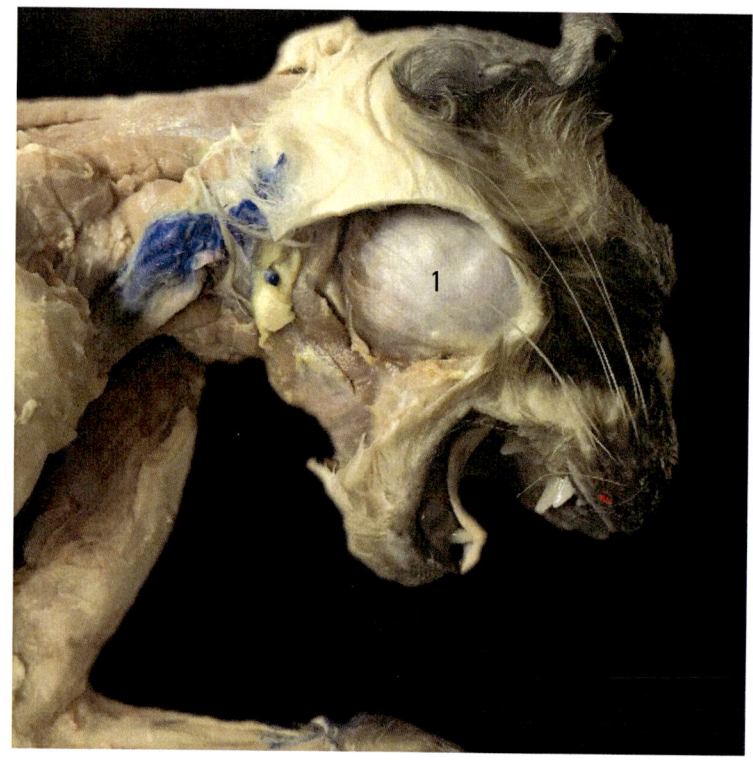

Figure 29. Lateral Head.

1. Masseter

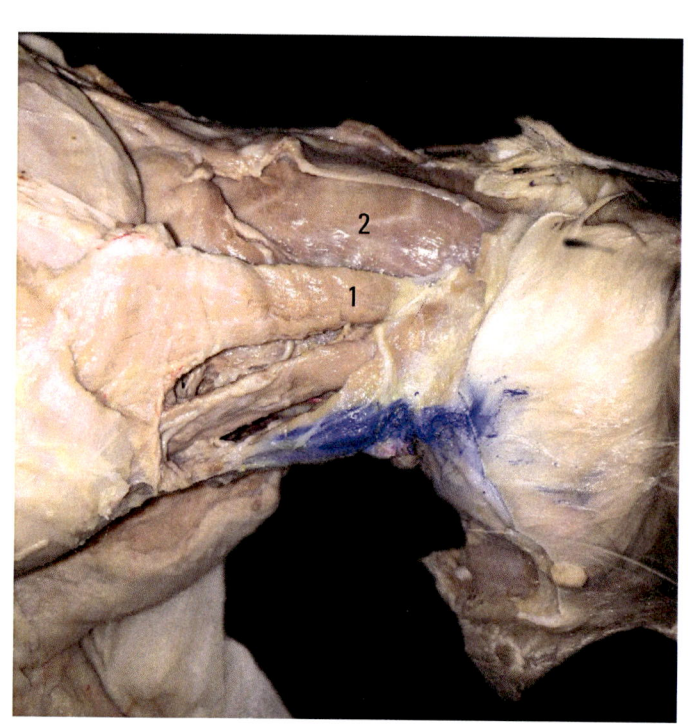

Figure 30. Lateral Neck.

1. Levator scapulae ventralis
2. Splenius

PART 1: MUSCLES

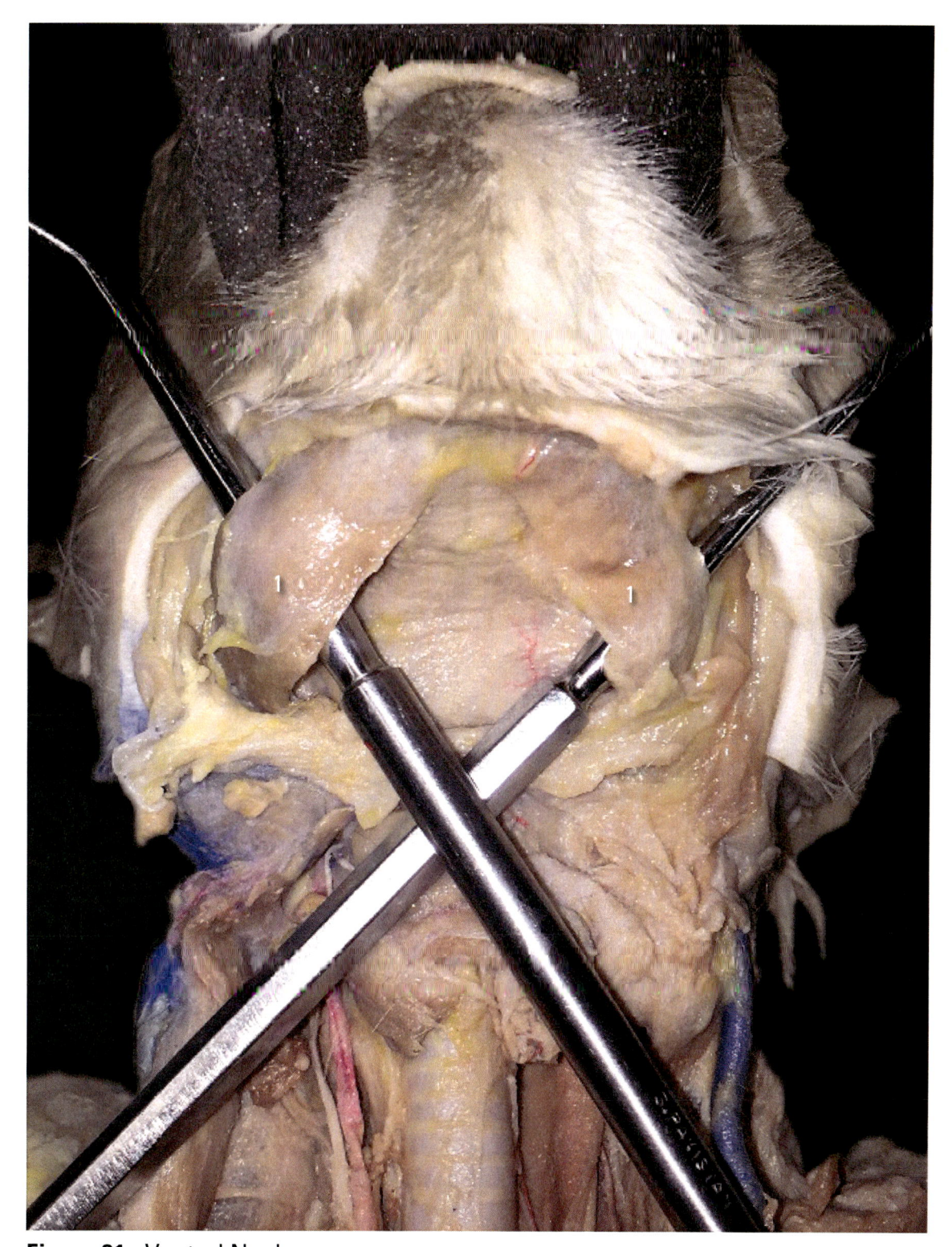

Figure 31. Ventral Neck.

1. Digastric

45

PART 1: MUSCLES

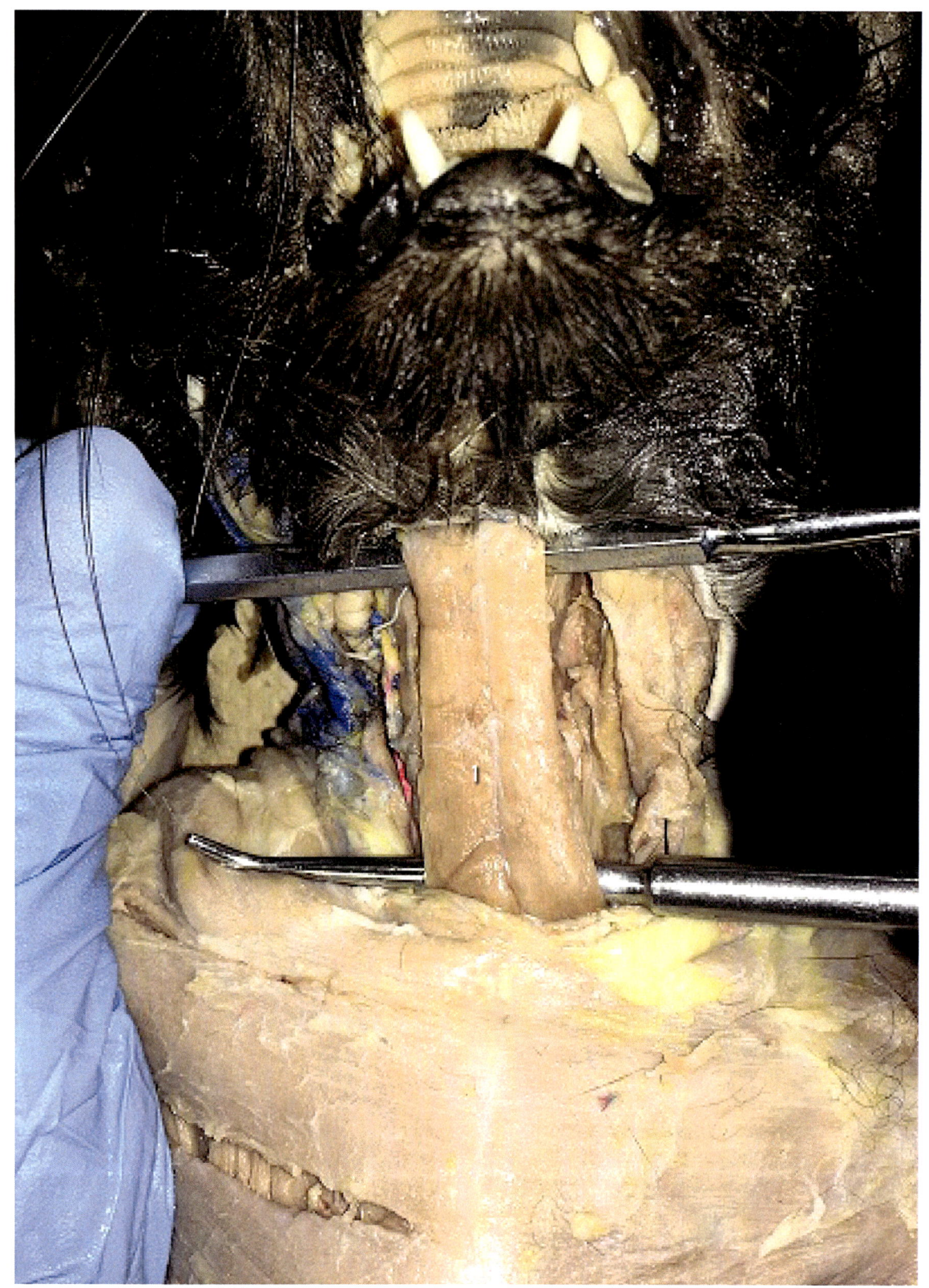

Figure 32. Ventral Neck.

1. Sternohyoid

46

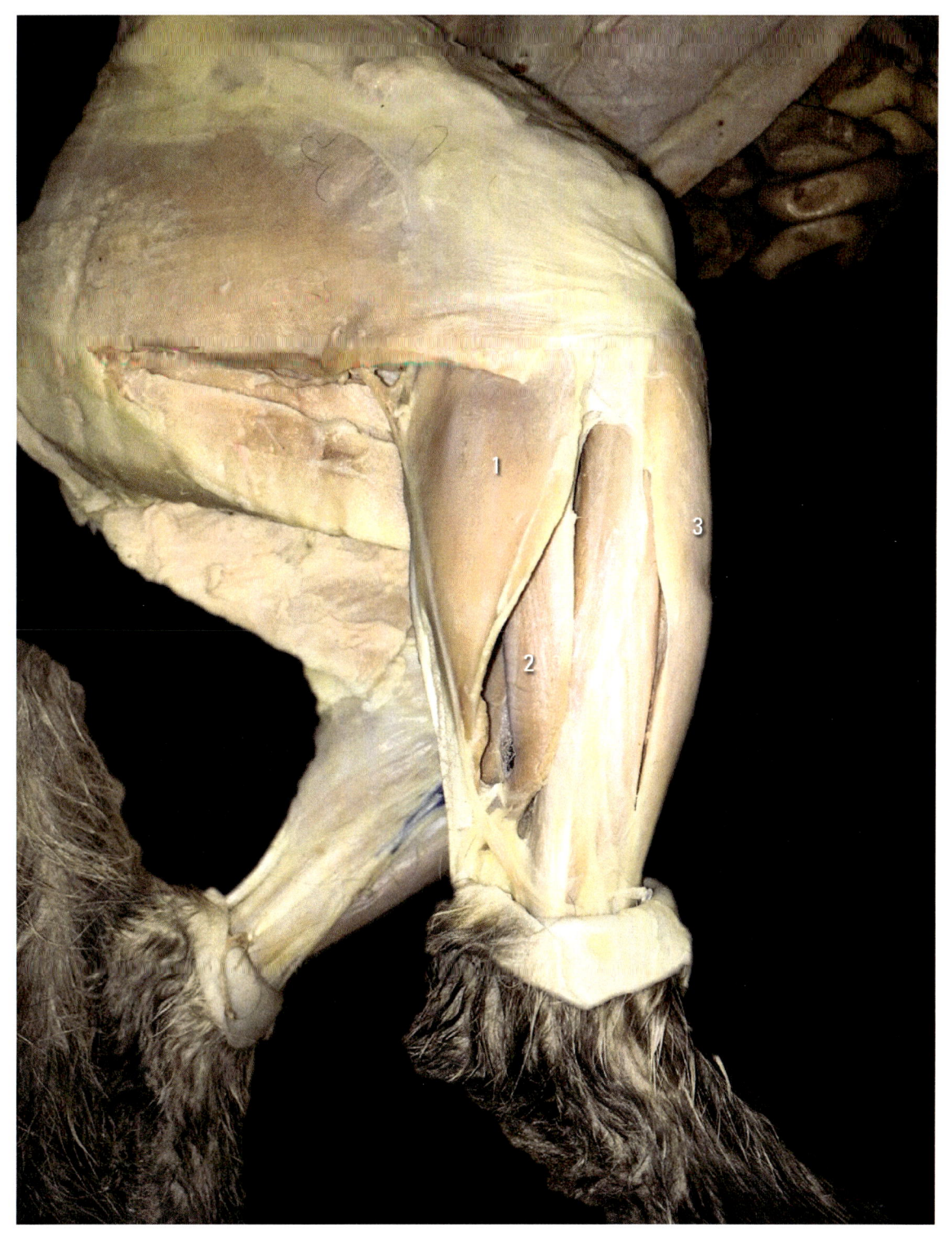

Figure 33. Lateral Leg.

1. Gastrocnemius
2. Soleus
3. Tibialis anterior

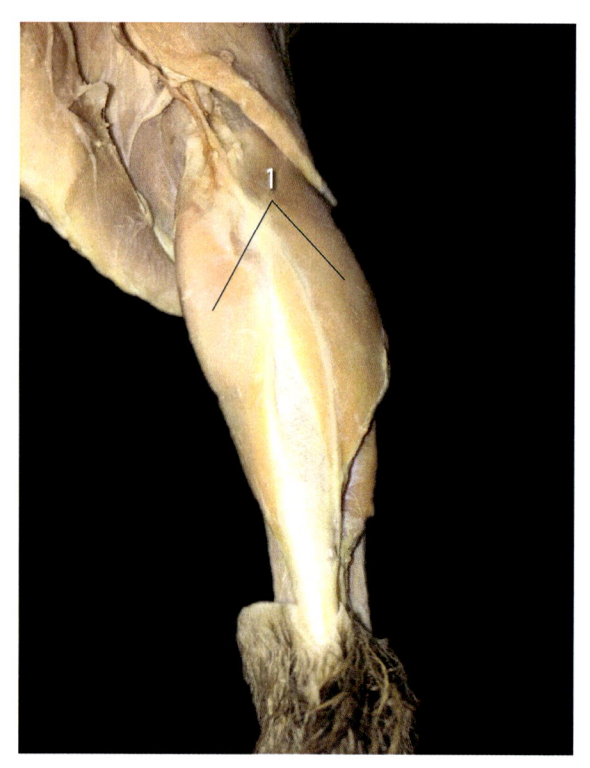

Figure 34. Posterior Leg.

1. Gastrocnemius

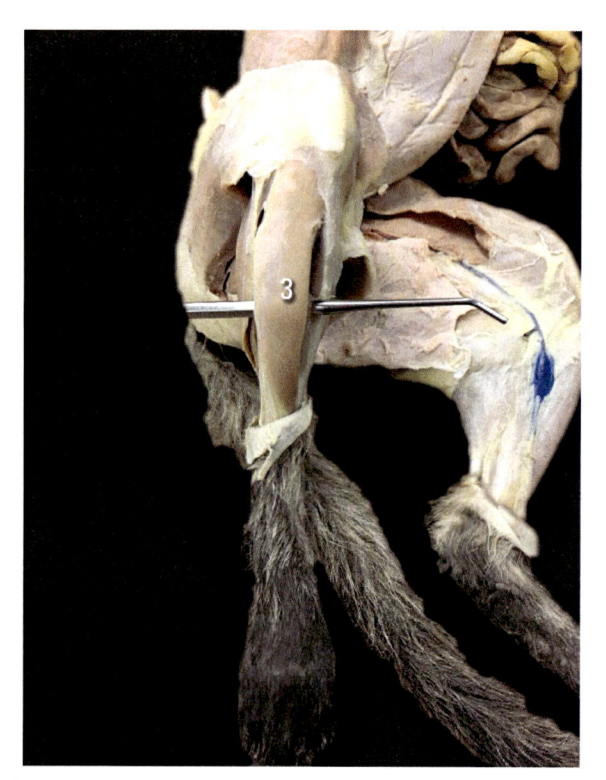

Figure 35. Anterior Leg.

3. Tibialis anterior

PART 2
ORGANS AND CIRCULATORY SYSTEM

ORGANS AND VESSELS LIST

ORGANS

THORACIC CAVITY

- Heart
- Trachea
- Esophagus
- Lungs
- Diaphragm

ABDOMINOPELVIC CAVITY

- Pancreas
- Spleen
- Stomach
- Liver
- Gall bladder
- Small intestines
  - Duodenum
  - Jejunum
  - Ileum
- Large intestines (colon)
  - Cecum
  - Ascending colon
  - Transverse colon
  - Descending colon
  - Sigmoid colon
- Kidneys
- Adrenal glands
- Ureters
- Urinary bladder
- Ovaries (female)
- Oviduct (female)
- Horns of uterus (female)
- Body of uterus (female)
- Vas deferens (male)
- Testes (male)

BLOOD VESSELS

SUPERIOR THORACIC/ARM ARTERIES

- Arch of aorta
- Thoracic aorta
- Brachiocephalic artery
- R/L Subclavian arteries
- R/L Common carotid arteries
- Axillary artery
- Brachial artery

SUPERIOR THORACIC/ARM VEINS

- Superior vena cava
- R/L Brachiocephalic veins
- R/L Subclavian veins
- Axillary vein
- Brachial vein
- External jugular vein
- Internal jugular vein
- Inferior vena cava

INFERIOR ABDOMINAL ARTERIES

- Abdominal aorta
- Celiac trunk (artery)
  - Hepatic artery
  - Left gastric artery
  - Splenic artery
- Superior mesenteric artery
- Renal artery
- Inferior mesenteric artery
- External iliac artery
- Internal iliac artery

INFERIOR ABDOMINAL VEINS

- Inferior vena cava
- Renal vein
- Common iliac vein
- External iliac vein
- Internal iliac vein

THIGH VESSELS

- Femoral artery
- Femoral vein

CIRCULATORY SYSTEM PATHWAYS

1. Arm
2. Head
3. Brain
4. Kidney
5. Leg
6. Liver
7. Spleen
8. Pancreas
9. Stomach
10. Upper Intestine
11. Lower Intestine

1. ARM

- Left ventricle
- Ascending aorta
- Arch of aorta
- Brachiocephalic artery
- Subclavian artery
- Axillary artery
- Brachial artery
- Capillaries of arm
- Brachial vein
- Axillary vein
- Subclavian vein
- Brachiocephalic vein
- Superior vena cava
- Right atrium

2. HEAD

- Left ventricle
- Ascending aorta
- Arch of aorta
- Brachiocephalic artery
- Right common carotid artery
- External carotid artery
- Capillaries of head
- External jugular vein
- Subclavian vein
- Brachiocephalic vein
- Superior vena cava
- Right atrium

3. BRAIN

- Left ventricle
- Ascending aorta
- Arch of aorta
- Brachiocephalic artery
- Subclavian artery
- Vertebral artery
- Basilar artery
- Circle of Willis
- Capillaries of brain
- Venous sinuses
- Internal jugular vein
- Brachiocephalic vein
- Superior vena cava
- Right atrium

4. KIDNEY

- Left ventricle
- Ascending aorta
- Arch of aorta
- Thoracic aorta
- Abdominal aorta
- Renal artery
- Smaller arteries and arterioles within the kidney
- Afferent arteriole to the glomerulus
- Efferent arteriole away from the glomerulus
- Peritubular capillaries around renal tubules
- Venules and smaller veins within the kidney
- Renal vein
- Inferior vena cava
- Right atrium

5. LEG

- Left ventricle
- Ascending aorta
- Arch of aorta
- Thoracic aorta
- Abdominal aorta
- Common iliac artery
- External iliac artery
- Femoral artery
- Capillaries of leg
- Femoral vein
- External iliac vein
- Common iliac vein
- Inferior vena cava
- Right atrium

6. LIVER

- Left ventricle
- Ascending aorta
- Arch of aorta
- Thoracic aorta
- Abdominal aorta
- Celiac artery
- Hepatic artery
- Capillaries of liver
- Small veins within liver
- Hepatic veins
- Inferior vena cava
- Right atrium

7. SPLEEN

- Left ventricle
- Ascending aorta
- Arch of aorta
- Thoracic aorta
- Abdominal aorta
- Celiac artery
- Splenic artery
- Capillaries of spleen
- Splenic vein
- Portal vein
- Small veins within liver
- Hepatic veins
- Inferior vena cava
- Right atrium

PART 2: ORGANS AND CIRCULATORY SYSTEM

8. PANCREAS

- Left ventricle
- Ascending aorta
- Arch of aorta
- Thoracic aorta
- Abdominal aorta
- Celiac artery
- Splenic artery
- Capillaries of pancreas
- Splenic vein
- Portal vein
- Small veins within liver
- Hepatic veins
- Inferior vena cava
- Right atrium

9. STOMACH

- Left ventricle
- Ascending aorta
- Arch of aorta
- Thoracic aorta
- Abdominal aorta
- Celiac artery
- Left gastric artery
- Capillaries of stomach
- Left gastric vein
- Portal vein
- Small veins within liver
- Hepatic veins
- Inferior vena cava
- Right atrium

10. UPPER INTESTINE

- Left ventricle
- Ascending aorta
- Arch of aorta
- Thoracic aorta
- Abdominal aorta
- Superior mesenteric artery
- Capillaries of upper intestine
- Superior mesenteric vein
- Portal vein
- Small veins within liver
- Hepatic veins
- Inferior vena cava
- Right atrium

11. LOWER INTESTINE

- Left ventricle
- Ascending aorta
- Arch of aorta
- Thoracic aorta
- Abdominal aorta
- Inferior mesenteric artery
- Capillaries of lower intestine
- Inferior mesenteric vein
- Splenic vein
- Portal vein
- Small veins within liver
- Hepatic veins
- Inferior vena cava
- Right atrium

PART 2: ORGANS AND CIRCULATORY SYSTEM

HUMAN CIRCULATORY SYSTEM PATHWAYS

ARM PATHWAY, ARTERIES

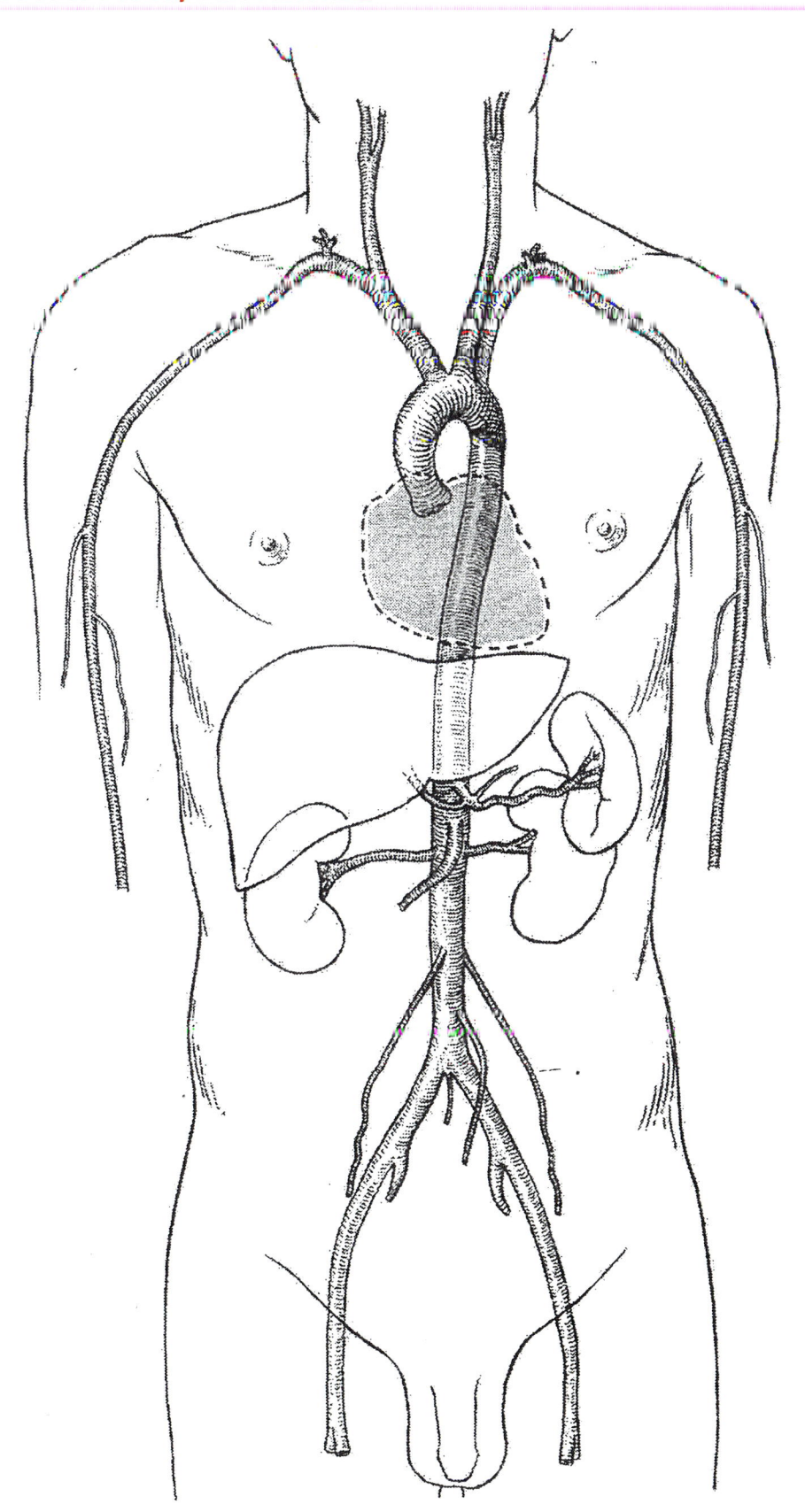

55

PART 2: ORGANS AND CIRCULATORY SYSTEM

ARM PATHWAY, VEINS

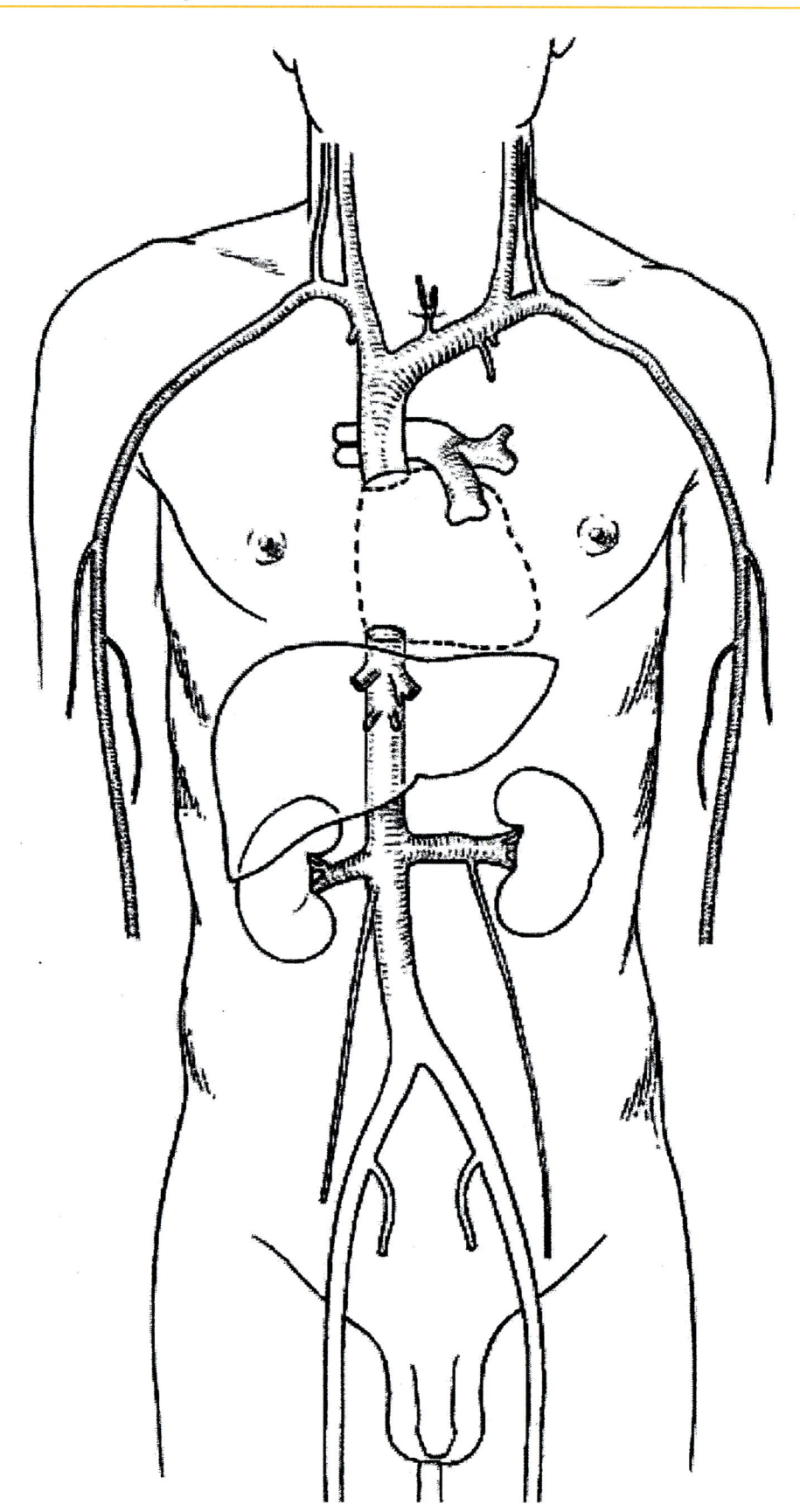

PART 2: ORGANS AND CIRCULATORY SYSTEM

HEAD PATHWAY, ARTERIES

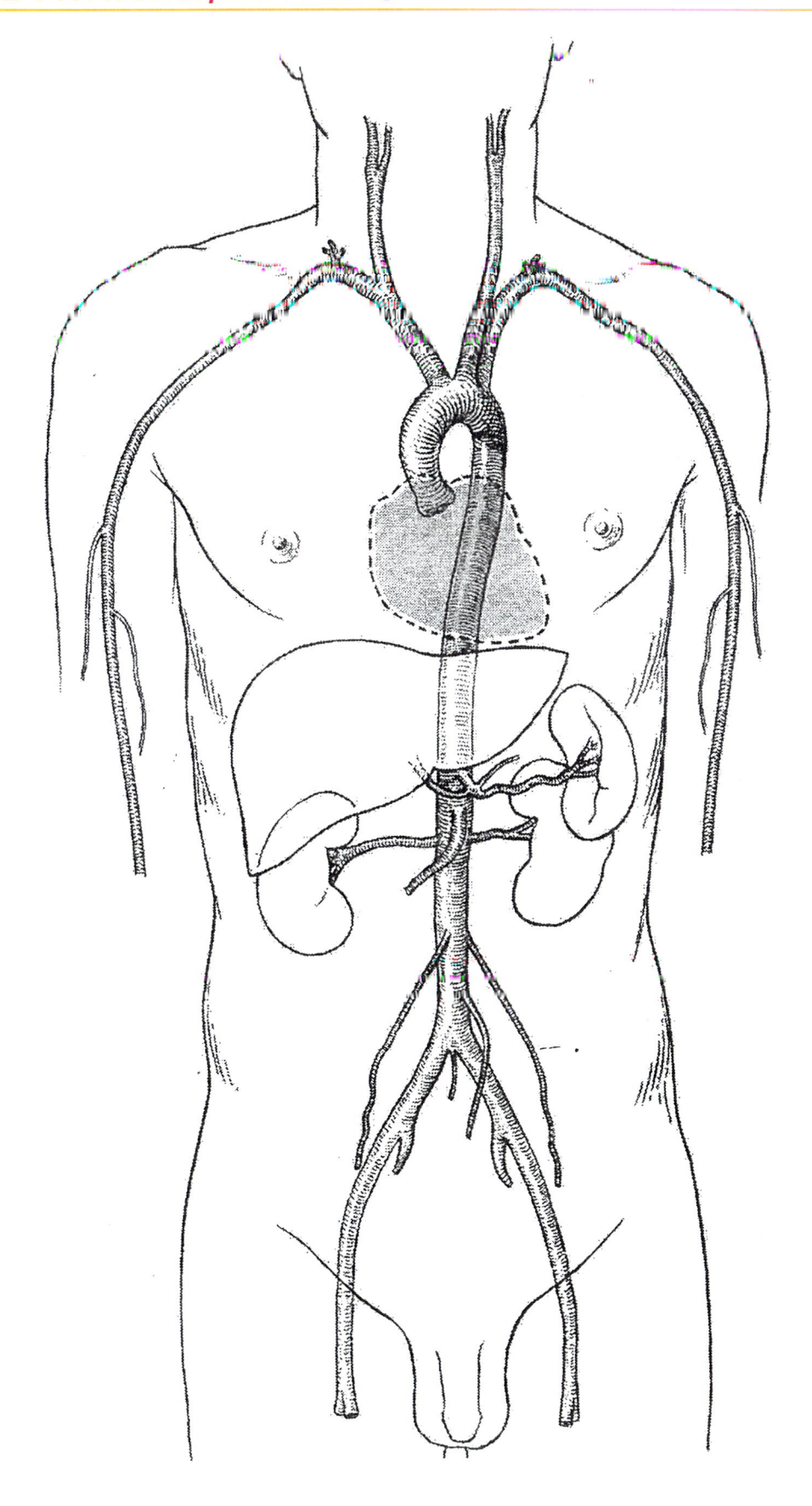

57

PART 2: ORGANS AND CIRCULATORY SYSTEM

HEAD PATHWAY, VEINS

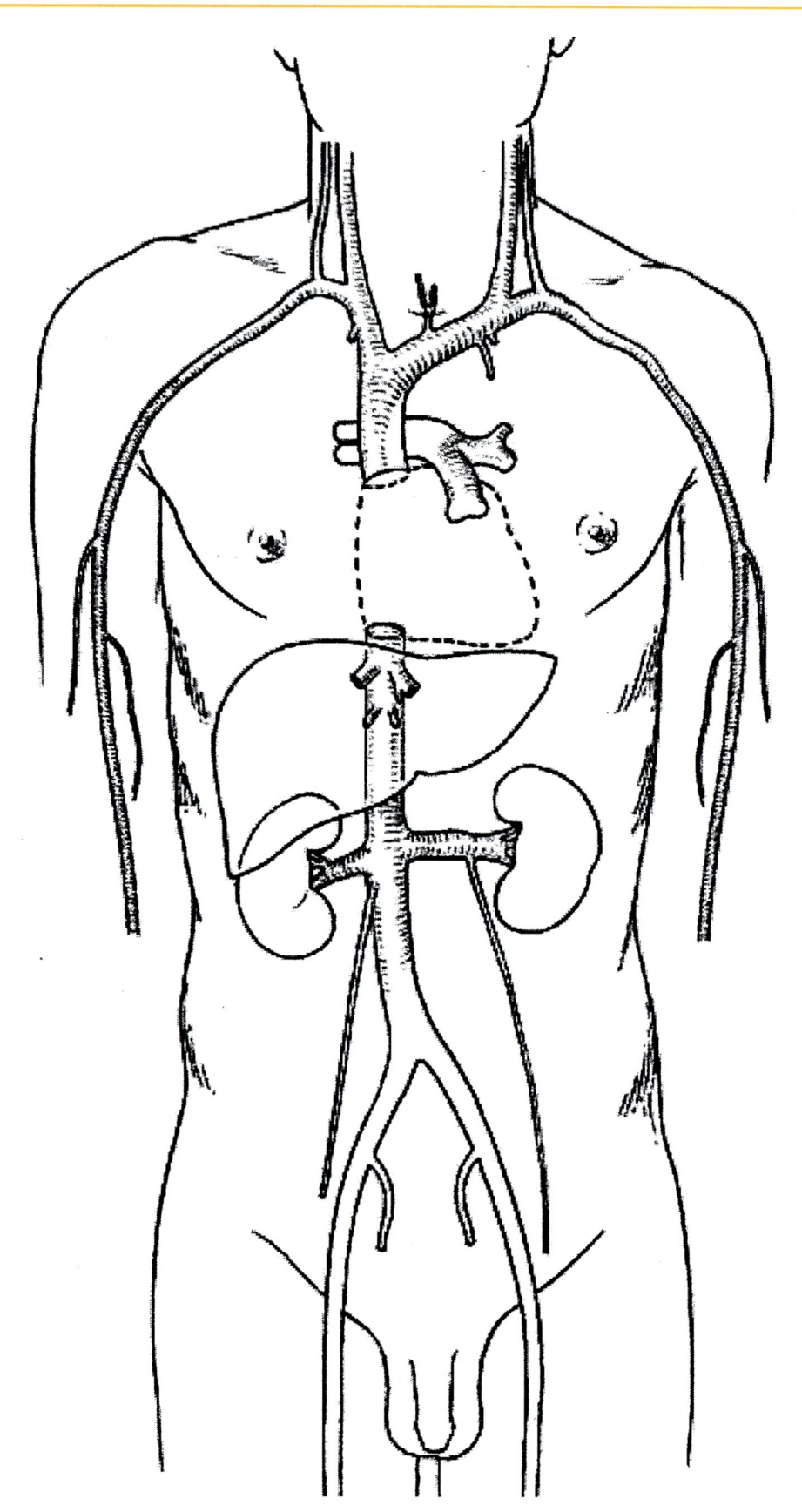

PART 2: ORGANS AND CIRCULATORY SYSTEM

BRAIN PATHWAY LATERAL, ARTERIES

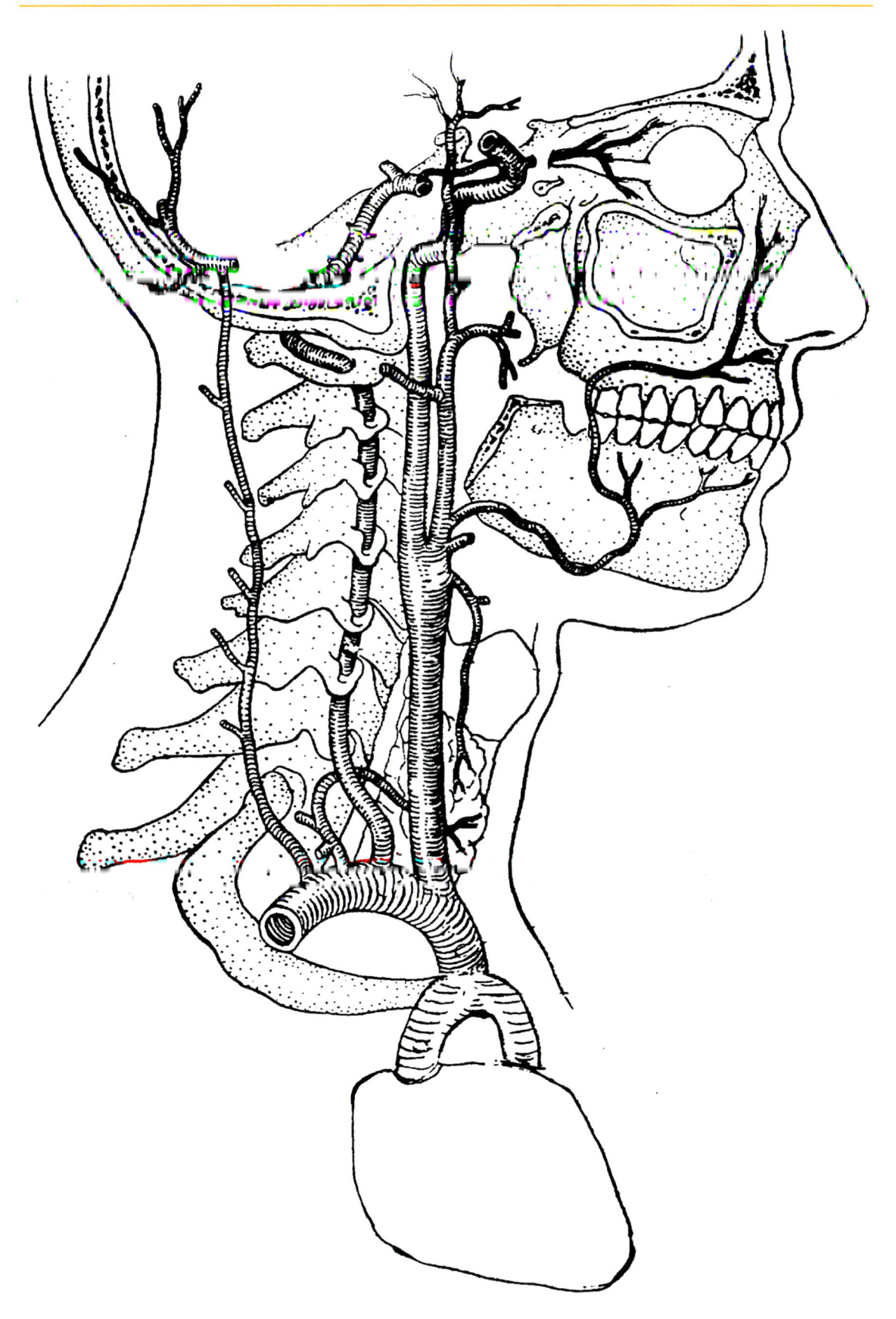

59

BRAIN PATHWAY INFERIOR, ARTERIES

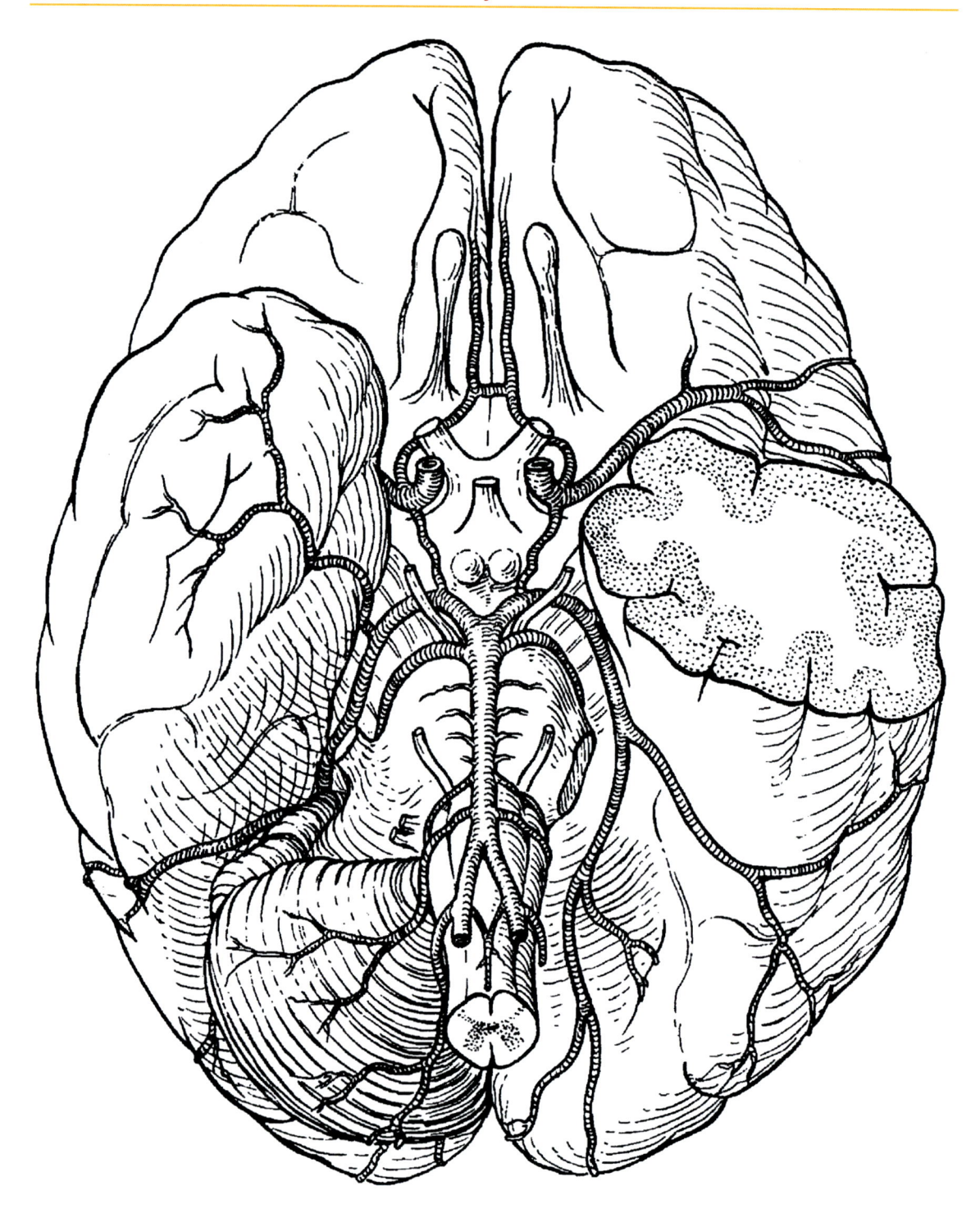

BRAIN PATHWAY LATERAL, VEINS

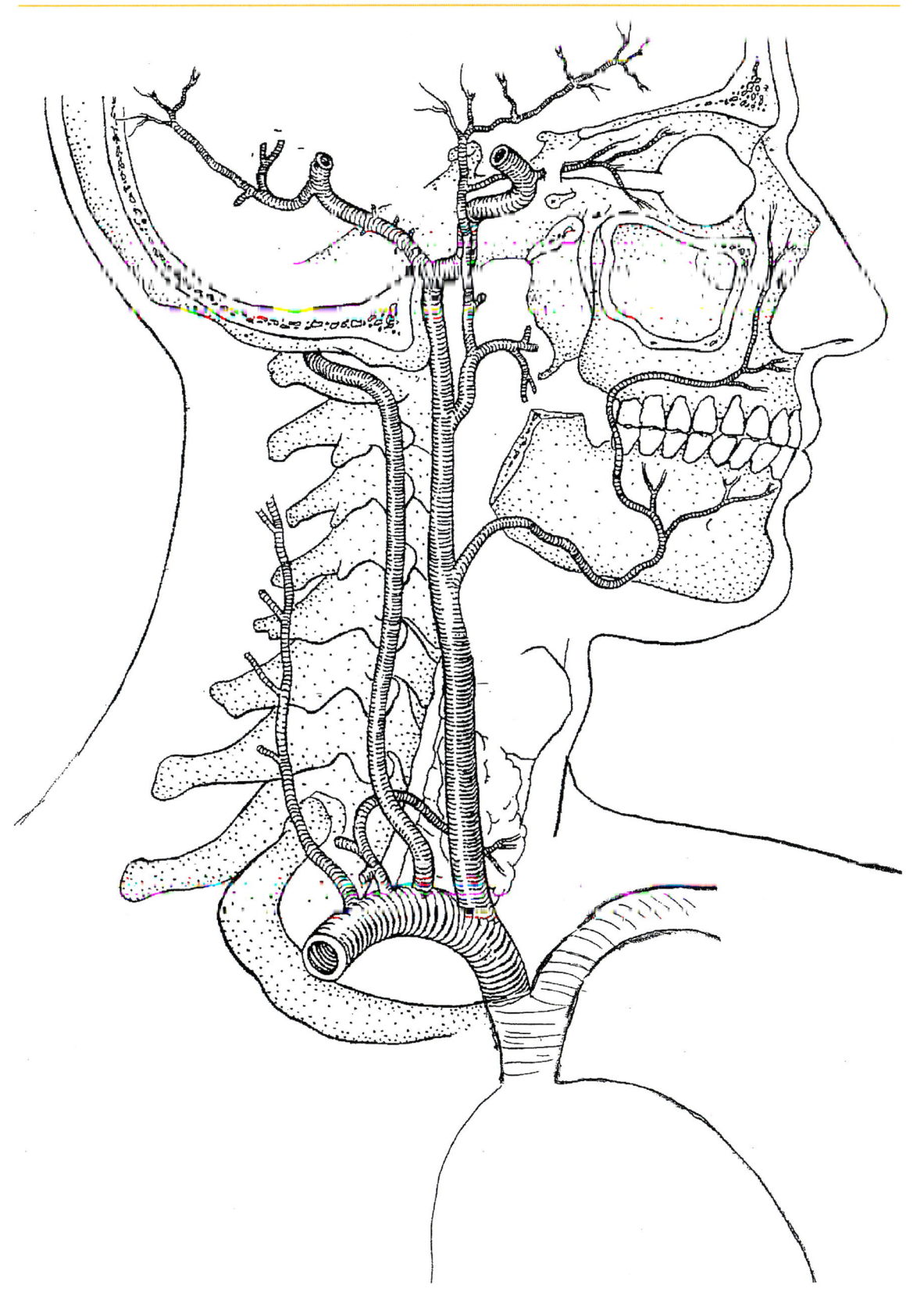

PART 2: ORGANS AND CIRCULATORY SYSTEM

KIDNEY PATHWAY, ARTERIES

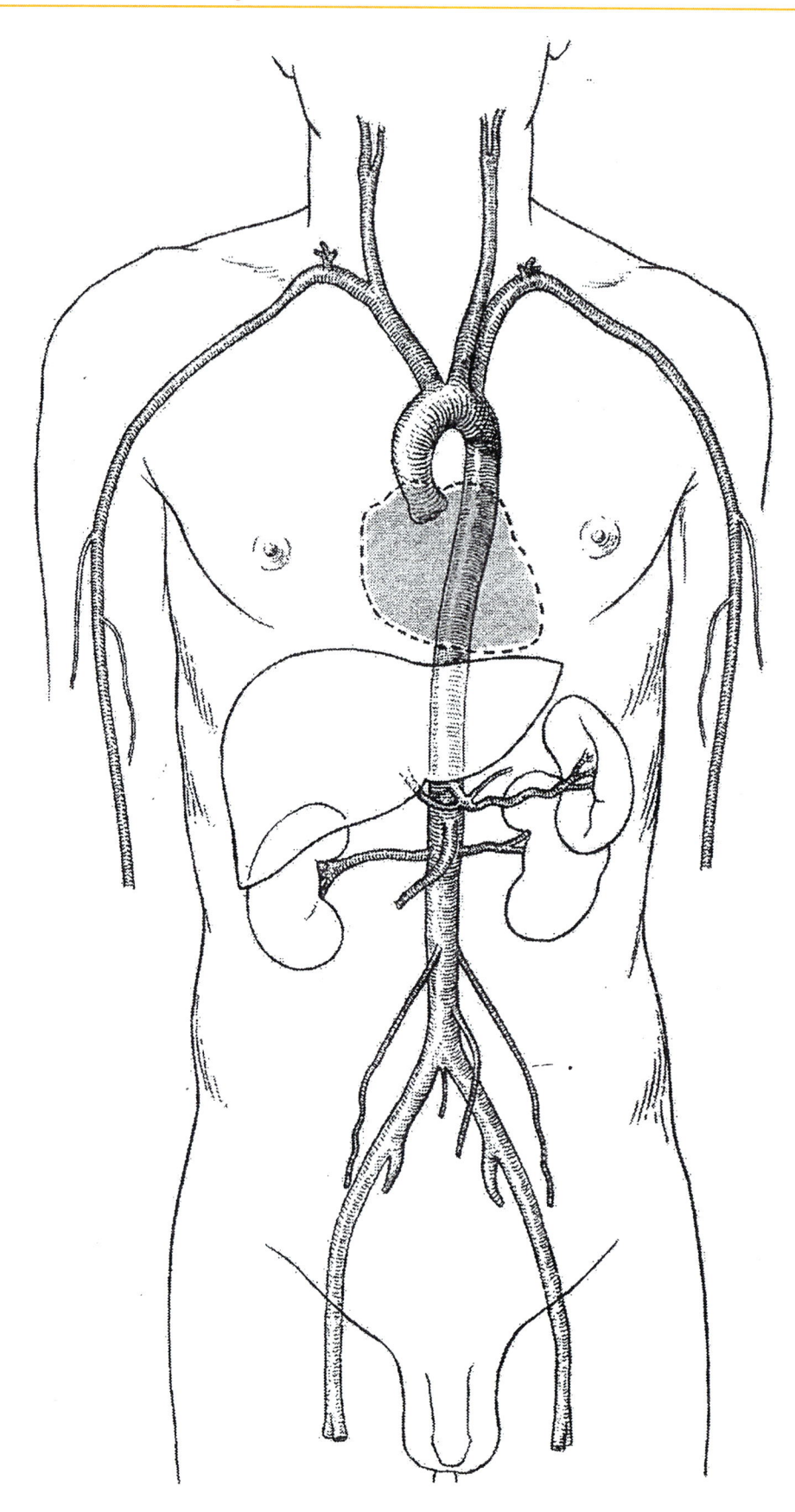

KIDNEY PATHWAY, NEPHRON

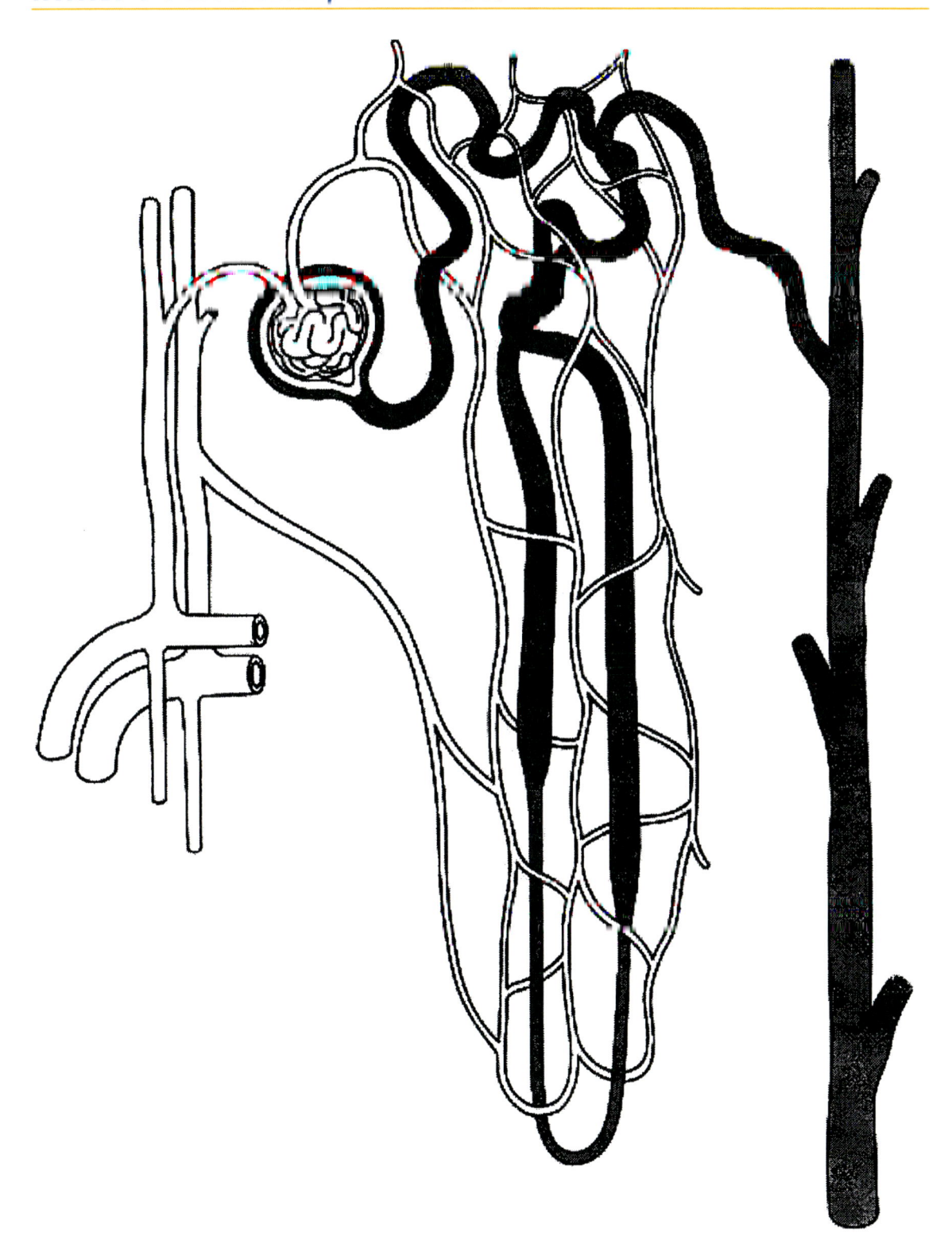

PART 2: ORGANS AND CIRCULATORY SYSTEM

KIDNEY PATHWAY, VEINS

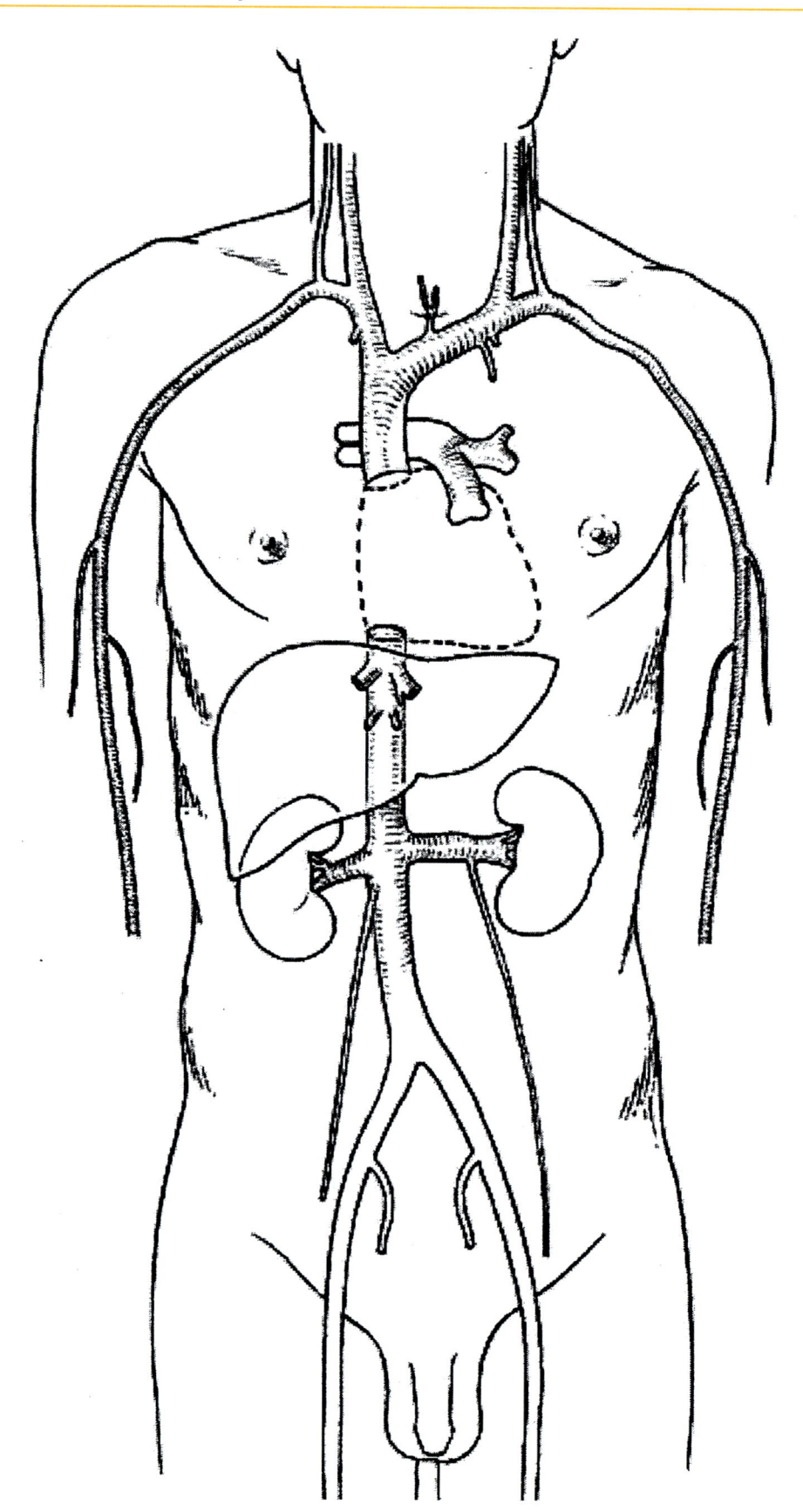

LEG PATHWAY, ARTERIES

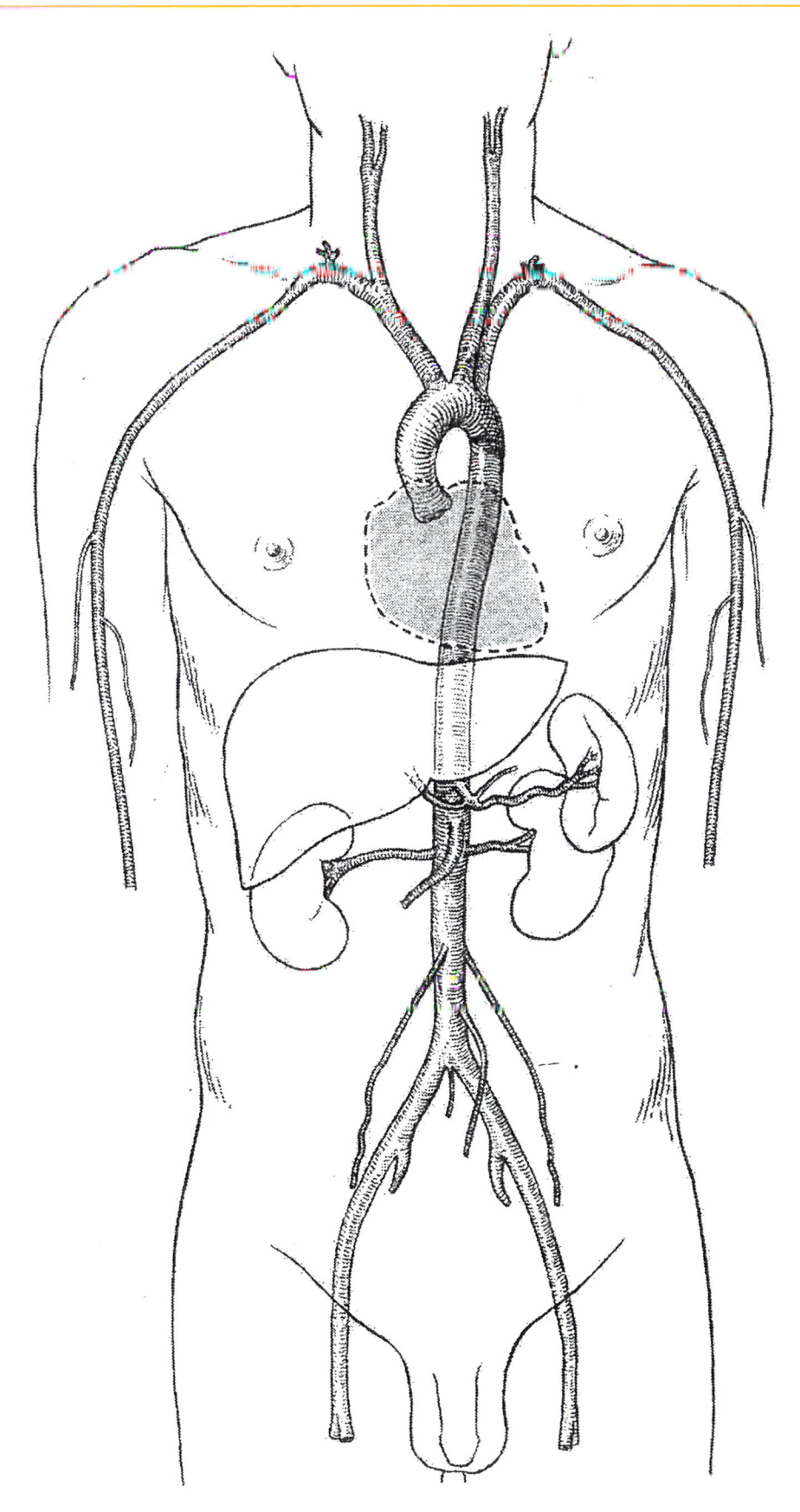

LEG PATHWAY, VEINS

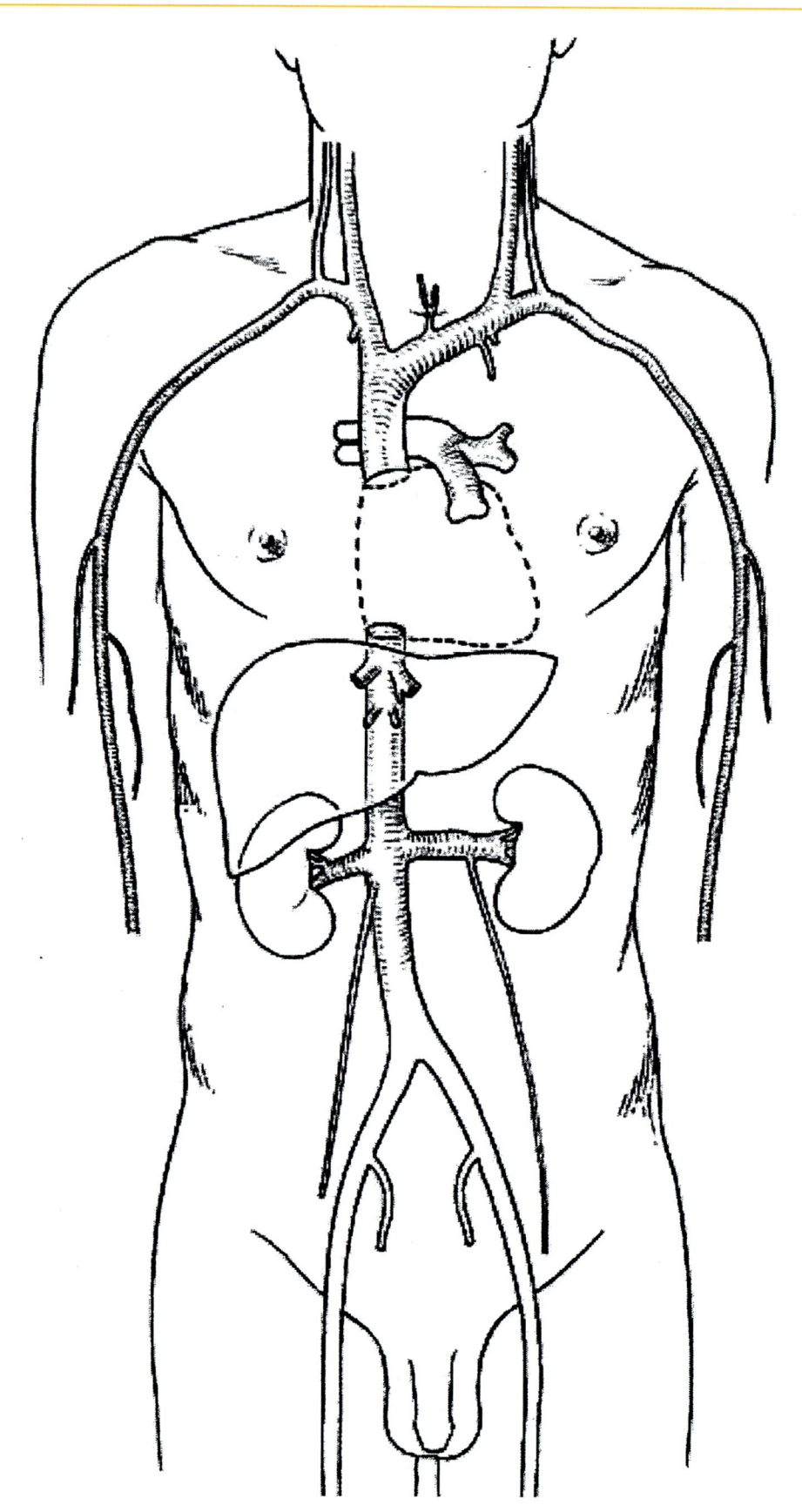

PART 2: ORGANS AND CIRCULATORY SYSTEM

LIVER PATHWAY, ARTERIES

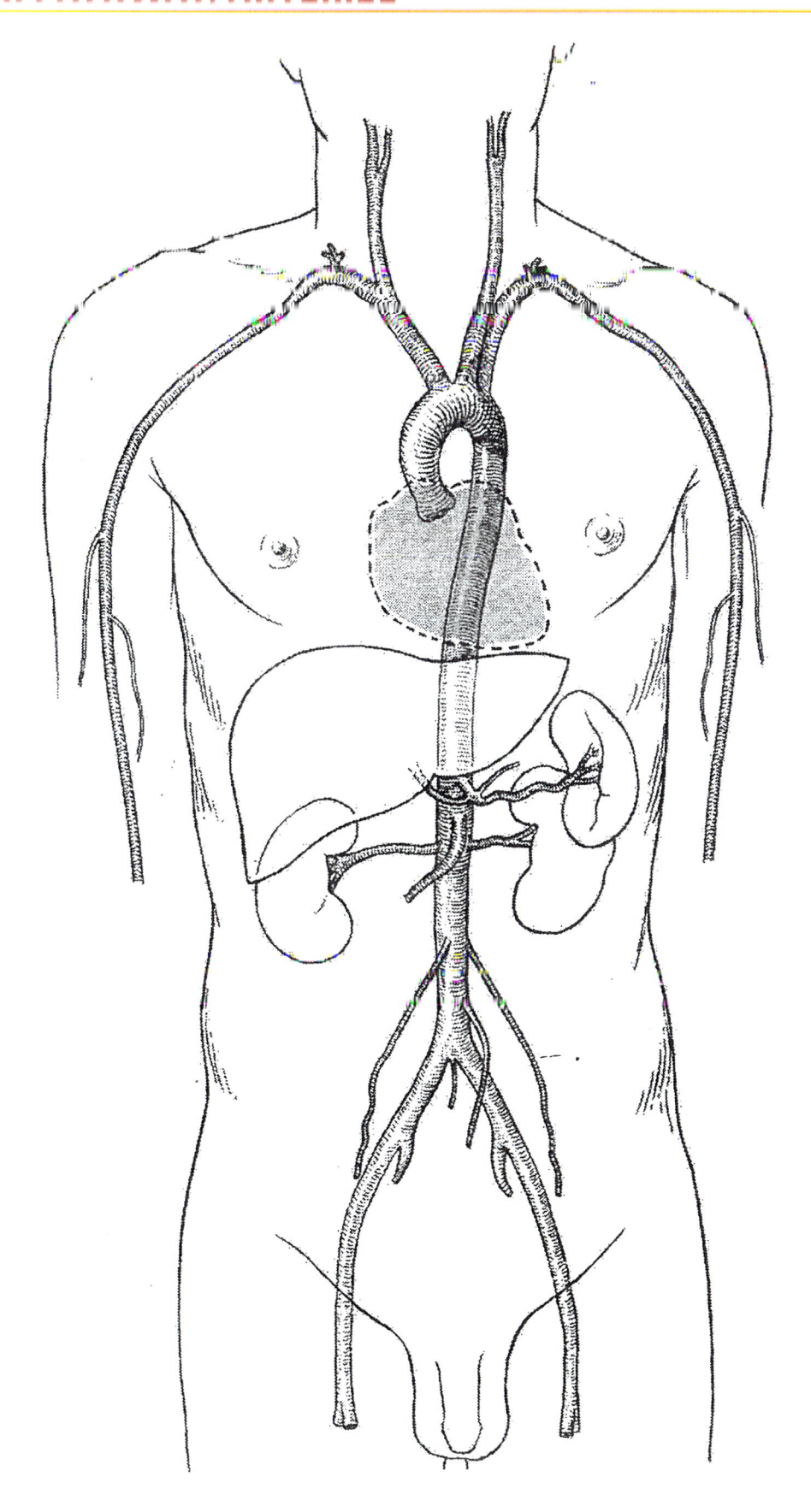

67

LIVER PATHWAY, HEPATIC (PORTAL) SYSTEM

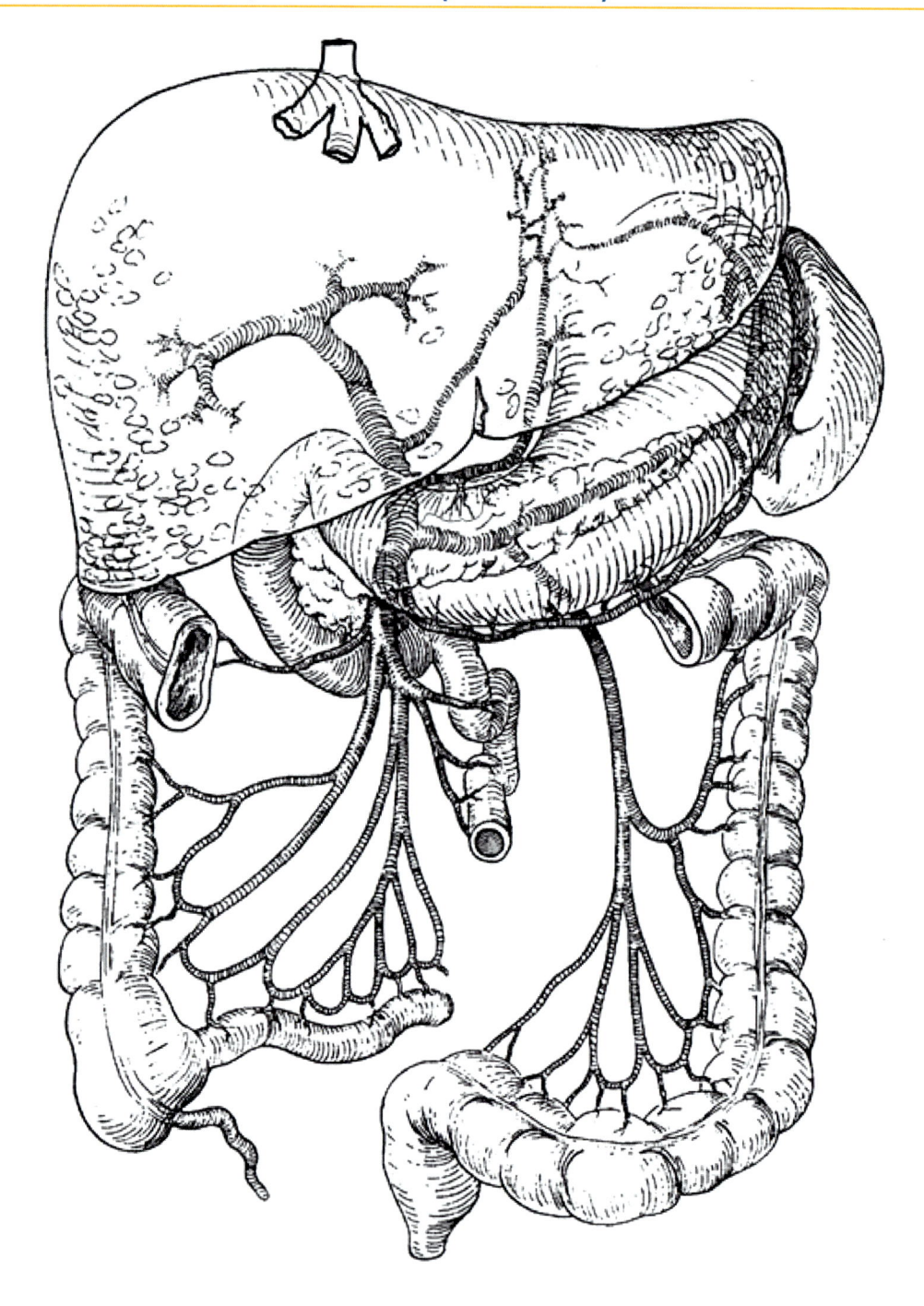

LIVER PATHWAY, VEINS

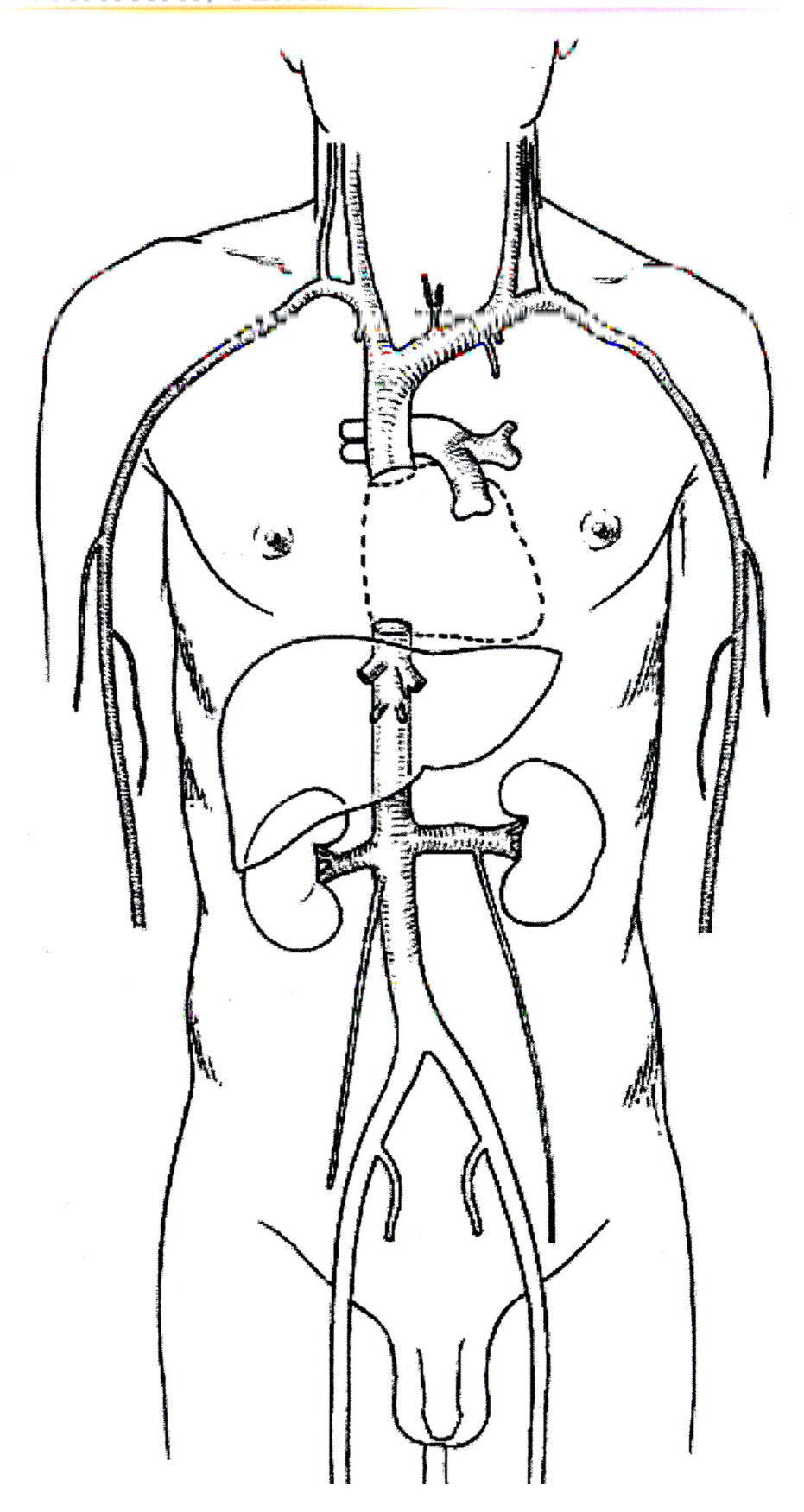

PART 2: ORGANS AND CIRCULATORY SYSTEM

SPLEEN PATHWAY, ARTERIES

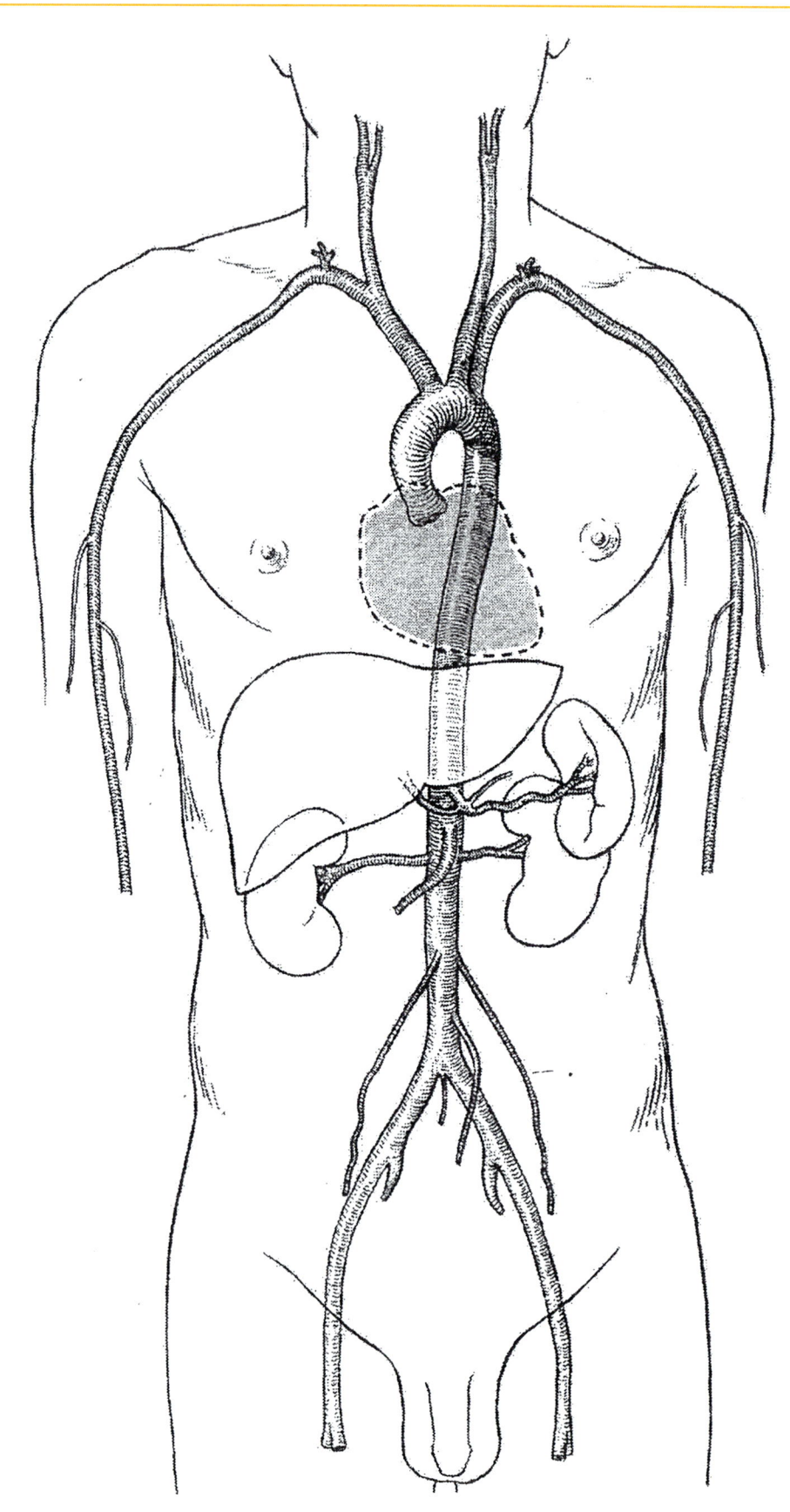

70

PART 2: ORGANS AND CIRCULATORY SYSTEM

SPLEEN PATHWAY, HEPATIC (PORTAL) SYSTEM

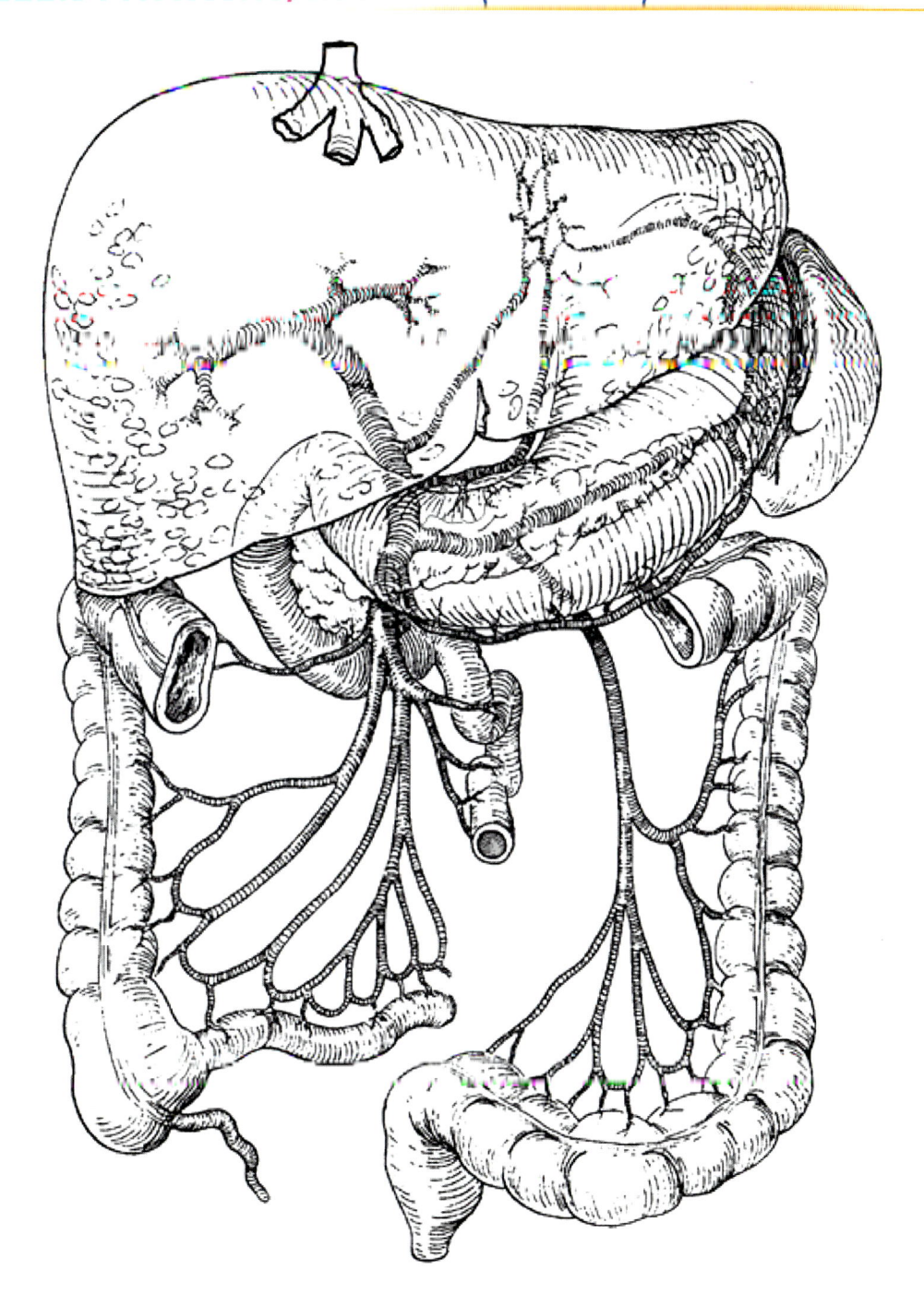

71

SPLEEN PATHWAY, VEINS

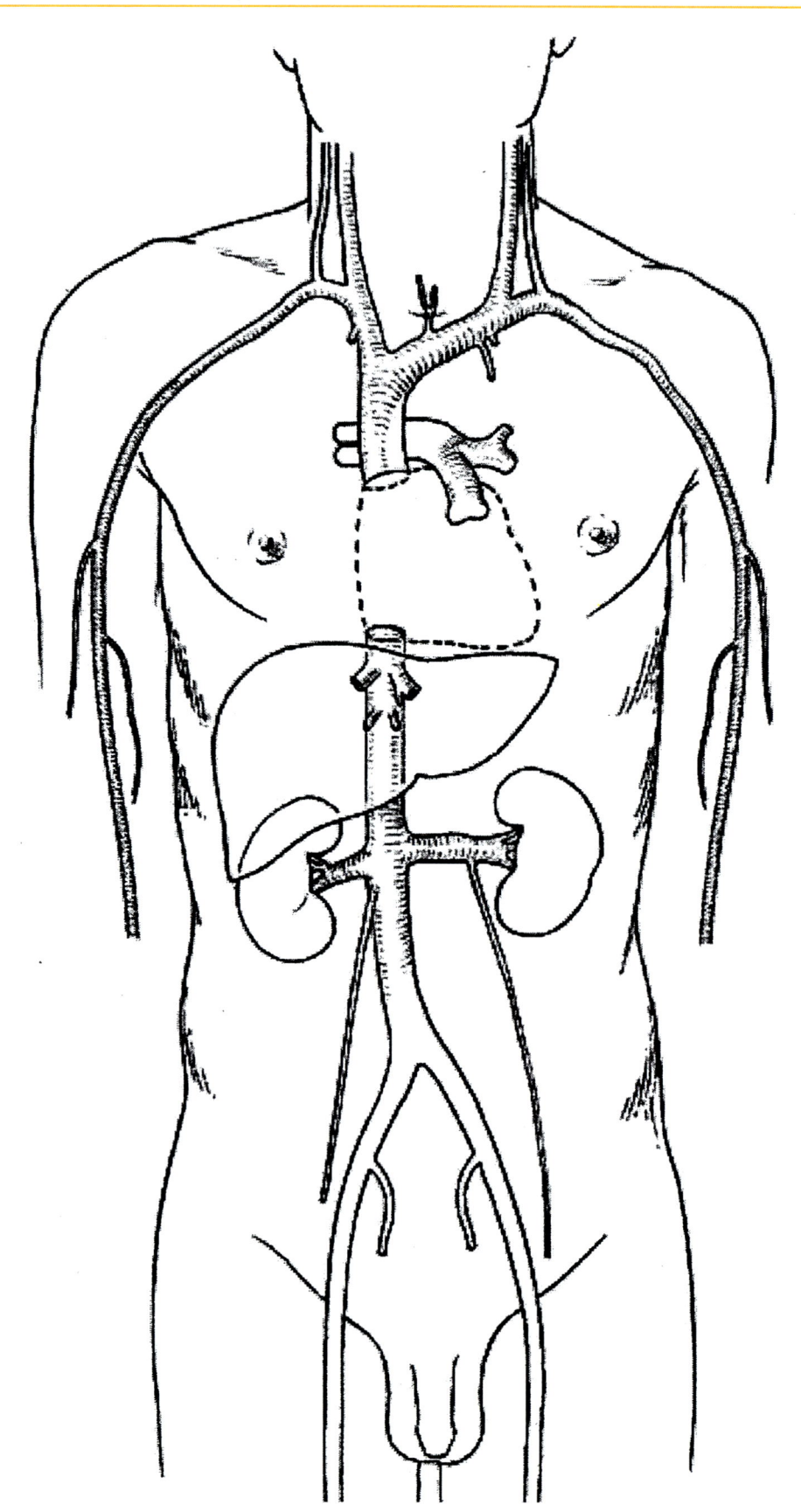

PANCREAS PATHWAY, ARTERIES

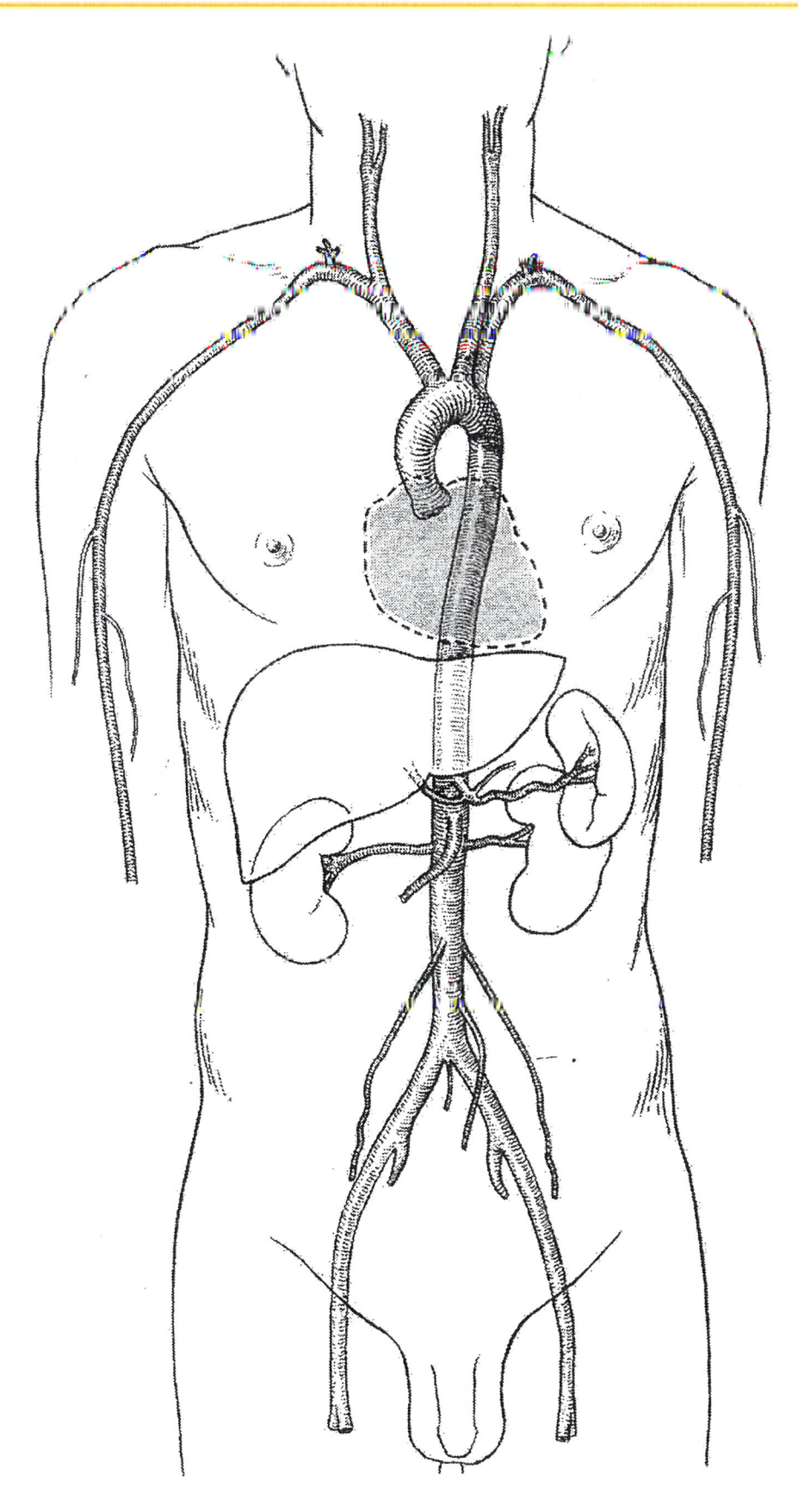

PART 2: ORGANS AND CIRCULATORY SYSTEM

PANCREAS PATHWAY, HEPATIC (PORTAL) SYSTEM

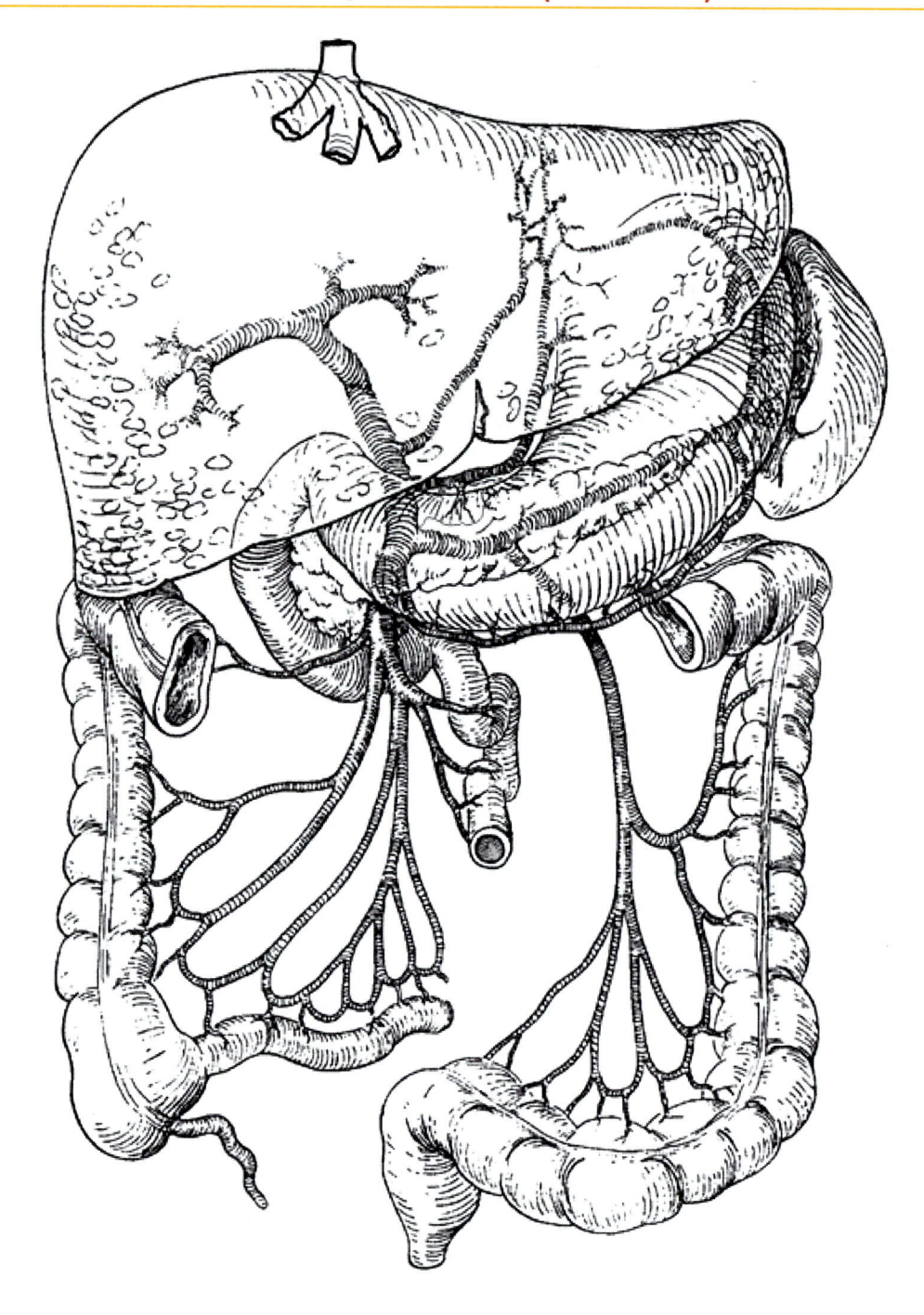

PART 2: ORGANS AND CIRCULATORY SYSTEM

PANCREAS PATHWAY, VEINS

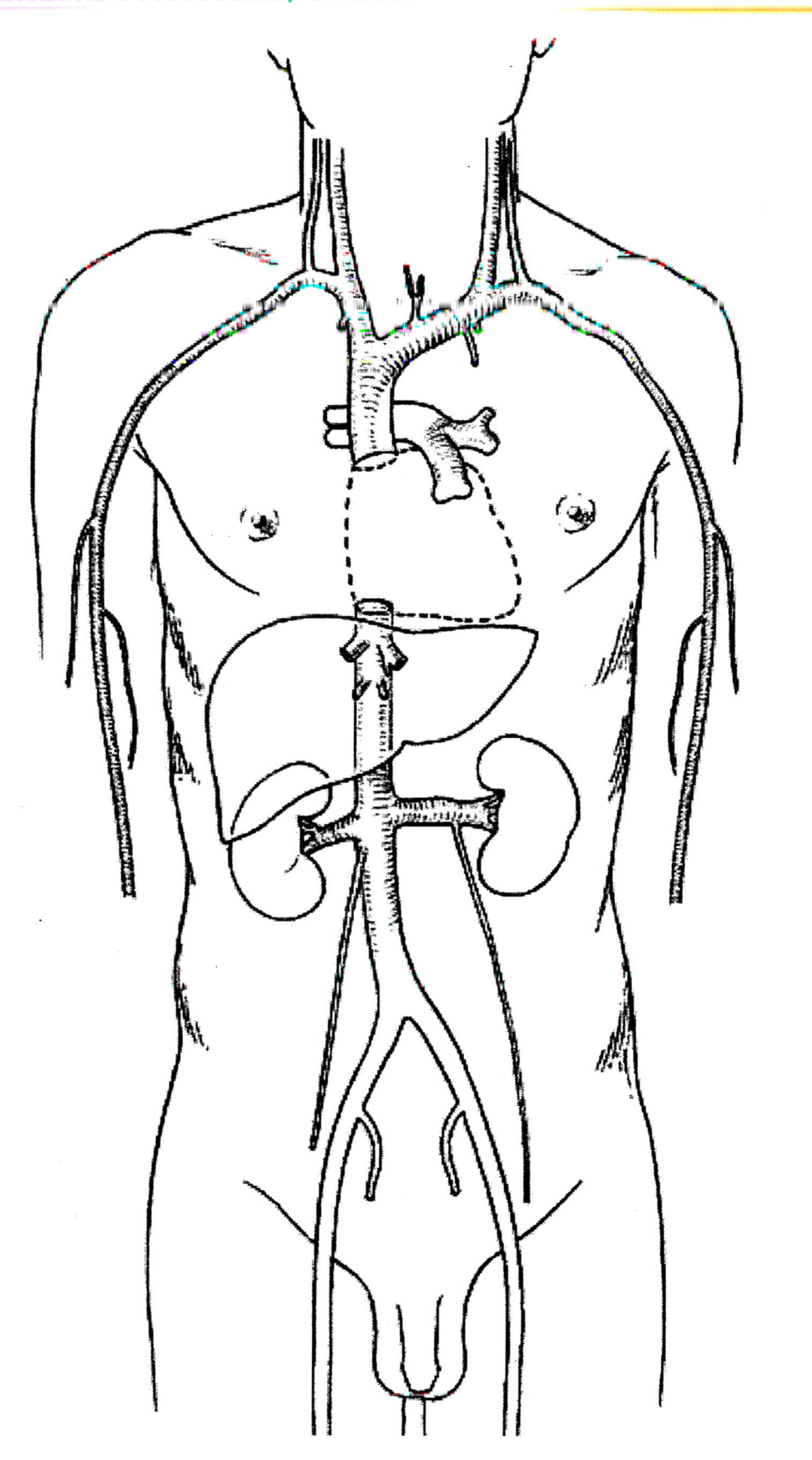

75

PART 2: ORGANS AND CIRCULATORY SYSTEM

STOMACH PATHWAY, ARTERIES

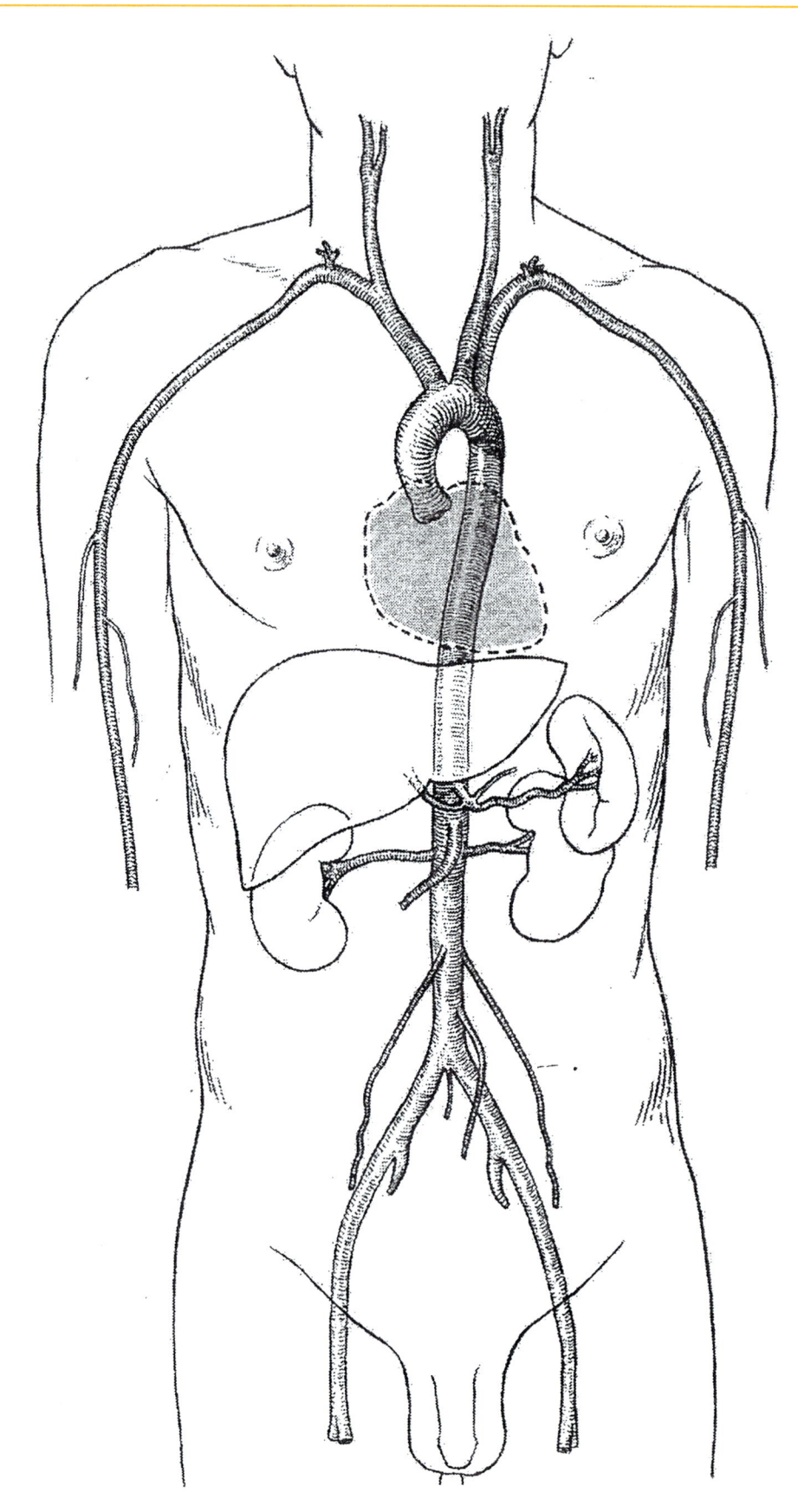

76

STOMACH PATHWAY, HEPATIC (PORTAL) SYSTEM

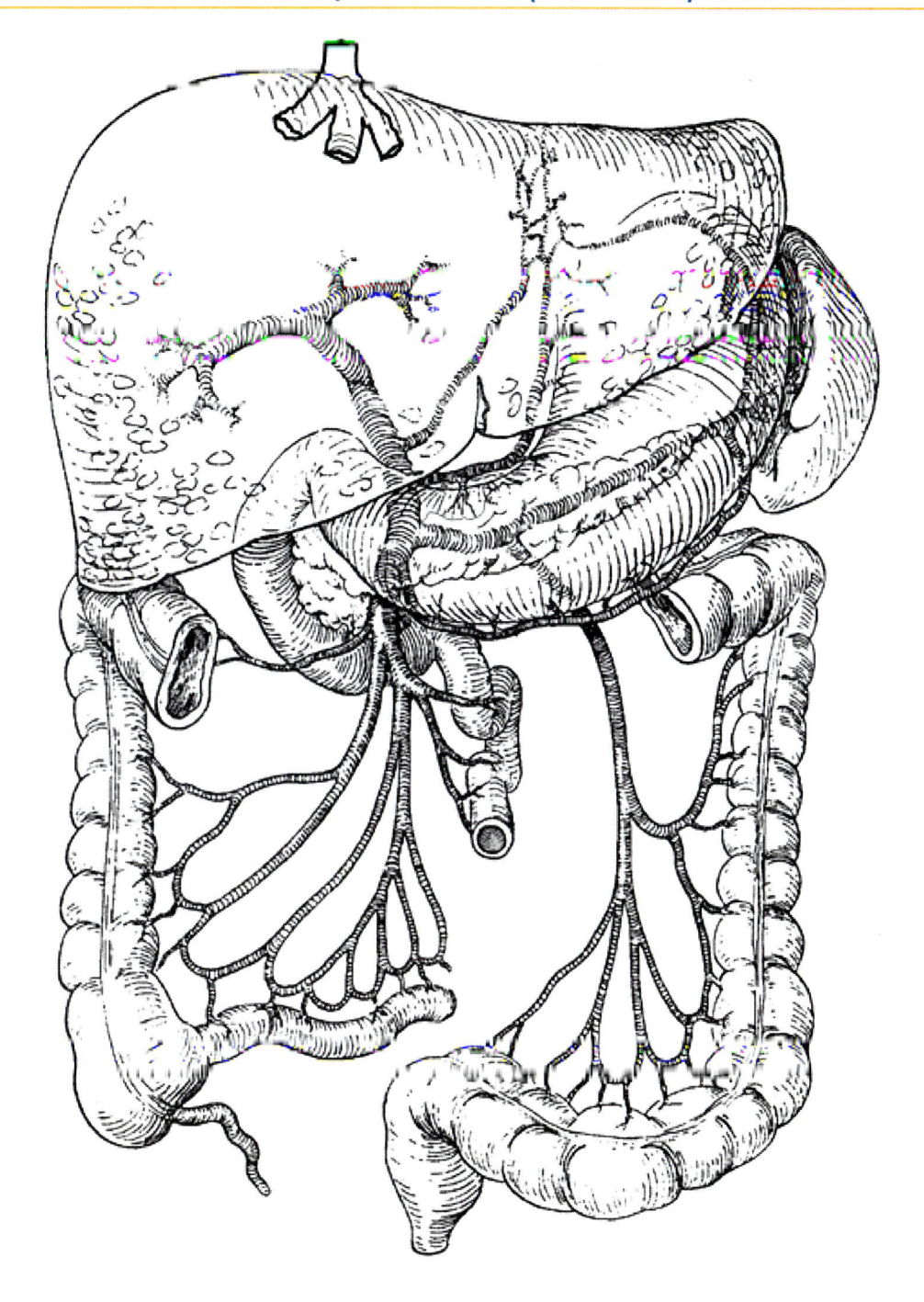

PART 2: ORGANS AND CIRCULATORY SYSTEM

STOMACH PATHWAY, VEINS

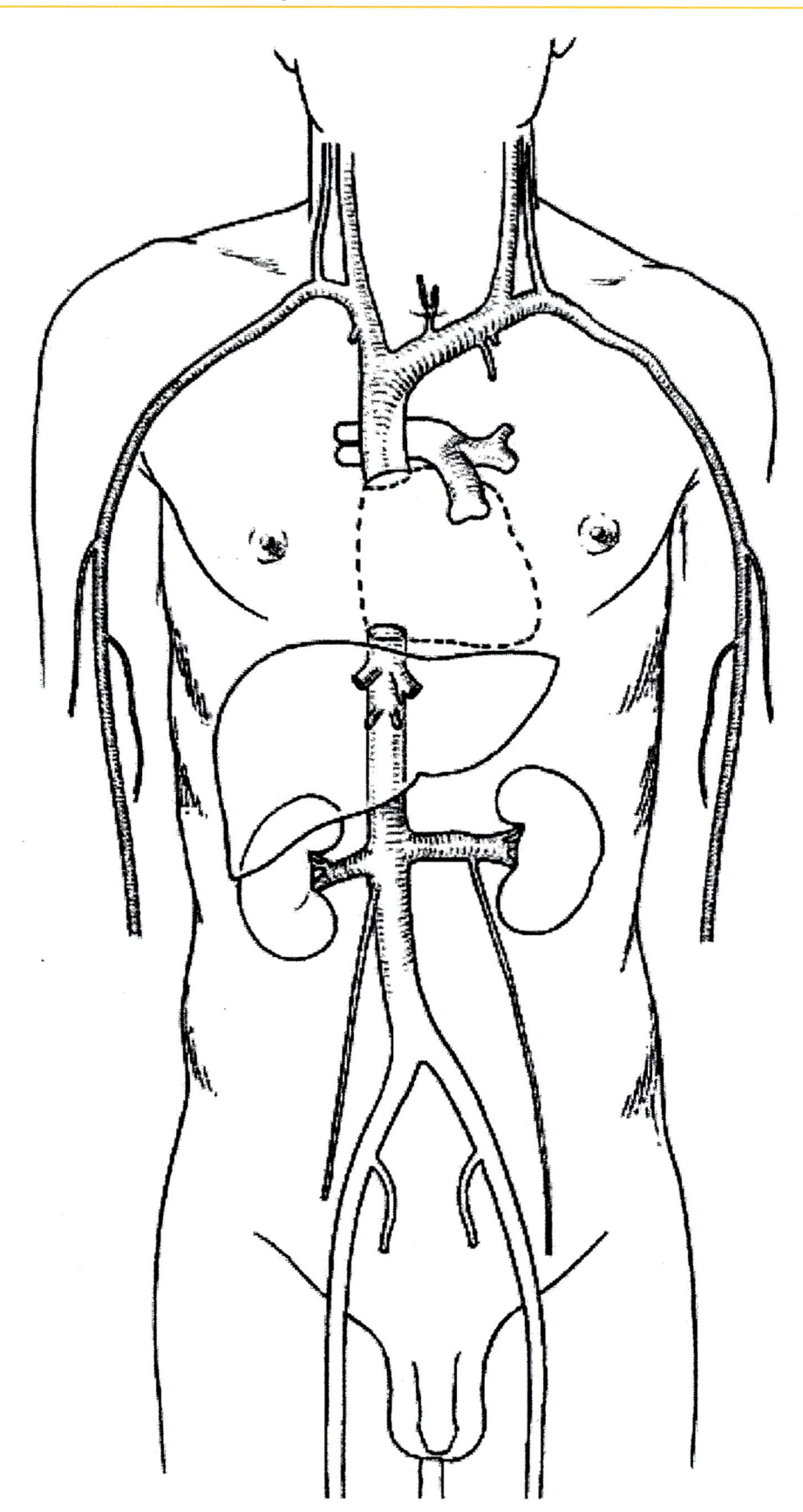

78

PART 2: ORGANS AND CIRCULATORY SYSTEM

UPPER INTESTINE PATHWAY, ARTERIES

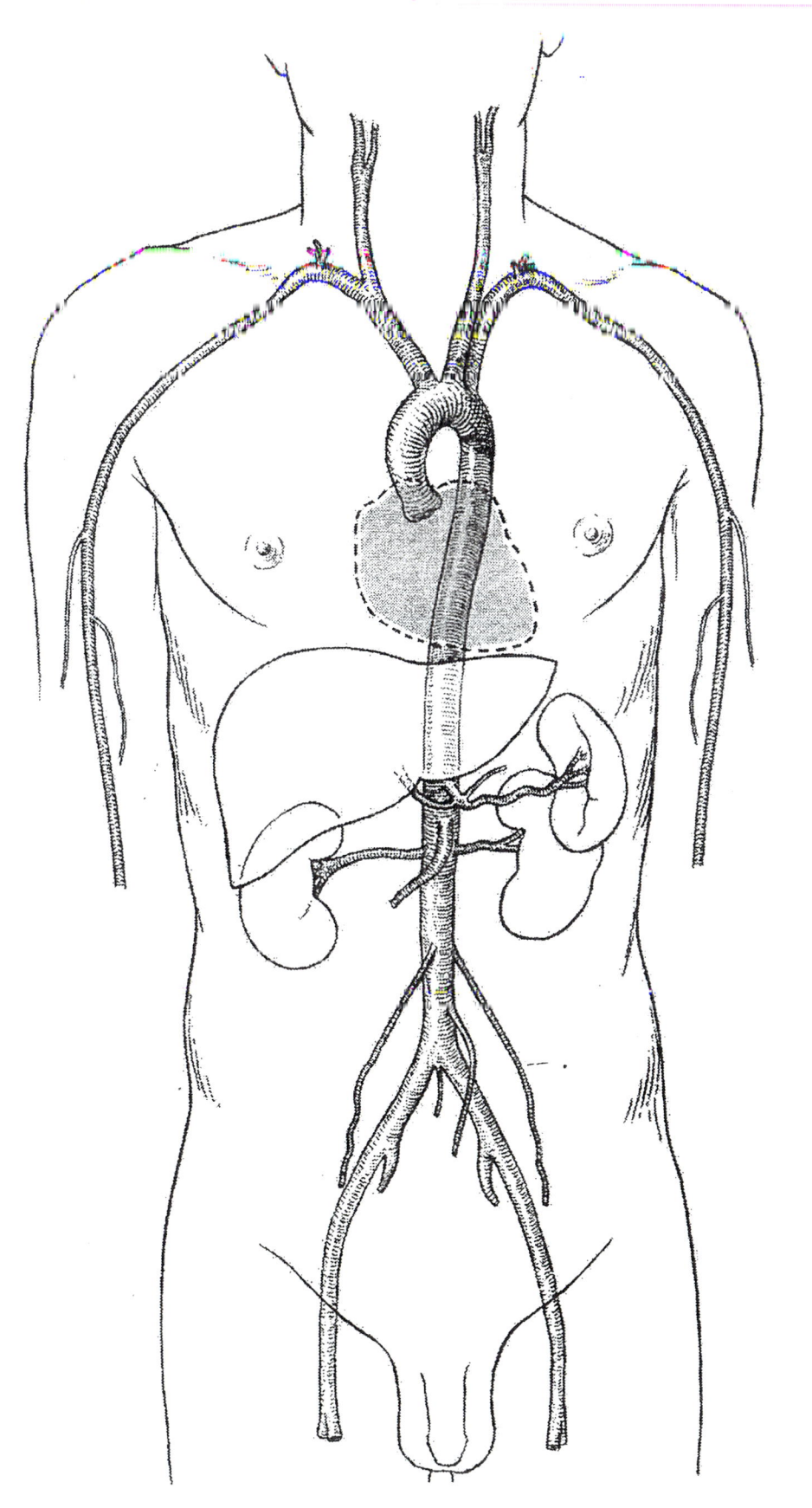

79

UPPER INTESTINE PATHWAY, HEPATIC (PORTAL) SYSTEM

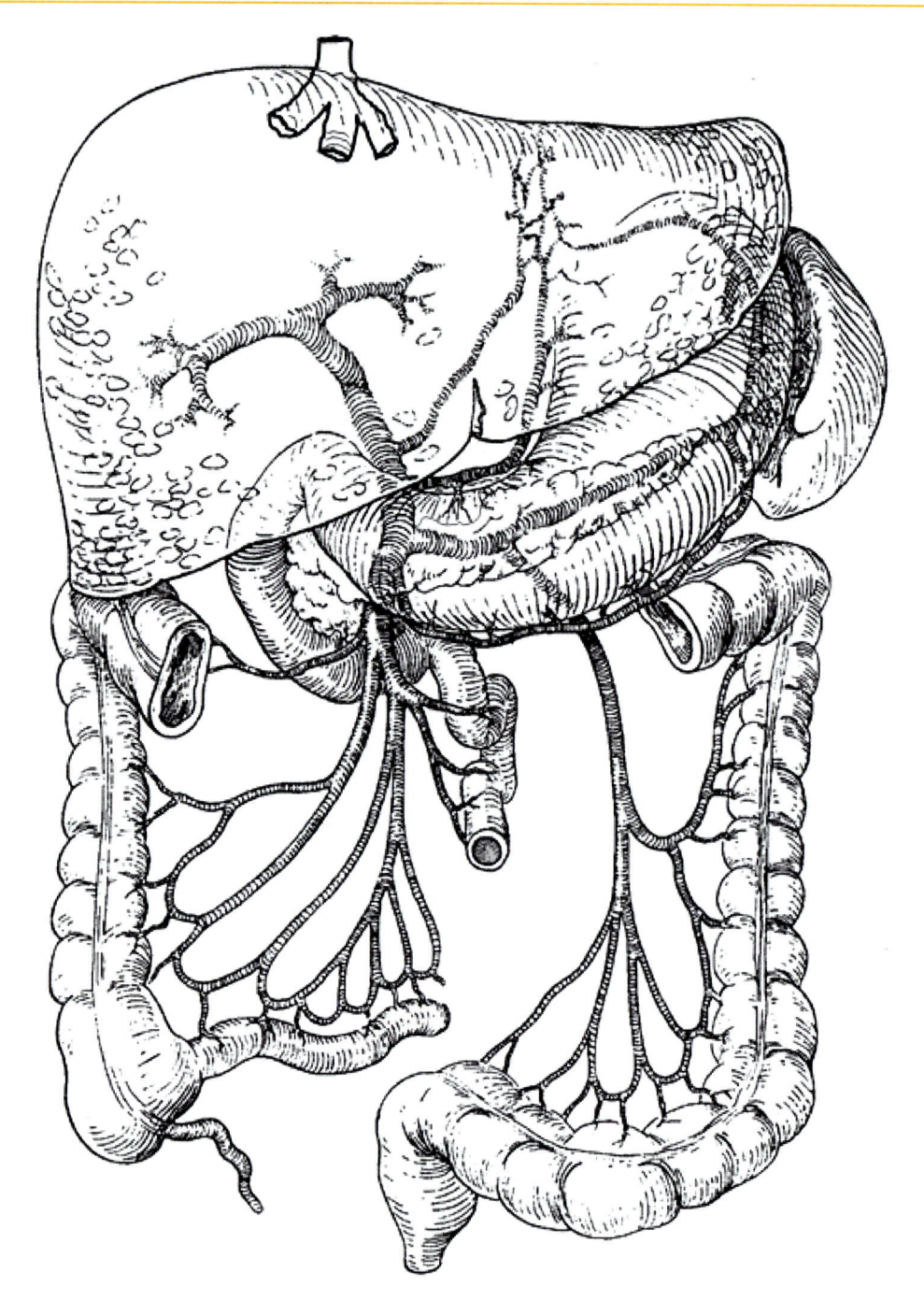

UPPER INTESTINE PATHWAY, VEINS

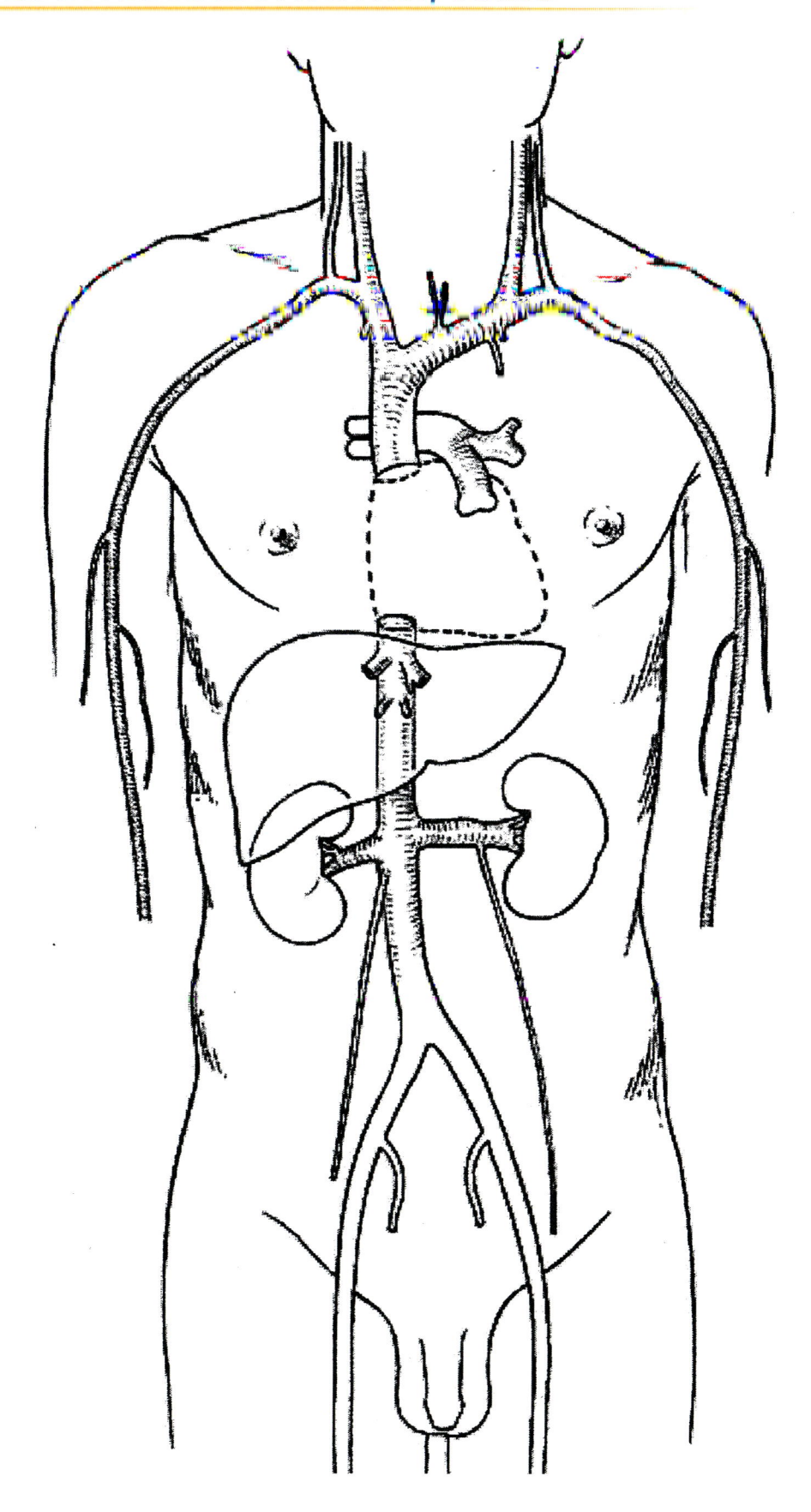

PART 2: ORGANS AND CIRCULATORY SYSTEM

LOWER INTESTINE PATHWAY, ARTERIES

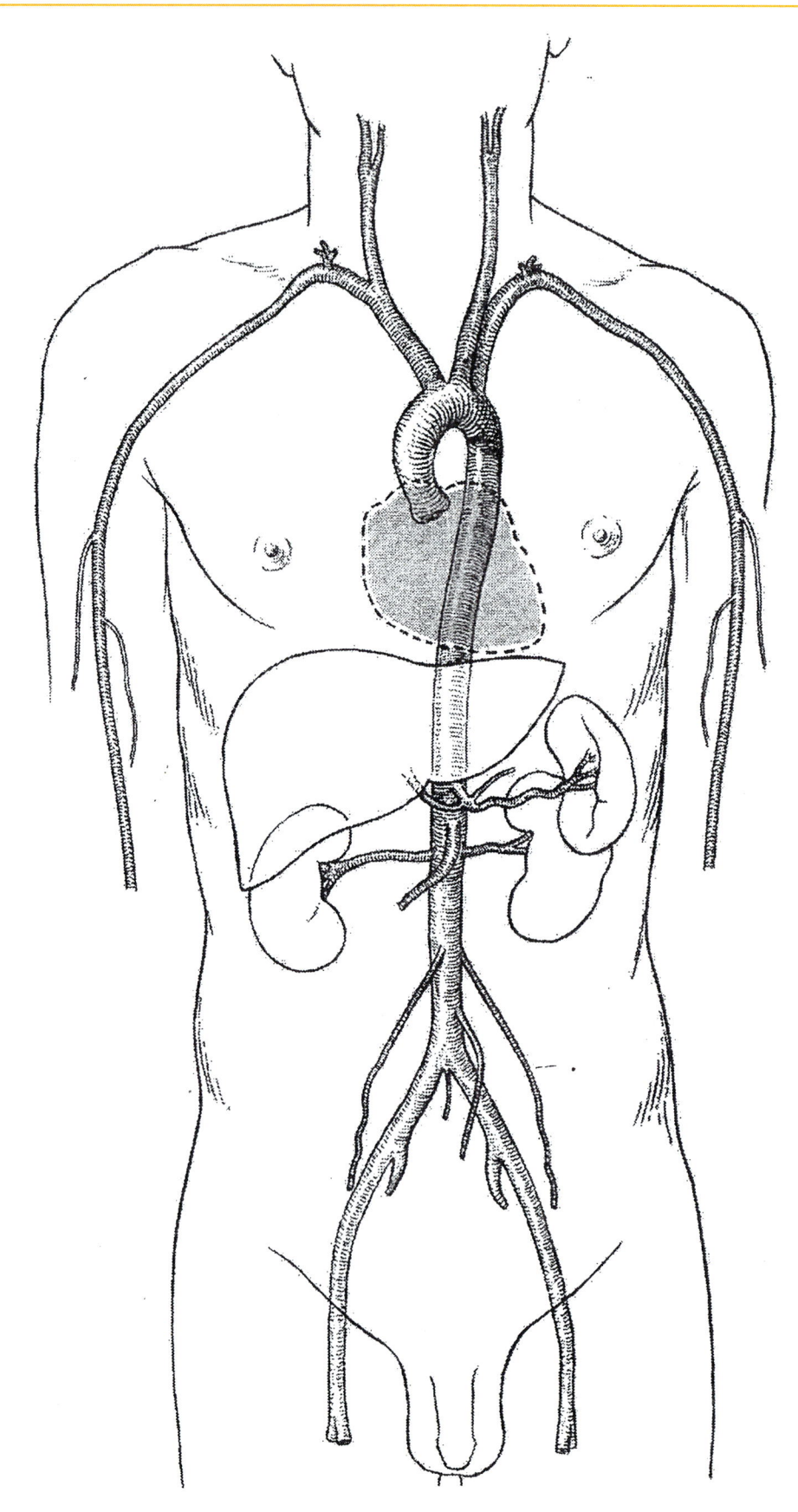

82

LOWER INTESTINE PATHWAY, HEPATIC (PORTAL) SYSTEM

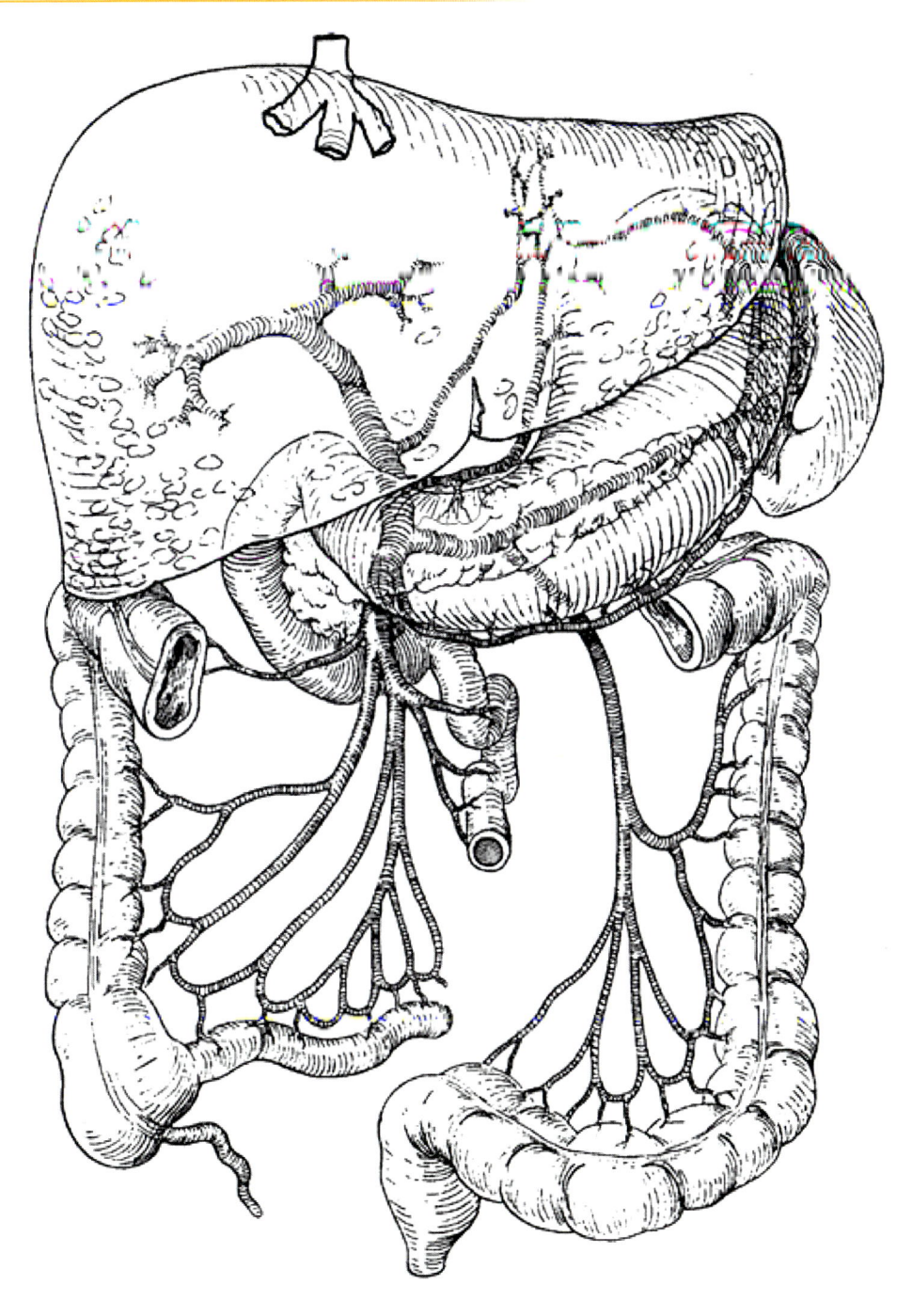

LOWER INTESTINE PATHWAY, VEINS

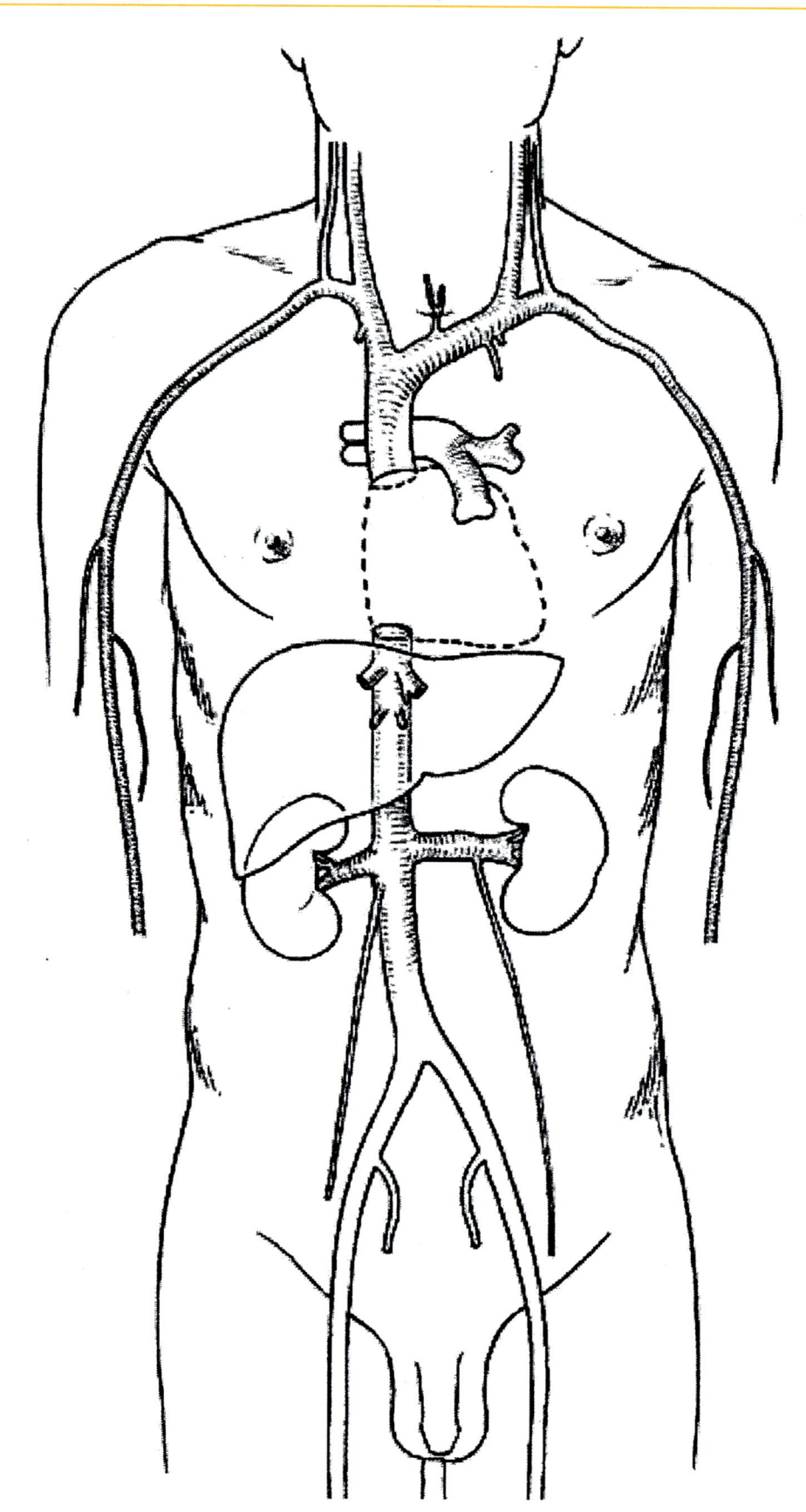

PART 2: ORGANS AND CIRCULATORY SYSTEM

CAT CIRCULATORY SYSTEM VESSELS

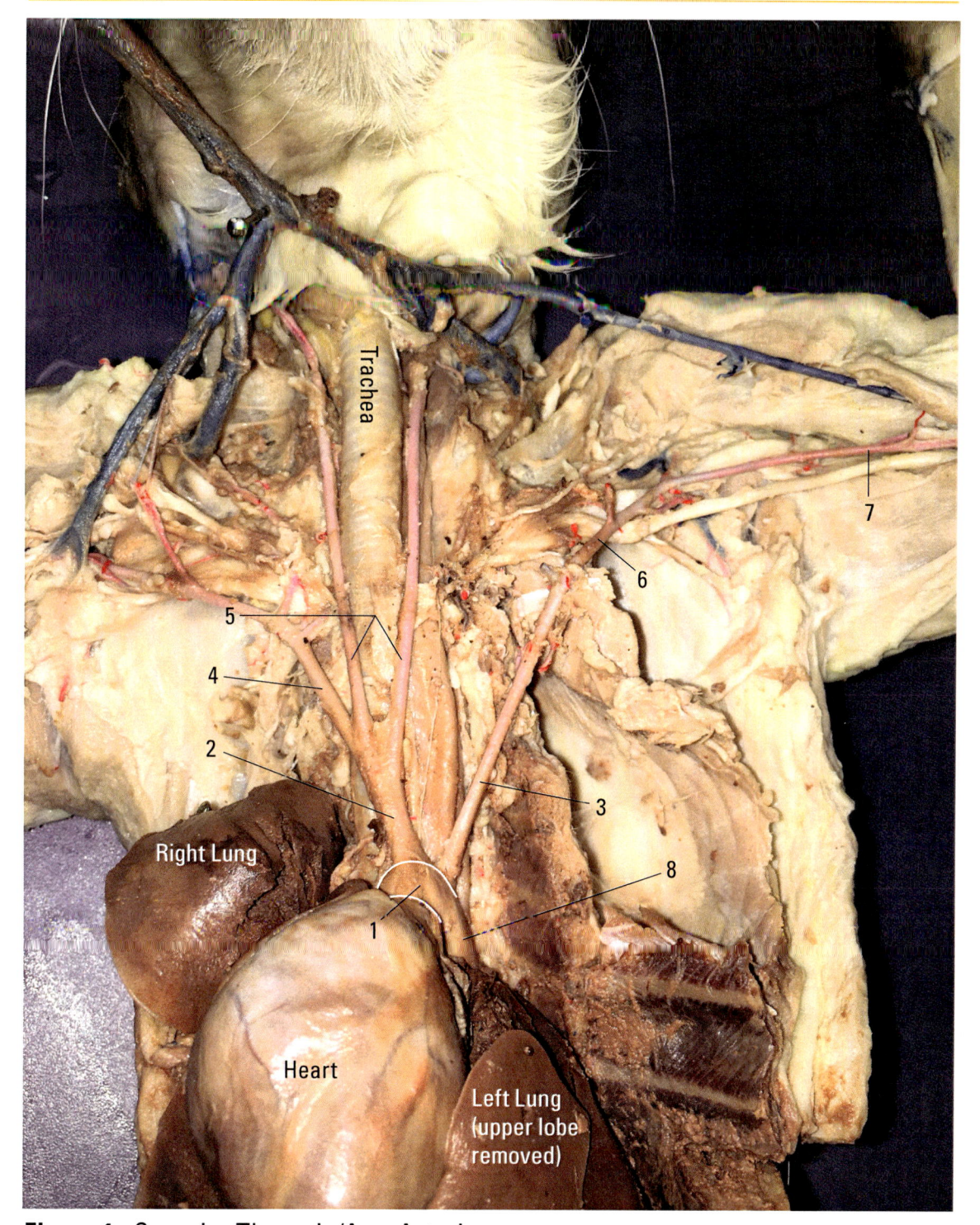

Figure 1. Superior Thoracic/Arm Arteries.

1. Arch of aorta
2. Brachiocephalic artery
3. L Subclavian artery
4. R Subclavian artery
5. R/L Common carotid arteries
6. L Axillary artery
7. L Brachial artery
8. Thoracic aorta

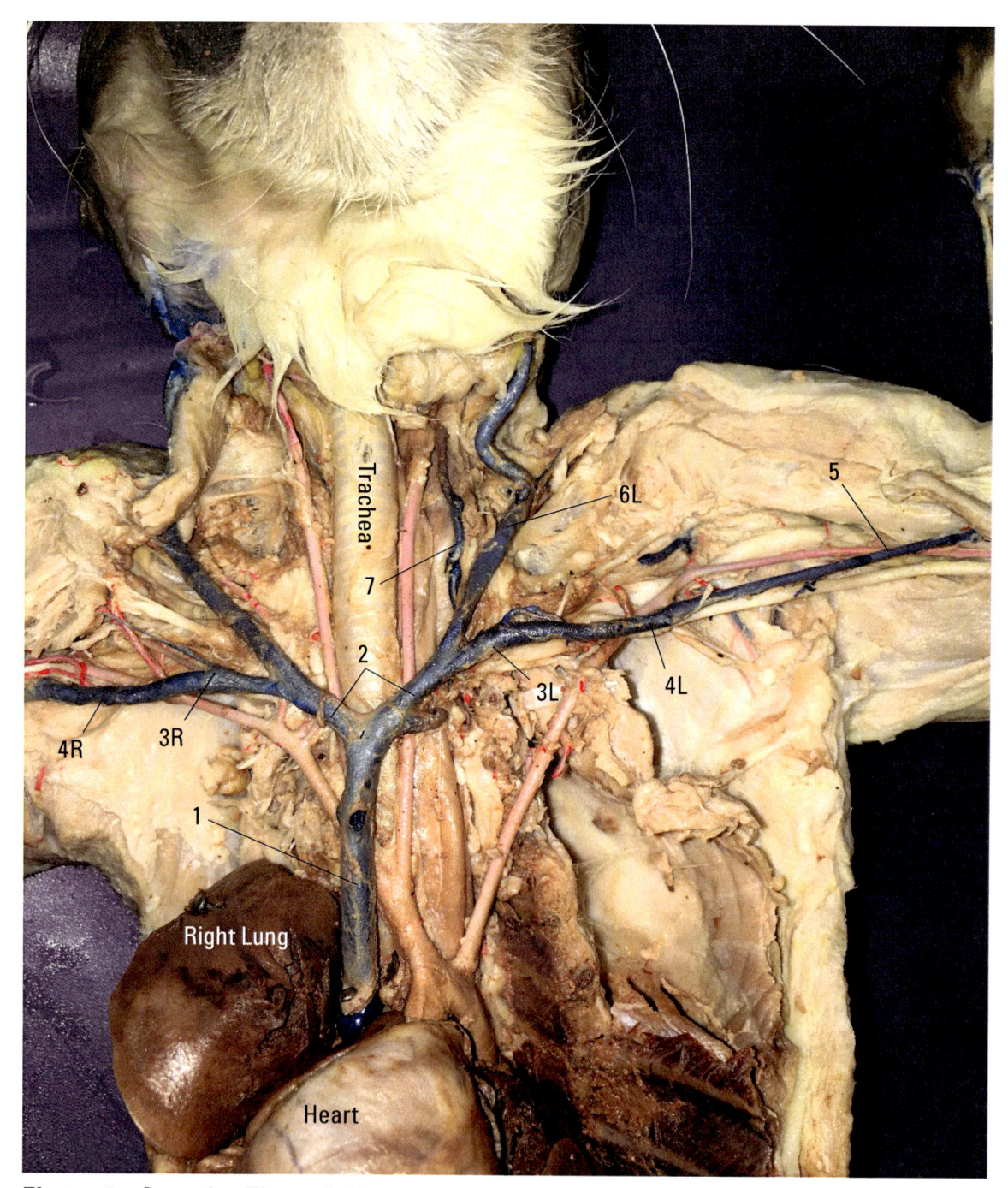

Figure 2. Superior Thoracic/Arm Veins.

1. Superior vena cava
2. R/L Brachiocephalic veins
3. R/L Subclavian veins
4. R/L Axillary vein
5. L Brachial vein
6. L External jugular vein
7. L Internal jugular vein

PART 2: ORGANS AND CIRCULATORY SYSTEM

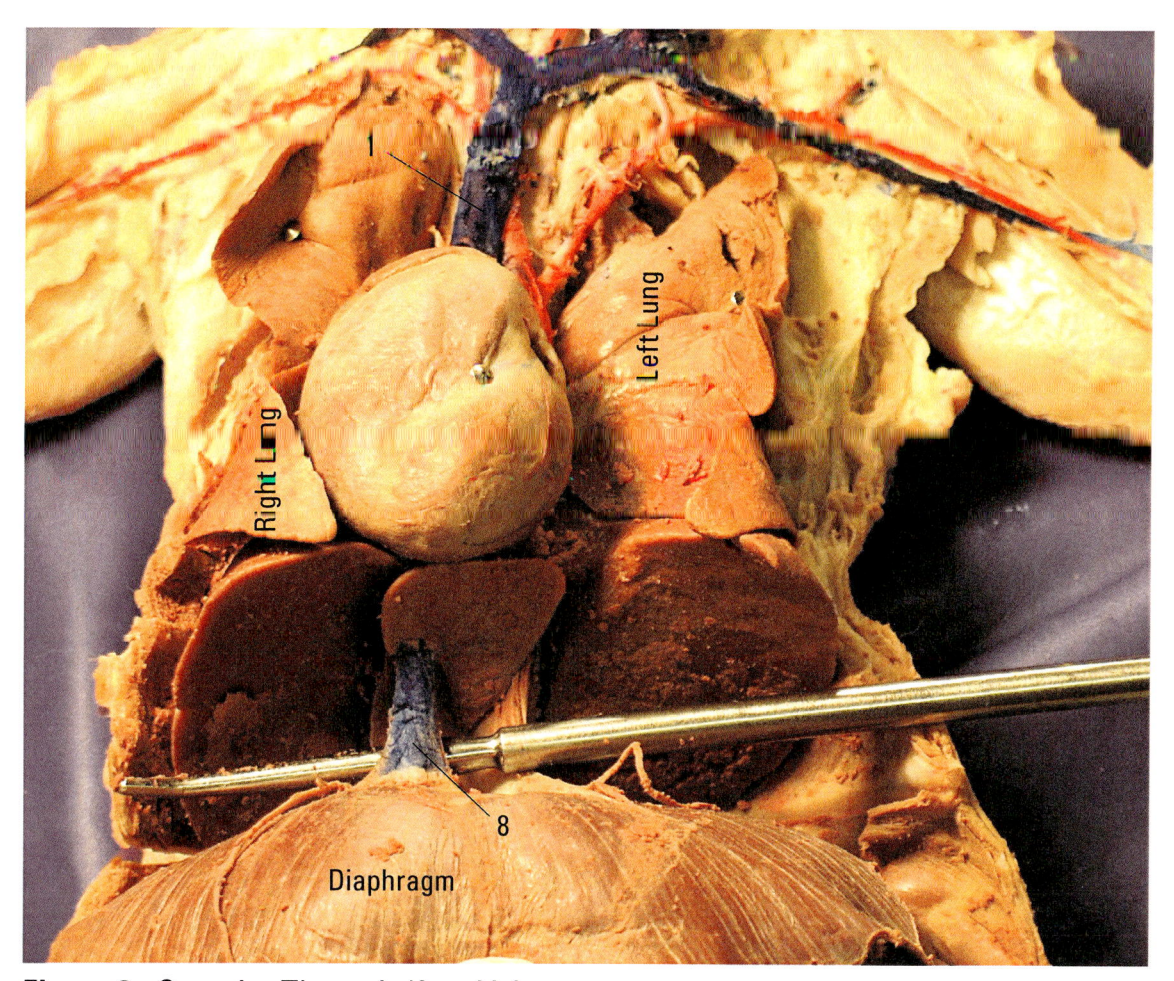

Figure 3. Superior Thoracic/Arm Veins.

1. Superior vena cava

8. Inferior vena cava

PART 2: ORGANS AND CIRCULATORY SYSTEM

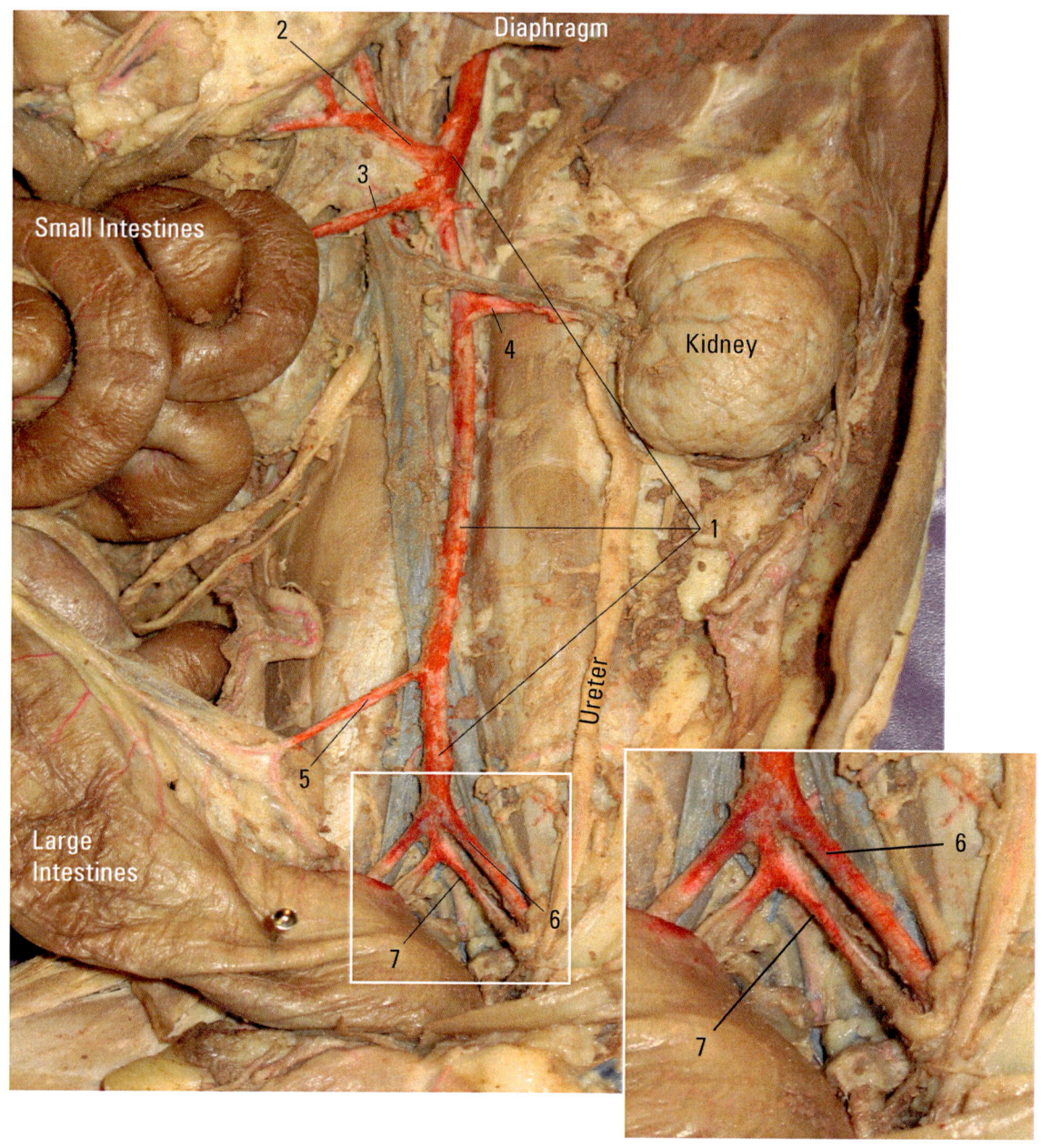

Figure 4. Inferior Abdominal Arteries.

1. Abdominal aorta
2. Celiac trunk (artery)
3. Superior mesenteric artery
4. Renal artery
5. Inferior mesenteric artery
6. External iliac artery
7. Internal iliac artery

PART 2: ORGANS AND CIRCULATORY SYSTEM

Retraction of the lungs exposes the thoracic and abdominal aorta in the photo to the right. An enlarged and labeled view of the celiac trunk, abdominal aorta, and their respective branches is shown below.

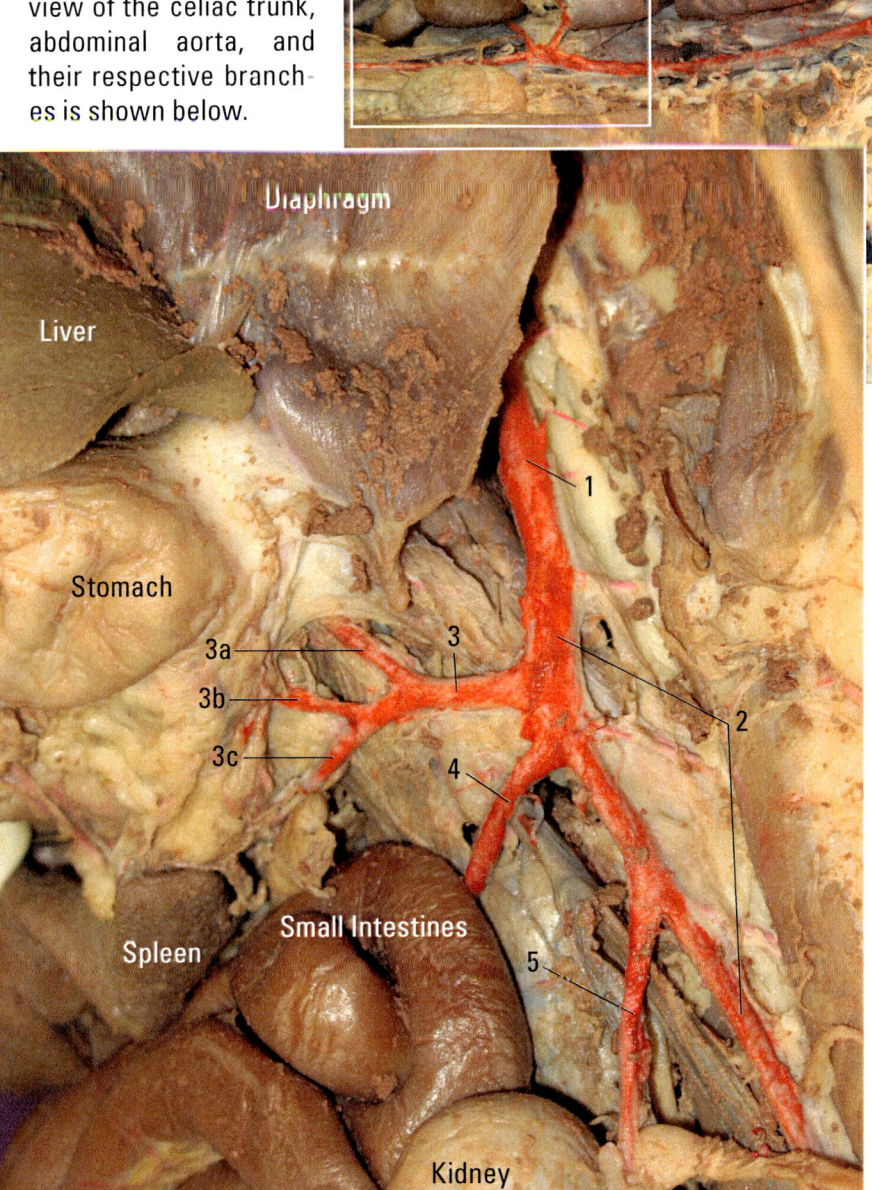

Figure 5. Inferior Abdominal Arteries: Celiac Trunk.

1. Thoracic aorta (Superior)
2. Abdominal aorta
3. Celiac trunk (artery)
    a. Hepatic artery
    b. Left gastric artery
    c. Splenic artery
4. Superior mesenteric artery
5. Renal artery

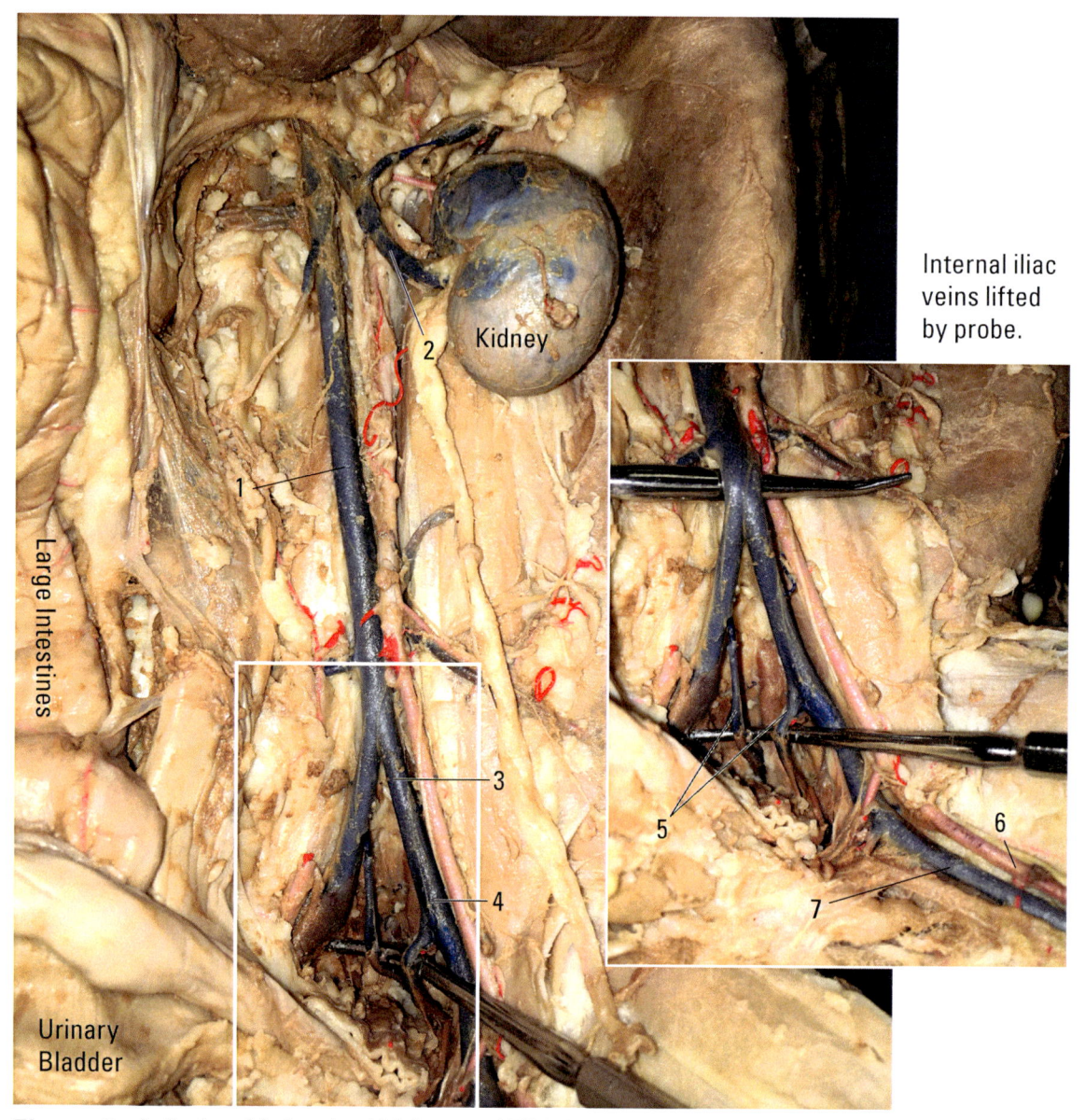

Figure 6. Inferior Abdominal Veins and Thigh Vessels.

Internal iliac veins lifted by probe.

INFERIOR ABDOMINAL VEINS
1. Inferior vena cava
2. Renal vein
3. Common iliac vein
4. External iliac vein
5. Internal iliac vein

THIGH VESSELS
6. Femoral artery
7. Femoral vein

PART 3
NERVOUS SYSTEM

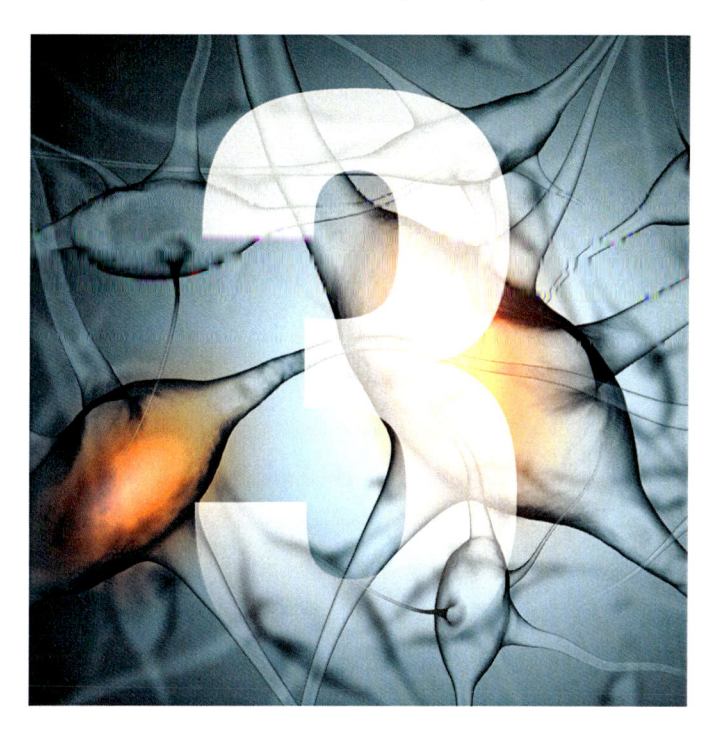

CENTRAL NERVOUS SYSTEM—THE BRAIN

EXERCISE

In this laboratory activity, you will identify and label structures on human brain diagrams and on a sheep brain specimen.

PART 1

Label each of the following diagrams of the **human brain.** Use the labeled diagrams to locate the structures on models of the human brain.

PART 2

Using two **sheep brain** specimens; one intact specimen, another sectioned sagittally, and referring to the diagrams in this module, identify the following structures.

- Abducens nerves
- Auditory nerves
- Cerebellum
- Cerebrum
- Corpus callosum
- Facial nerves
- Fourth ventricle
- Frontal lobe
- Gyri
- Lateral ventricle
- Longitudinal fissure
- Mammillary body
- Massa intermedia
- Medulla oblongata

- Midbrain
- Occipital lobe
- Oculomotor nerves
- Olfactory nerves
- Optic chiasma
- Optic nerves
- Parietal lobe
- Pineal gland
- Pons
- Spinal cord
- Sulci
- Third ventricle
- Trigeminal nerves

PART 3: NERVOUS SYSTEM

HUMAN BRAIN

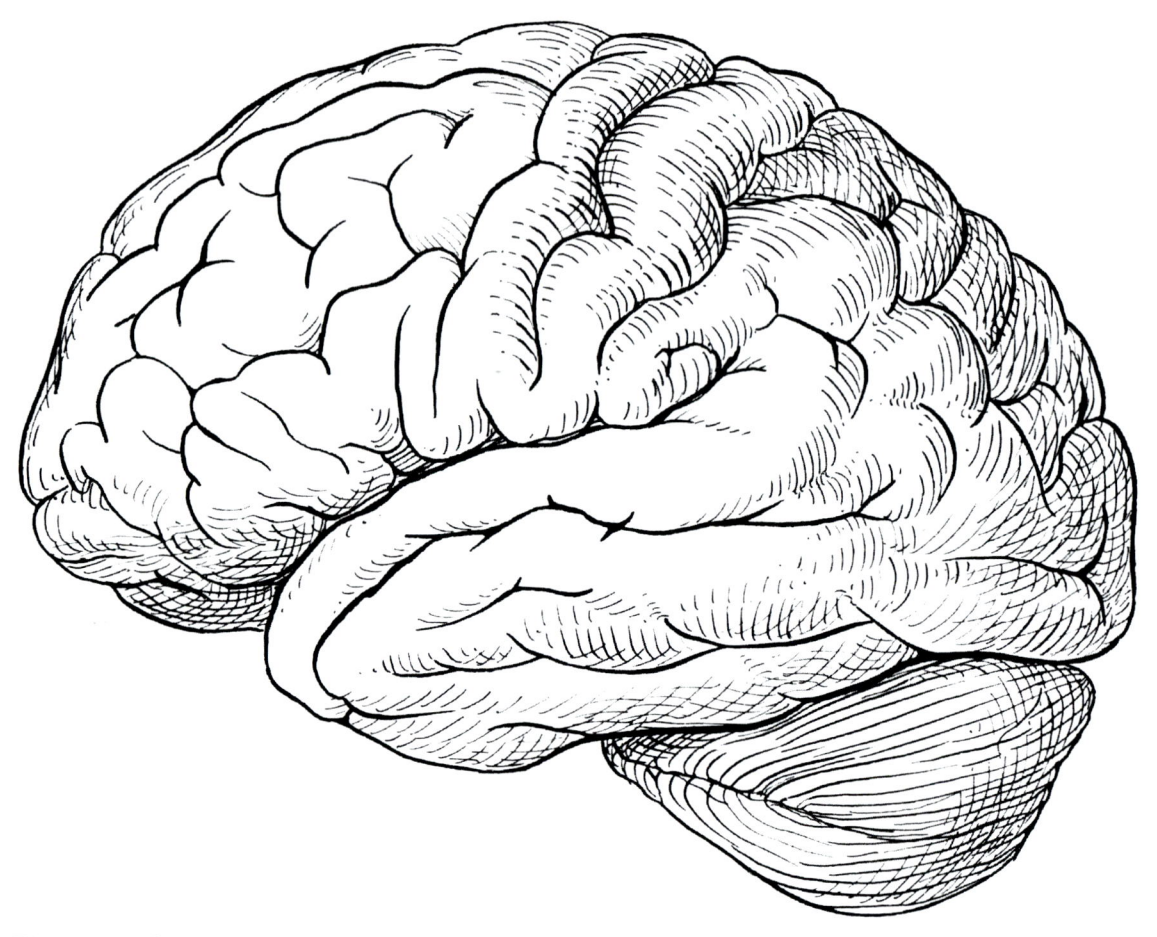

Figure 1. Cerebrum—External, Lateral, Left.

Locate the following structures:

- Cerebellum
- Central sulcus
- Frontal lobe
- Lateral sulcus
- Parietal lobe
- Parieto-occipital sulcus
- Occipital lobe
- Precentral gyrus
- Postcentral gyrus
- Temporal lobe
- Transverse fissure

HUMAN BRAIN

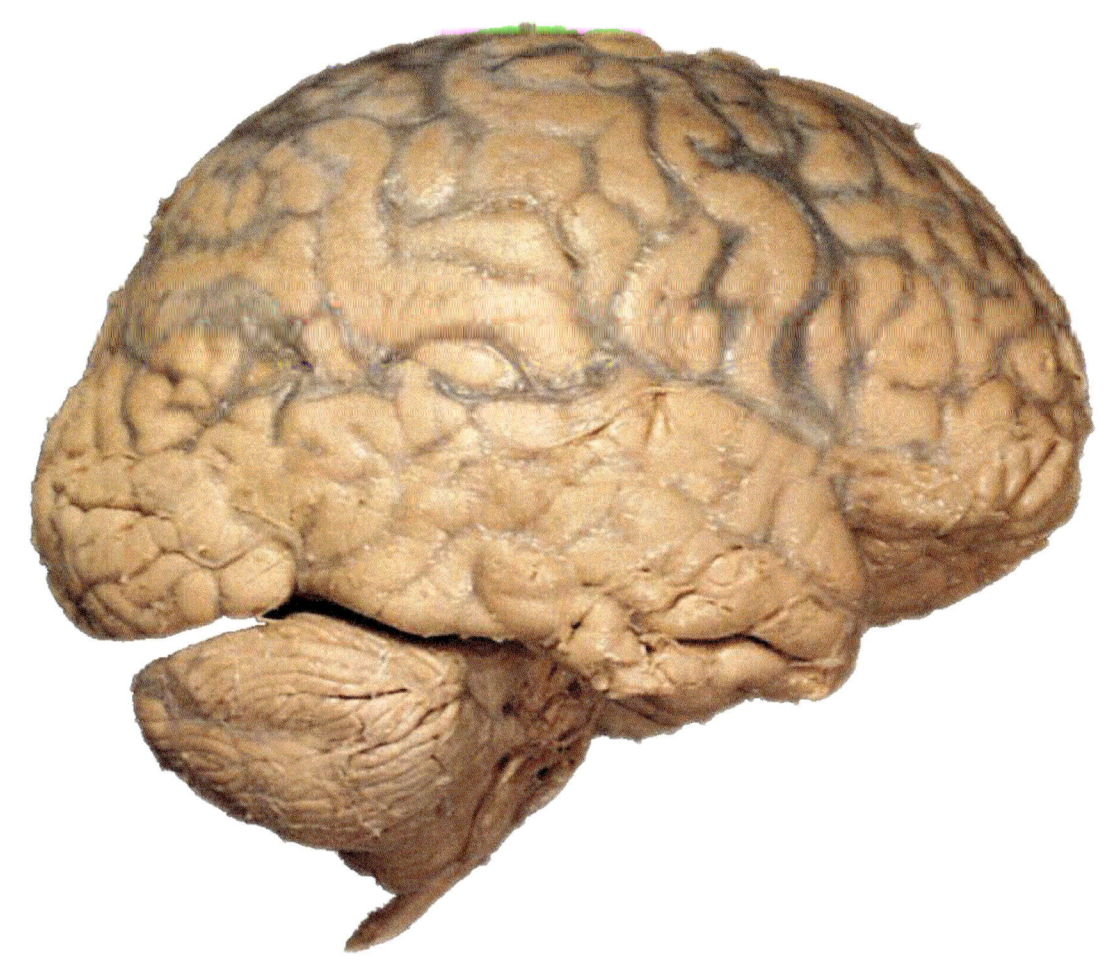

Figure 2. Cerebrum—External, Lateral, Right.

PART 3: NERVOUS SYSTEM

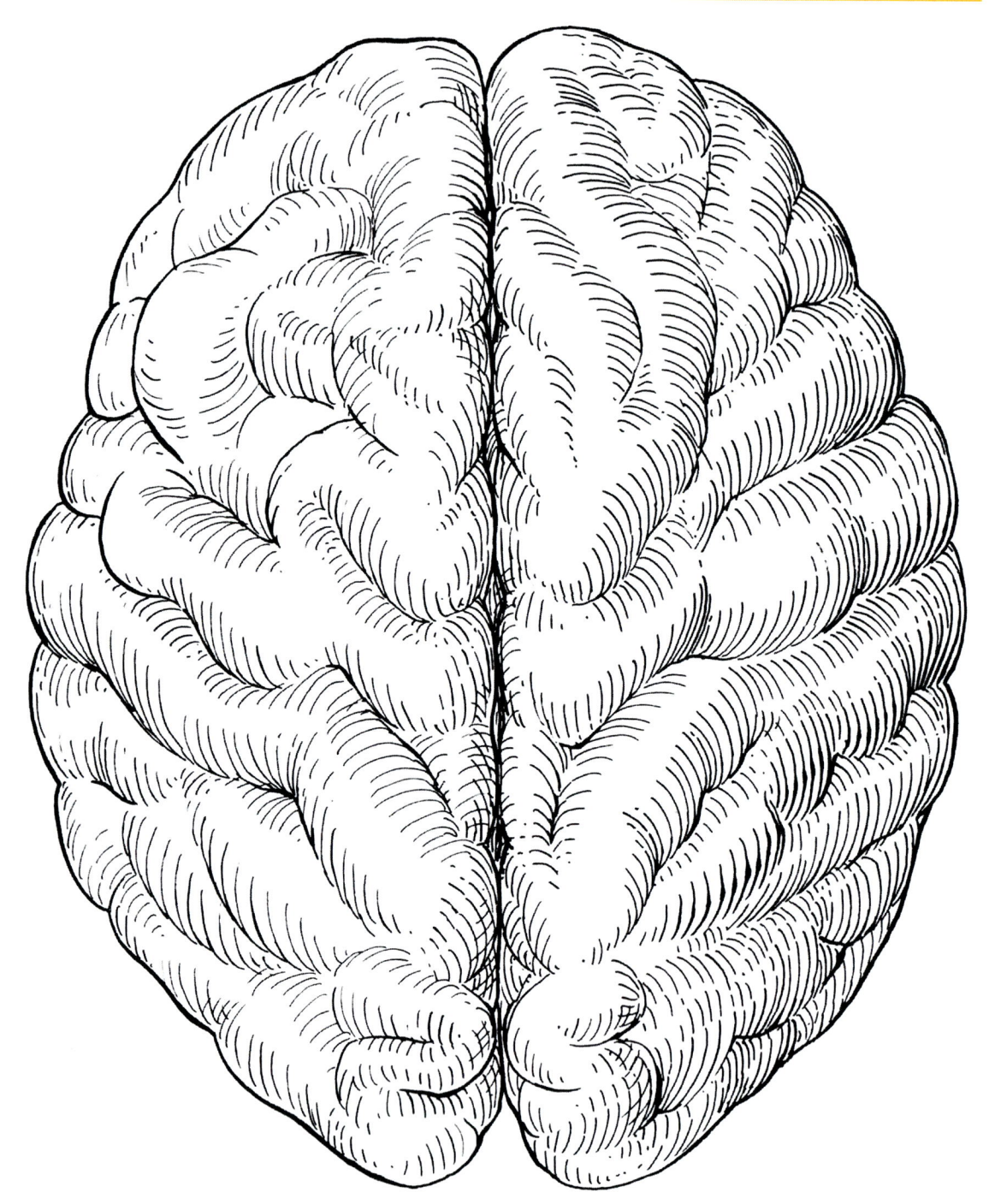

HUMAN BRAIN

Figure 3. Cerebrum—External, Superior.

Locate the following structures:
- Central sulcus
- Frontal lobe
- Longitudinal fissure
- Occipital lobe
- Parietal lobe
- Precentral gyrus
- Postcentral gyrus

HUMAN BRAIN

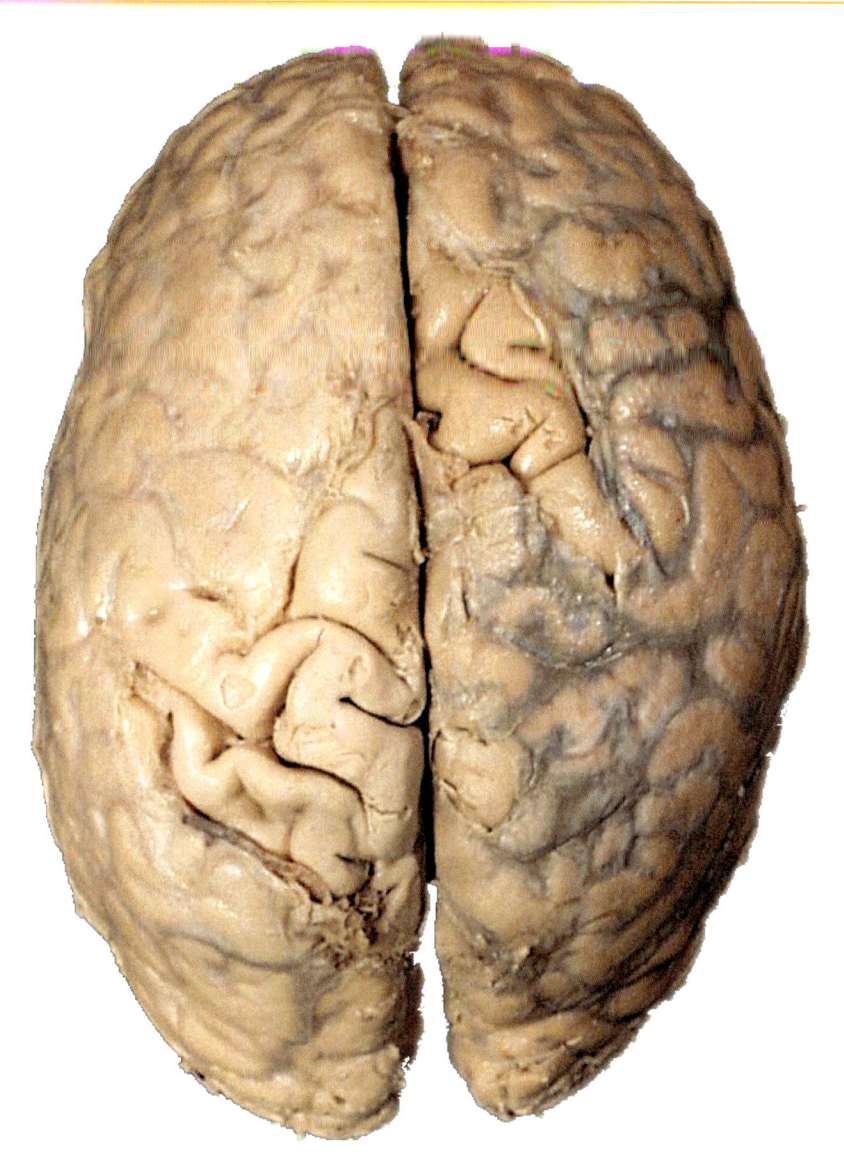

Figure 4. Cerebrum—External, Superior.

PART 3: NERVOUS SYSTEM

HUMAN BRAIN

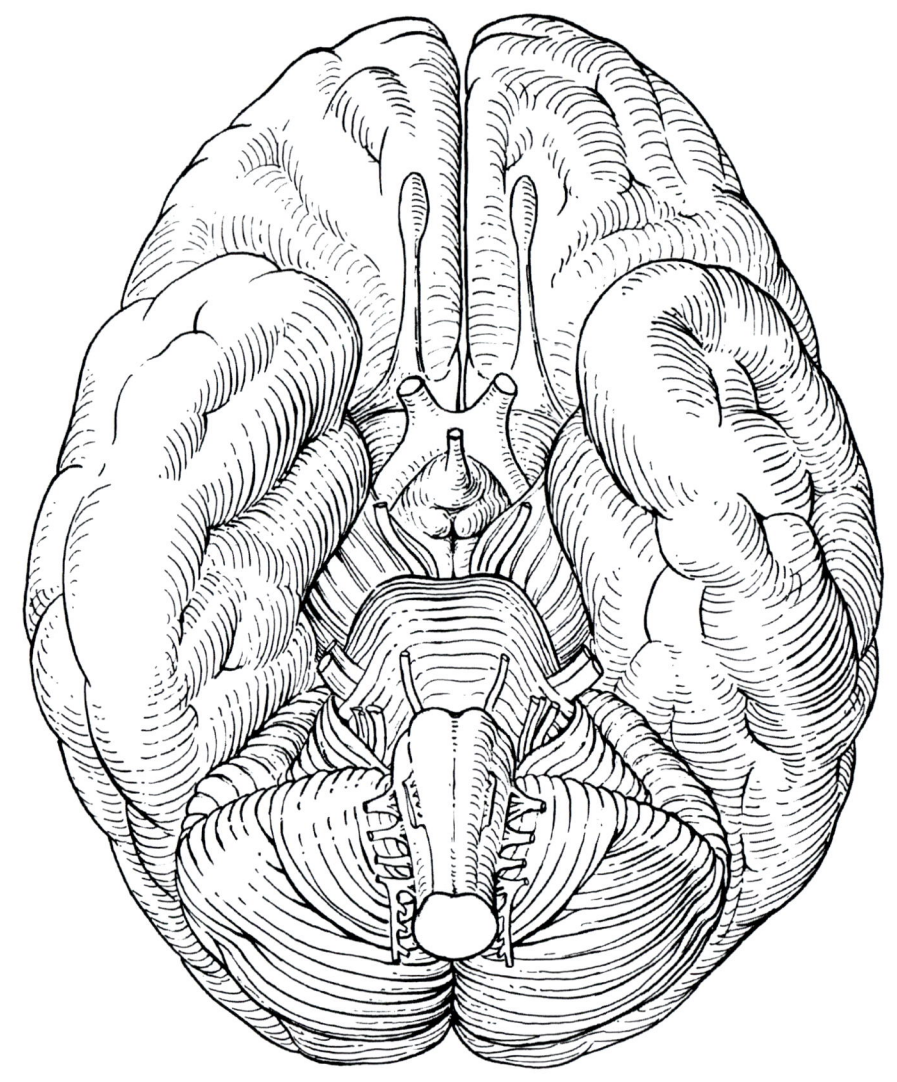

Figure 5. Cerebrum—External, Inferior.

Locate the following structures:

- Cerebellum
- Cerebral peduncle of midbrain
- Frontal lobe
- Mammillary body
- Medulla oblongata
- Olfactory bulbs
- Optic chiasma
- Pons
- Spinal cord
- Temporal lobe

Locate cranial nerves listed below as per instructor:

- (I) Olfactory nerve
- (II) Optic nerve
- (III) Oculomotor nerve
- (IV) Trochlear nerve
- (V) Trigeminal nerve
- (VI) Abducens nerve
- (VII) Facial nerve
- (VIII) Vestibulocochlear nerve
- (IX) Glossopharyngeal nerve
- (X) Vagus nerve
- (XI) Accessory nerve
- (XII) Hypoglossal nerve

HUMAN BRAIN

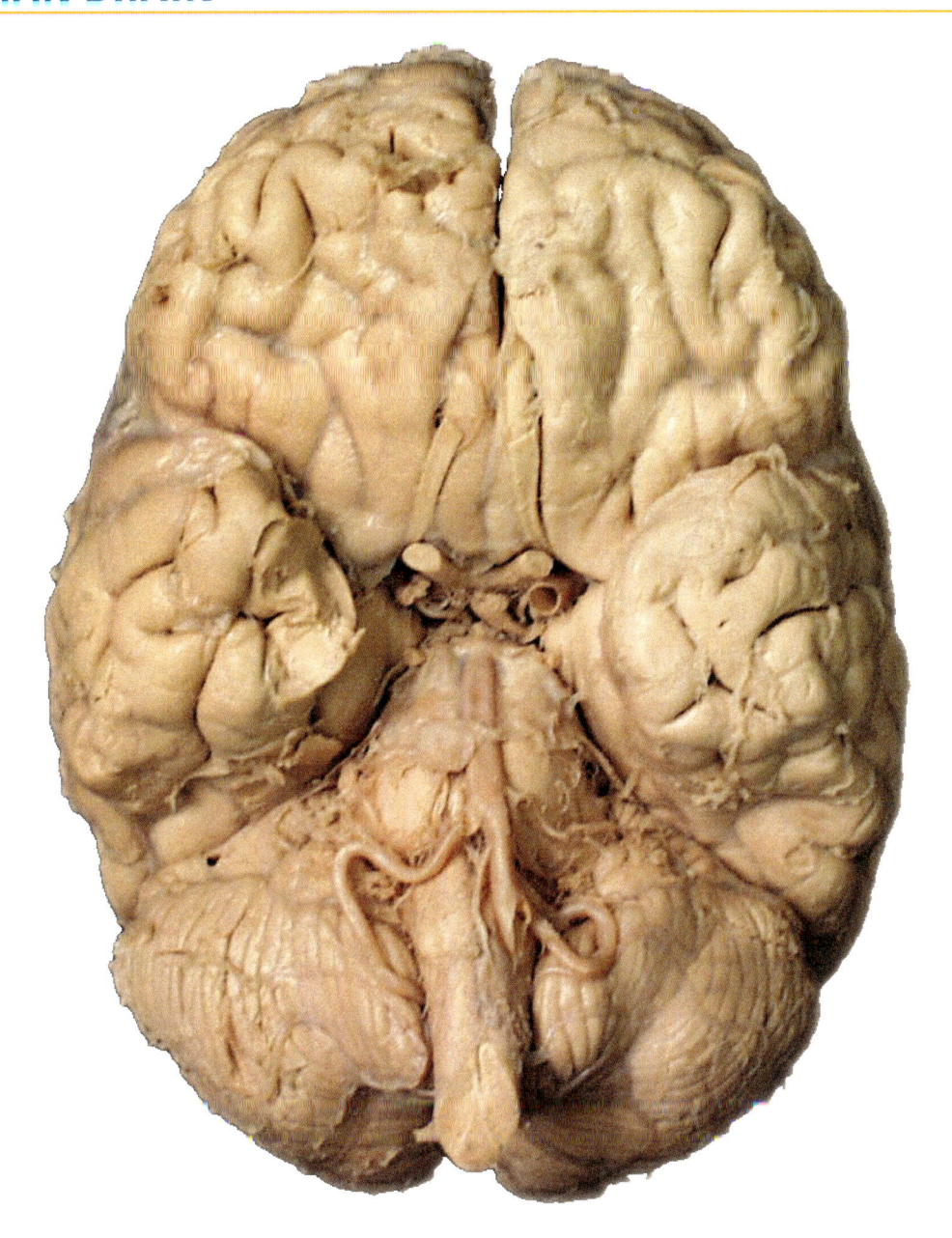

Figure 6. Cerebrum—External, Inferior.

PART 3: NERVOUS SYSTEM

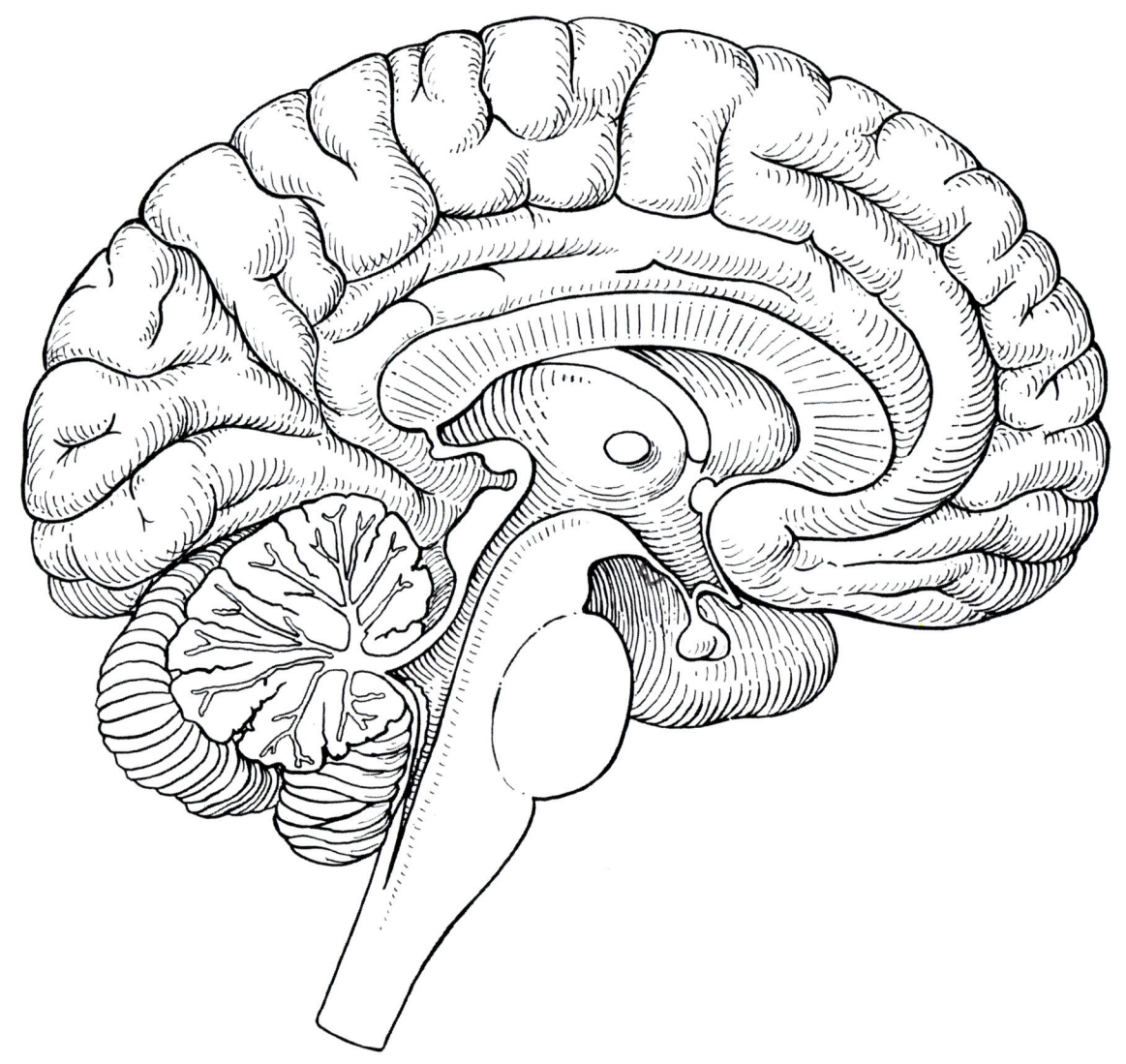

HUMAN BRAIN

Figure 7. Cerebrum—Mid-Sagittal, Right.

Locate the following structures:

- Arachnoid
- Central canal
- Cerebellum
- Cerebral aqueduct
- Cerebral nuclei (basal ganglia)
- Cerebral peduncle
- Cerebrum
- Corpora quadrigemina
- Corpus callosum
- Cortex (gray matter)
- Diencephalon
- Dura mater
- Fourth ventricle
- Infundibulum
- Interventricular foramen (foramen of Monro)
- Lateral ventricle
- Massa intermedia
- Medulla oblongata
- Midbrain
- Pia mater
- Pineal body
- Pituitary gland
- Pons
- Spinal cord
- Subarachnoid space
- Subdural space
- Third ventricle
- Tracts (white matter)
- mammillary body

PART 3: NERVOUS SYSTEM

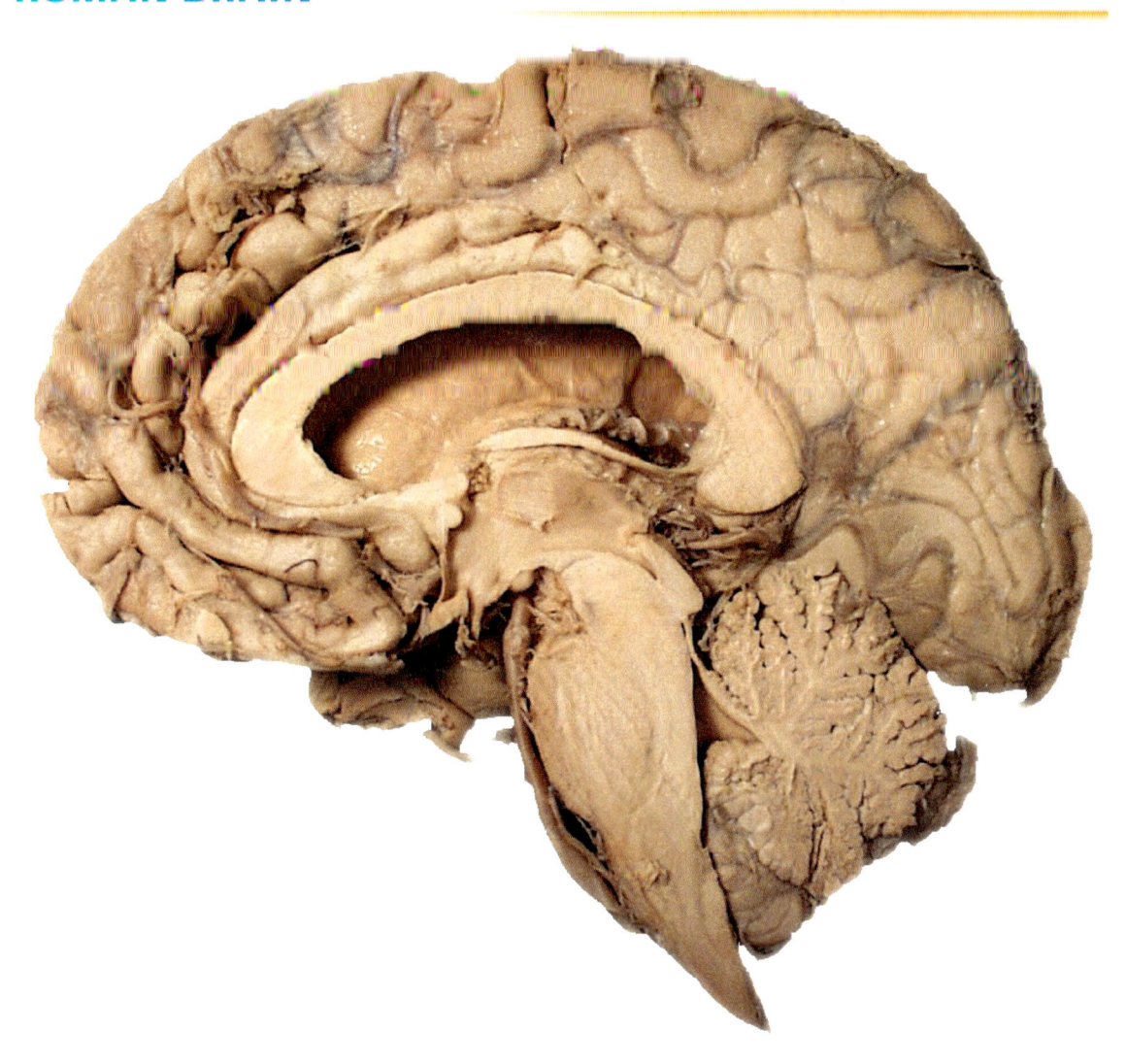

HUMAN BRAIN

Figure 8. Cerebrum—Mid-Sagittal, Left.

PART 3: NERVOUS SYSTEM

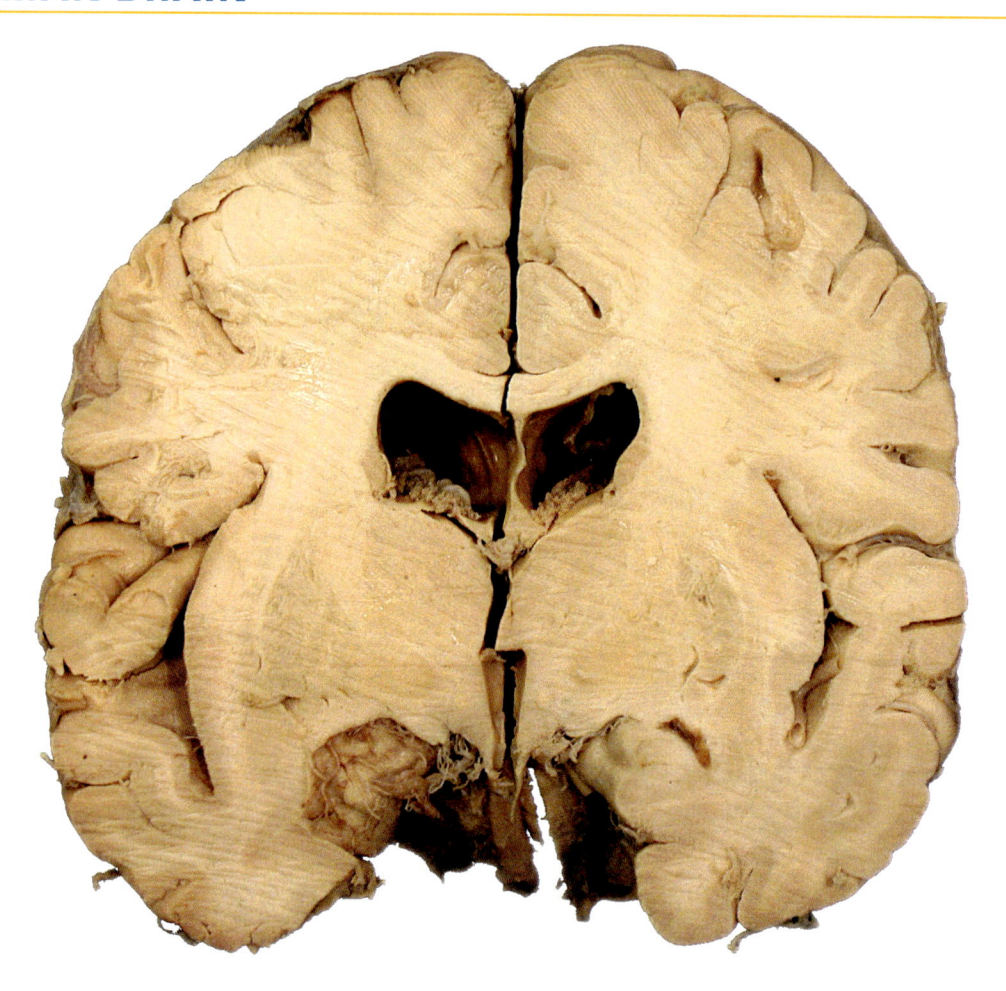

HUMAN BRAIN

Figure 9. Cerebrum—Coronal.

Locate the following structures:

- Basal ganglia
- Cerebellum
- Cerebral cortex
- Corpus callosum
- Insula
- Lateral fissure
- Lateral ventricles
- Longitudinal fissure
- Pons
- Spinal cord
- Thalamus
- Third ventricle

SHEEP BRAIN

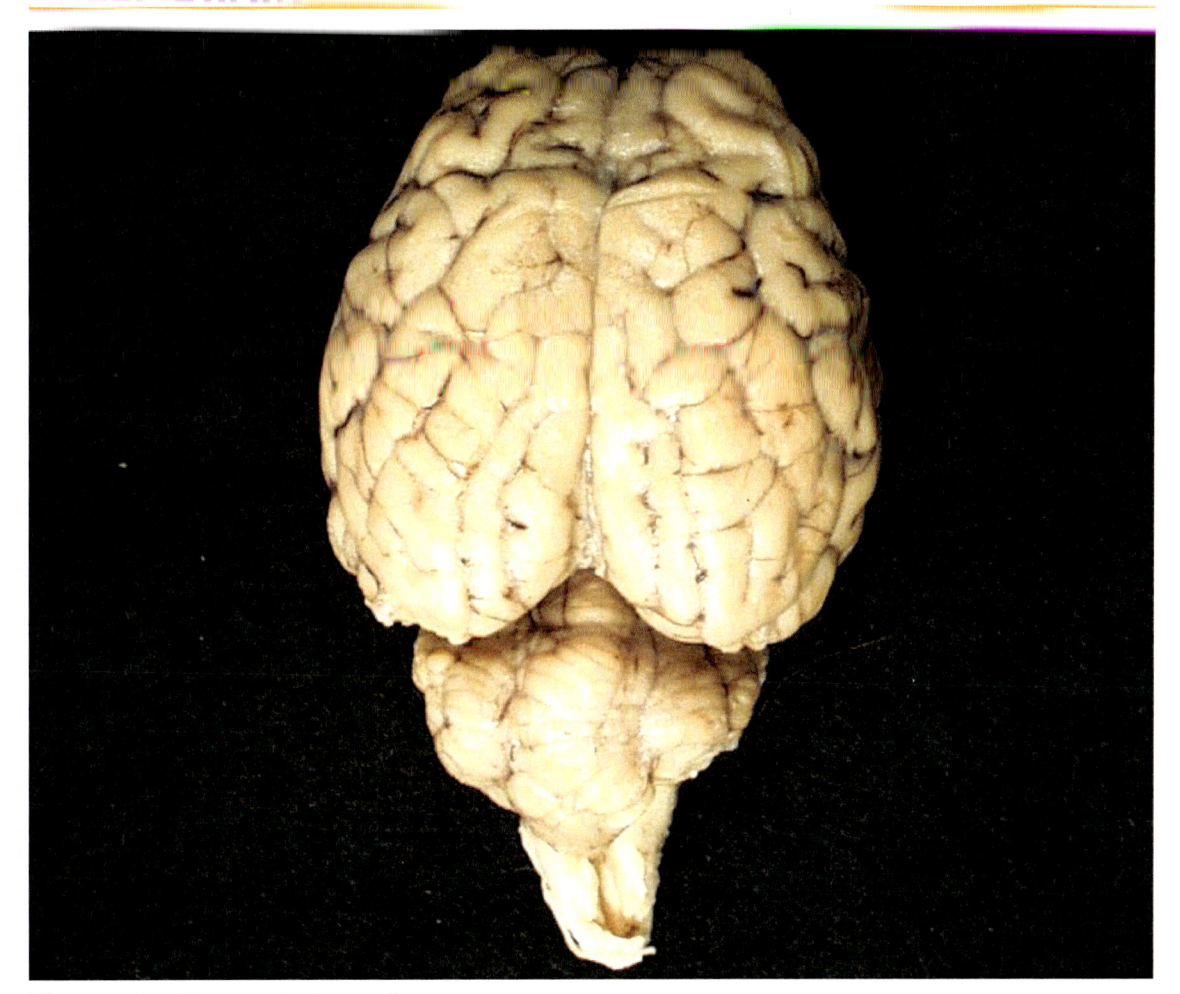

Figure 10. External, Superior.

Locate the following structures:
- Cerebellum
- Cerebrum
- Frontal lobe
- Gyri
- Longitudinal fissure
- Occipital lobe
- Parietal lobe
- Spinal cord
- Sulci

SHEEP BRAIN

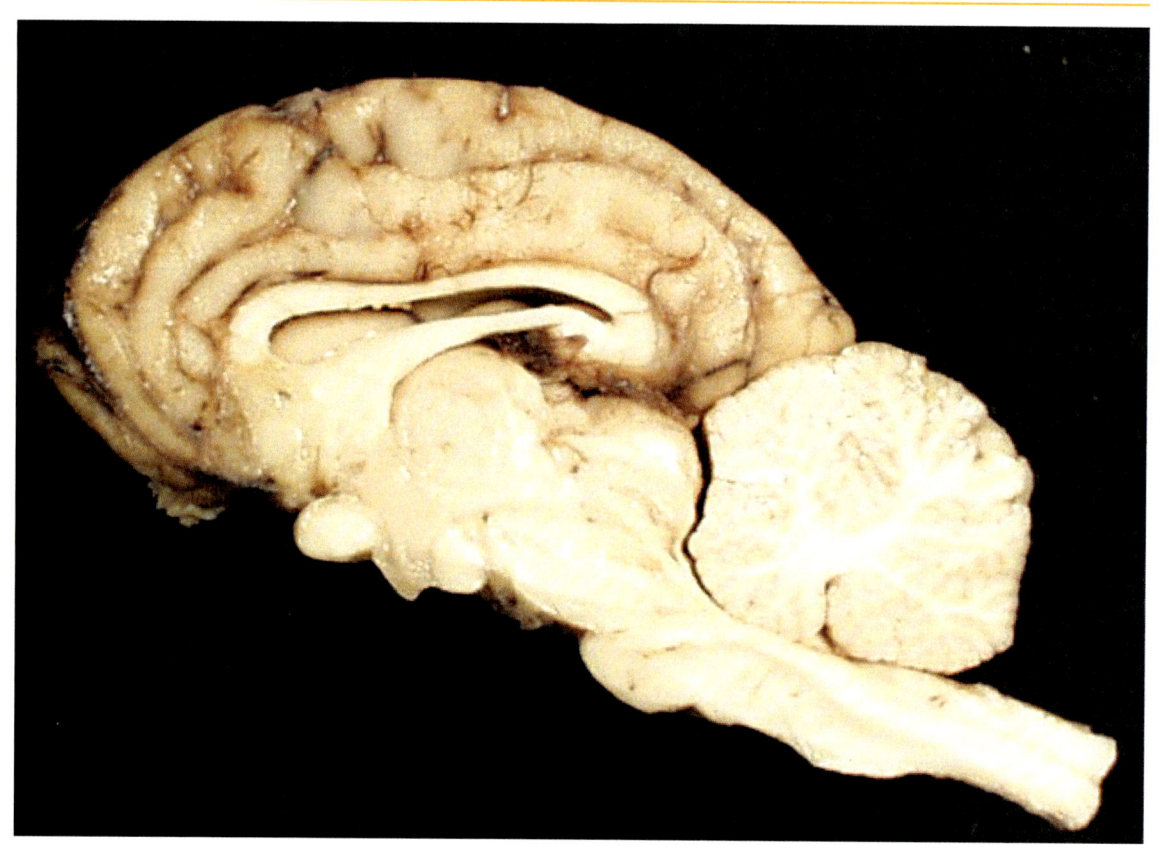

Figure 11. Mid-Sagittal, Left.

Locate the following structures:

- Cerebellum
- Cerebrum
- Corpus callosum
- Lateral ventricle
- Fourth ventricle
- Mammillary body
- Massa intermedia
- Medulla oblongata
- Midbrain
- Pineal gland
- Pituitary gland
- Pons
- Spinal cord
- Third ventricle

CENTRAL NERVOUS SYSTEM— THE SPINAL CORD

INTRODUCTION

The spinal cord serves as an important highway conducting both **sensory (afferent) impulses** from receptors to the brain and **motor (efferent) impulses** down from the brain to effectors. It is somatic and autonomic in its motor function since it transmits impulses not only to skeletal muscles but also to smooth muscle, cardiac muscle, and glandular epithelium.

A deep, wide groove called **anterior median fissure** runs lengthwise down the anterior side of the spinal cord. The **posterior median sulcus,** a narrower, shallower furrow, runs down the posterior side.

The outer portion of the spinal cord contains **myelinated fibers** arranged in three large bundles called **columns (funiculi)** on each lateral side. Each column is subdivided into smaller bundles of fibers known as **tracts (fasciculi).** Since these nerve fibers are **myelinated,** this is the white matter of the spinal cord.

Gray matter, arranged in an H-shaped formation, is found at the center of the spinal cord, and it is made up of unmyelinated dendrites and **neuron cell bodies (ncbs)** of interneurons and motor neurons. Three protrusions of this gray matter are located on each lateral side, and they are called the **horns.** The crossbar of the H is known as the **gray commissure,** which contains the central canal running lengthwise down through the spinal cord. **Cerebrospinal fluid (CSF)** is found within the central canal.

A total of 31 pairs of spinal nerves come off the spinal cord. Each of these nerves is said to be mixed, since it contains both sensory fibers and motor fibers. The entire nerve could be analogous to a large electrical cable, within which there are bundles of electrical wires. Some of the wires are afferent, running alongside of other wires that are efferent.

At a nerve's attachment to the spinal cord, the sensory fibers split away from the motor fibers. Sensory neurons enter the cord from the posterior side via the dorsal root, while motor neurons exit the cord from the anterior side by means of the ventral root. The ncbs of the sensory fibers are found within a bulging structure called the **dorsal root ganglion.** There is no ventral root ganglion; instead, the ncbs of the motor fibers are located within the spinal cord itself. If the motor fiber is somatic, its ncb is found within the anterior gray horn; however if it is autonomic, its ncb is within the lateral gray horn.

EXERCISE

SPINAL CORD MICROSCOPIC ANATOMY

View a cross-sectioned spinal cord microscope slide and identify the following structures:

- White matter
- Gray matter
- Spinal nerve roots

SPINAL CORD MACROSCOPIC ANATOMY

Examine a spinal cord cross-section model and identify the following structures:

- Anterior median fissure
- Posterior median sulcus
- Anterior (ventral) column
- Lateral column
- Posterior (dorsal) column
- Anterior (ventral) horn
- Lateral horn
- Posterior (dorsal) horn
- Gray commissure
- Central canal
- Posterior (dorsal) root ganglion
- Posterior (dorsal) root
- Anterior (ventral) root

PERIPHERAL NERVOUS SYSTEM— AUTONOMIC NERVOUS SYSTEM

EXERCISE

All autonomic nervous system structures listed below are to be identified on the following illustrations.

Use a blue pencil for sympathetic division structures and a red pencil for parasympathetic division structures.

Bold structures below are to be also identified on cat.

SYMPATHETIC DIVISION (THORACOLUMBAR DIVISION) STRUCTURES

- Superior cervical ganglion
- Middle cervical ganglion
- Inferior cervical ganglion
- **Greater splanchnic nerve**
- **Lesser splanchnic nerve**
- Lumbar splanchnic nerve
- **Celiac ganglion**
- **Superior mesenteric ganglion**
- Inferior mesenteric ganglion
- Celiac plexus
- Superior mesenteric plexus
- Hypogastric plexus
- Cardiac plexus
- Pulmonary plexus
- Ventral root
- Spinal nerve
- White ramus
- Gray ramus
- **Sympathetic trunk—Sympathetic chain** *(On the cat, be able to identify the nerve in both the thoracic cavity and abdominopelvic cavity.)*
- Splanchnic nerve
- Collateral ganglion (prevertebral ganglion)

PARASYMPATHETIC DIVISION (CRANIOSACRAL DIVISION) STRUCTURES

- Oculomotor (III) nerve
- Facial (VII) nerve
- Glossopharyngeal (IX) nerve
- **Vagus (X) nerve** *(On the cat, be able to identify the nerve in both the neck area and where the nerve passes through the diaphragm in the thoracic cavity.)*
- Ciliary ganglion
- Pterygopalatine ganglion
- Submandibular ganglion
- Otic ganglion
- Pelvic splanchnic nerves

107

PART 3: NERVOUS SYSTEM

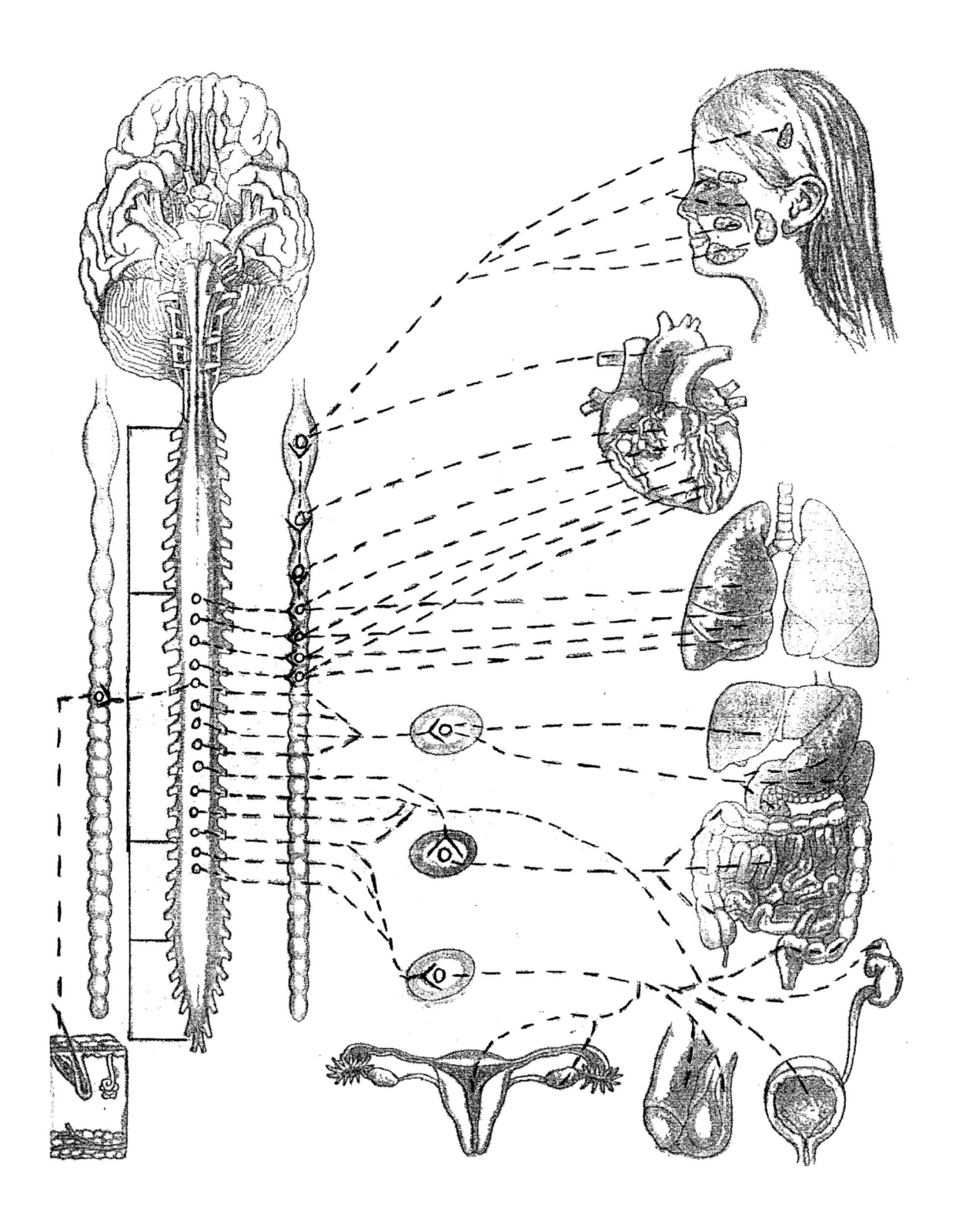

Figure 12. Sympathetic Division (Thoracolumbar Division).

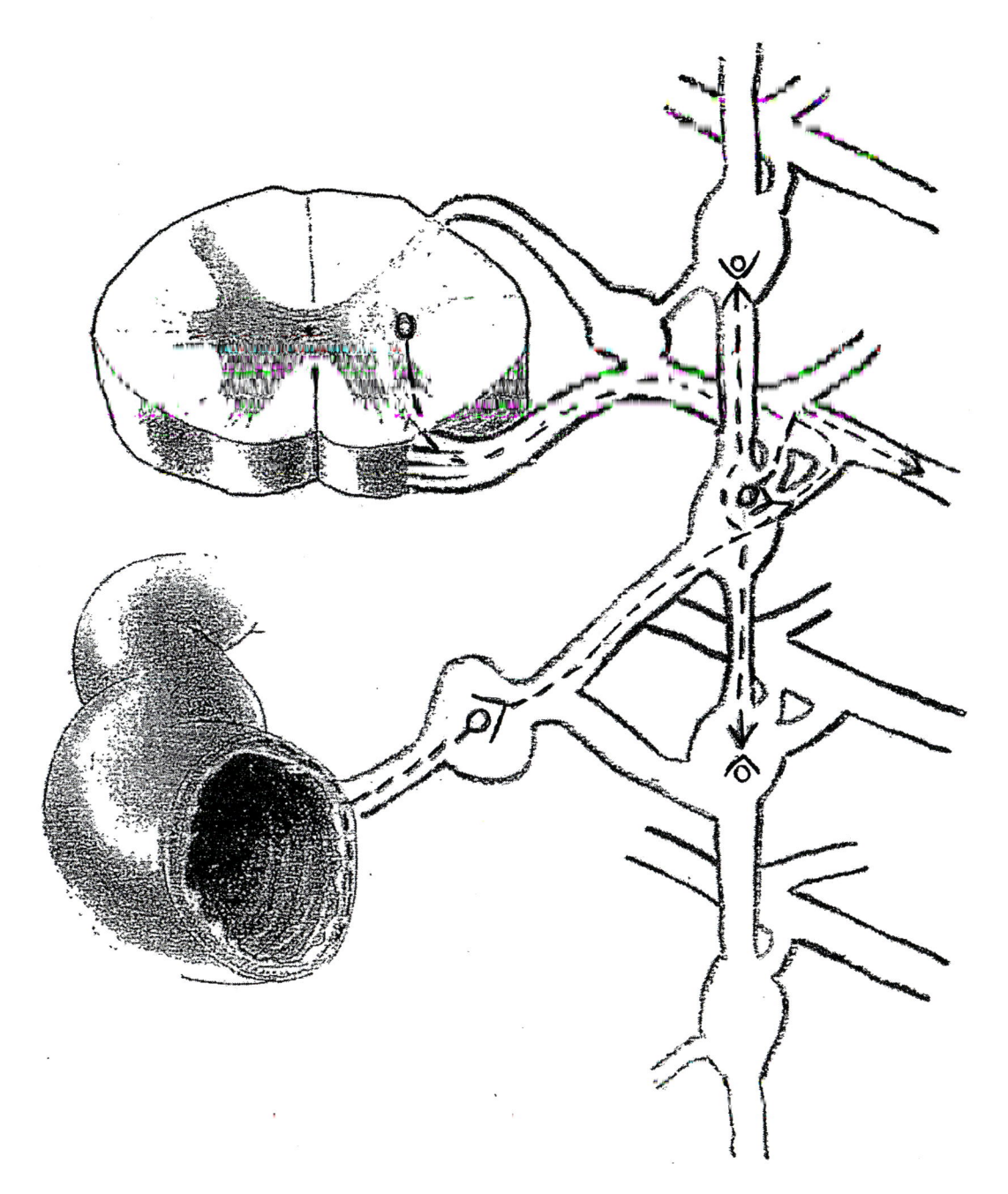

Figure 13. Sympathetic Division (Thoracolumbar Division).

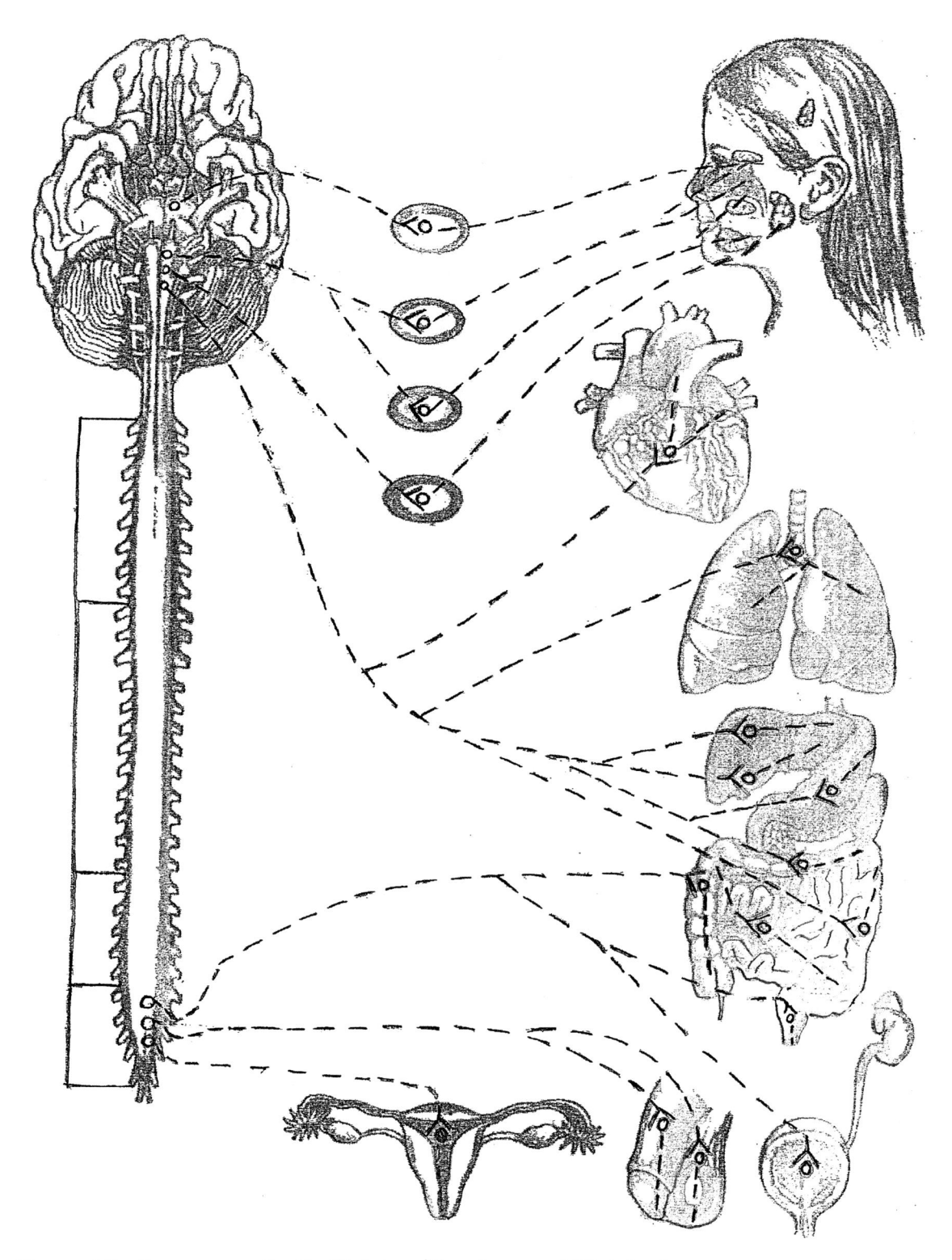

Figure 14. Parasympathetic Division (Craniosacral Division).

CAT NERVOUS SYSTEM GUIDE

- **Phrenic nerve:** identifiable in the cervical plexus (right side of thoracic cavity aspect)—travels lateral and in close proximity to the vagus nerve from lower neck through the thorax to the innervation at the diaphragm.

- **Vagus nerve:** identifiable in the brachial plexus and thoracic cavity (right side of thoracic cavity aspect)—travels parallel to common carotid artery and next to trachea, travels down through thoracic cavity and passes through diaphragm.

- **Radial nerve:** identifiable in the brachial plexus (ventral upper limb aspect)—lateral (and largest) of three parallel nerves in the plexus; travels to the side of the radius—on lateral (thumb) side of lower arm.

- **Median nerve:** identifiable in the brachial plexus (ventral upper limb aspect)—middle of three parallel nerves; travels with the brachial artery between radius and ulna—to the digits.

- **Ulnar nerve:** identifiable in the brachial plexus (ventral upper limb aspect)—medial of three parallel nerves; crosses the medial epicondyle of the humerus and travels to the side of the ulna—on medial (5th finger) side of lower arm.

- **Femoral nerve:** identifiable in the lumbosacral plexus (ventral pelvic cavity aspect)—large nerve, penetrates abdominal wall, deep to ventral thigh muscles.

- **Obturator nerve:** identifiable in the lumbosacral plexus (ventral pelvic cavity aspect)—smaller nerve, passes through obturator foramen, deep to ventral thigh muscles, superior to femoral nerve.

- **Sciatic (ischiatic) nerve:** identifiable in the lumbosacral plexus (lateral thigh aspect)—largest nerve in the plexus, travels over (and innervates) the lateral muscles of the thigh. Divides at the knee.

- **Tibial nerve:** identifiable in the lumbosacral plexus (lateral thigh aspect)—*deep* branch of the sciatic nerve, travels to the side of the tibia—medial side of lower leg; innervates muscle of the lower leg.

- **Common fibular (peroneal) nerve:** identifiable in the lumbosacral plexus (lateral thigh aspect)—*superficial* branch of the sciatic nerve, travels to the side of the fibula—lateral side of lower leg; innervates muscle of the lower leg down to the digits.

- **Sympathetic trunk:** located head to tail but easily located in the thoracic and lumbosacral trunk region; very thin nerve strands lying deep on the ventral surface of the vertebral column, in thoracic region travels parallel to the thoracic aorta.

PART 4
SPECIAL SENSES

EAR

ANATOMY

- The **outer ear** consists of the **pinna** and the **external acoustic meatus,** extending through the temporal bone to the **tympanic membrane.**

- The **middle ear** cavity contains three ear ossicles (bones): **malleus, incus, stapes.**

- The **eustachian tube** extends from the nasopharynx to the middle ear, assisting in equalizing pressure on both sides of the tympanic membrane.

- The **inner ear** contains two primary parts: the **bony labyrinth** and the **membranous labyrinth.**

- The **bony labyrinth** consists of the **cochlea, vestibule, semicircular canals.**
- The membranous **labyrinth** consists of the **cochlear duct** (within cochlea), **utricle** and **saccule** (within vestibule), and **membranous semicircular canals** (within semicircular canals).

HEARING

- Sound waves enter external acoustic meatus.
- Vibrations strike **tympanic membrane,** which in turn vibrates.
- The **malleus,** then **incus,** then **stapes** vibrate passing the vibrations through middle ear cavity.
- Stapes strikes **oval window,** setting up vibrations in **perilymph** of cochlea which is the fluid between the cochlea and the cochlear duct.
- The cochlear duct and its internal fluid, **endolymph,** also start to vibrate. The cochlear duct is coiled like a snail's shell, with a shelf-like membrane, called the **tectorial membrane** dividing it into an upper chamber and lower chamber. The lower chamber, called the **basilar membrane,** contains embedded hair cells, the **organ of Corti.**
- The basilar membrane vibrates, causing the hairs of the organ of Corti to strike the overlying tectorial membrane.
- The hair cells are bent which initiates the nerve impulse.

EQUILIBRIUM

- **Static equilibrium** is the position of the body in relation to gravity, involving the **utricle** and **saccule.**
- **Dynamic equilibrium** is the position of the body in relation to sudden changes in position, involving the membranous semicircular canals.
  - Utricle, saccule and membranous semicircular canals all contain fluid. Endolymph and hair cells are embedded in this gelatinous membrane.
  - These structures also contain tiny calcium carbonate stones called **otoliths.**
  - Changes in position of the head cause endolymph and otoliths to move.
  - This movement results in the hair cells being bent.
  - Bending of the hair cells initiates the nerve impulse.

PART 4: SPECIAL SENSES

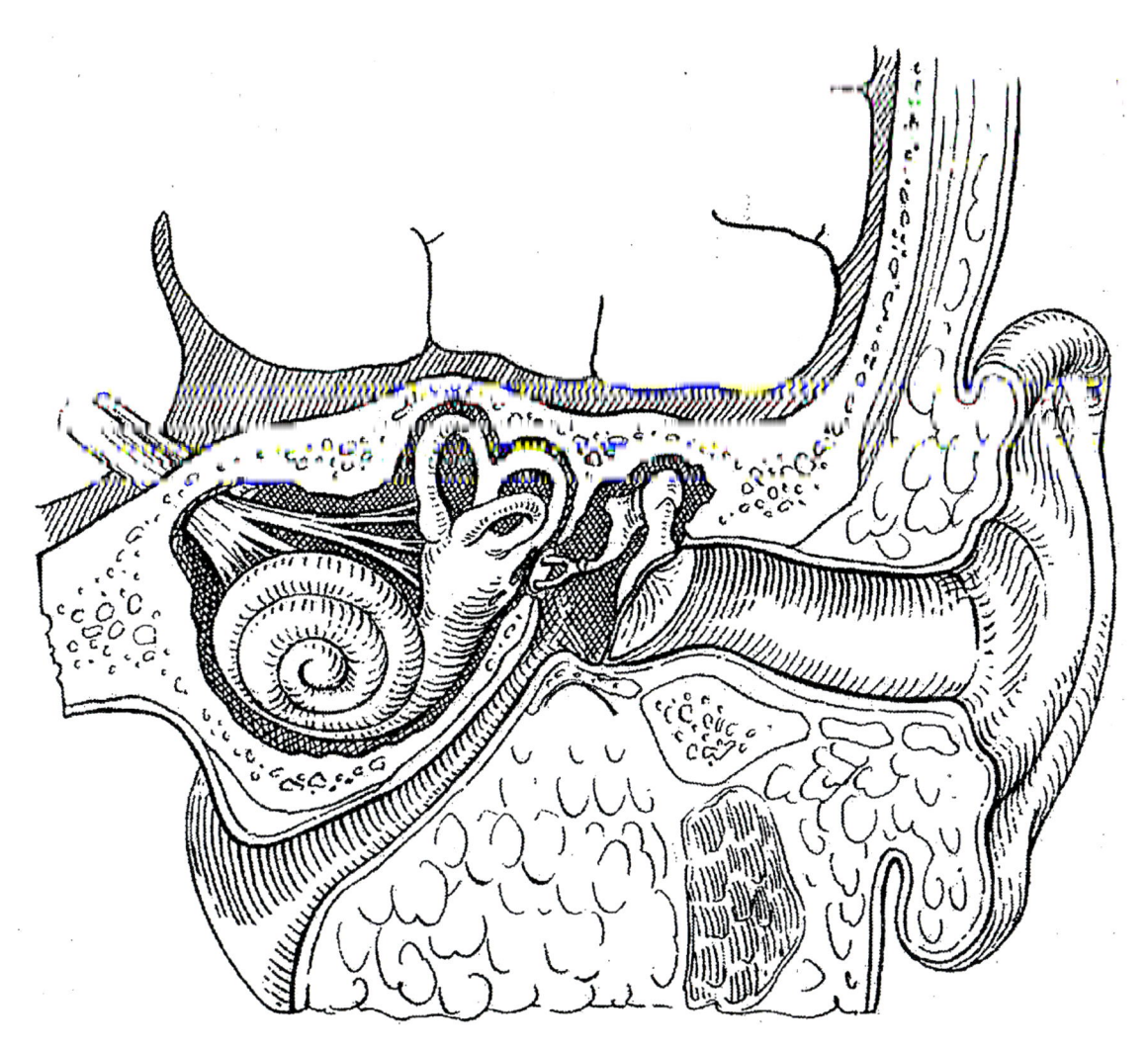

Figure 1. The Ear.

Locate the following structures:

- Pinna (auricle)
- Helix
- Lobule
- External auditory canal
- Tympanic membrane
- Malleus
- Incus
- Stapes
- Temporal bone
- Oval window
- Round window
- Semicircular canal
- Cochlea
- Vestibulocochlear (VIII) nerve
    - Vestibular branch
    - Cochlear branch
- Auditory (eustachian) tube

EYE

INTRODUCTION

BASIC LAYERS

- The **sclera** is tough, fibrous and the outermost layer which gives support to the eyeball. There is an anterior and a posterior portion. The **cornea** is the anterior transparent portion. The remainder is white and opaque.

- The **choroid** is the middle layer, deeply pigmented and highly vascularized. The anterior portion is modified into the **ciliary body** and **ciliary muscle.** The choroid layer is attached to the suspensory ligaments which extend to the **lens,** pulling on the lens to change its shape.

- The anterior portion of this middle layer is the **iris** with its circular and radial fibers which regulate the amount of light entering the eye.

- The **retina** is the innermost layer where the receptors for visions are located. The retina covers only the posterior portion of the internal cavity of the eye.

MUSCLES

- The **external (extrinsic) muscles** are six small muscles controlled by the oculomotor, trochlear, and abducens cranial nerves.

- The **internal (intrinsic) muscles** are associated with the ciliary muscle controlling the lens and iris regulating light entering the eye.

OTHER STRUCTURES

- The **conjunctiva** is a mucous membrane which lines the eyelid (palpebral portion) and continues over the cornea (bulbar portion).

- The **lacrimal gland,** located at the upper, lateral corner of the eye produces tears containing **lysozyme,** a bacteria-killing enzyme.

- The **aqueous humor** is a thin, watery fluid located in the anterior cavity between the cornea and the lens. The aqueous humor is constantly being produced and replenished. This fluid refracts light entering the eye. It also carries nutrients to and wastes from the cornea.

- The **vitreous humor** is a thick, gelatin-like substance located in the posterior cavity between the lens and the retina. This fluid helps to maintain the eyeball's shape and retinal position. It refracts some light but is not constantly produced or replenished.

PHOTORECEPTORS

- **Rods** are utilized for night vision. These receptors contain **rhodopsin** (visual purple) which is formed by a combination of retinene and opsin. Light rays cause the breakdown of rhodopsin to retinene and opsin which initiates the nerve impulse. In darkness, rhodopsin is reformed.

- **Cones** are utilized in daytime and color vision. These receptors also contain photosensitive pigments. However, stronger light is necessary for the breakdown of these pigments. It is theorized that three types of cones exist: red, blue, and green. Stimulating combinations of these receptors results in color differentiation.

EXERCISE

COW EYE DISSECTION

Carefully trim the fat tissue and muscle from around the circumference of the eyeball. With fat and muscle removed, the organ should appear as a dark gray ball with a thin muscle apron around the circumference and the optic nerve protruding posteriorly.

1. Make a coronal cut in the middle of the eyeball. With scissors, divide the eyeball into anterior and posterior halves.

2. Identify these structures:

    a. Anterior portion of the eye

    - **Cornea:** thick, translucent anterior membrane
    - **Pupil:** open slit, aperture
    - **Iris:** circular, black membrane (posterior surface is grooved)
    - **Aqueous humor:** watery fluid, anterior to the lens, may be reduced in volume or drained away
    - **Lens:** hard, transparent, orange oval structure

    b. Posterior portion of the eye (carefully remove the vitreous humor)

    - **Retina:** thin, transparent, fragile yellow membrane
    - **Choroid:** dark, greenish/blue membrane superficial to the retina
    - **Sclera:** thick, gray, tough outer layer superficial to the choroid
    - **Optic nerve**
    - **Vitreous chamber:** cavity inside eyeball posterior to the lens
    - **Vitreous humor:** stiff, jelly-like fluid filling the vitreous chamber

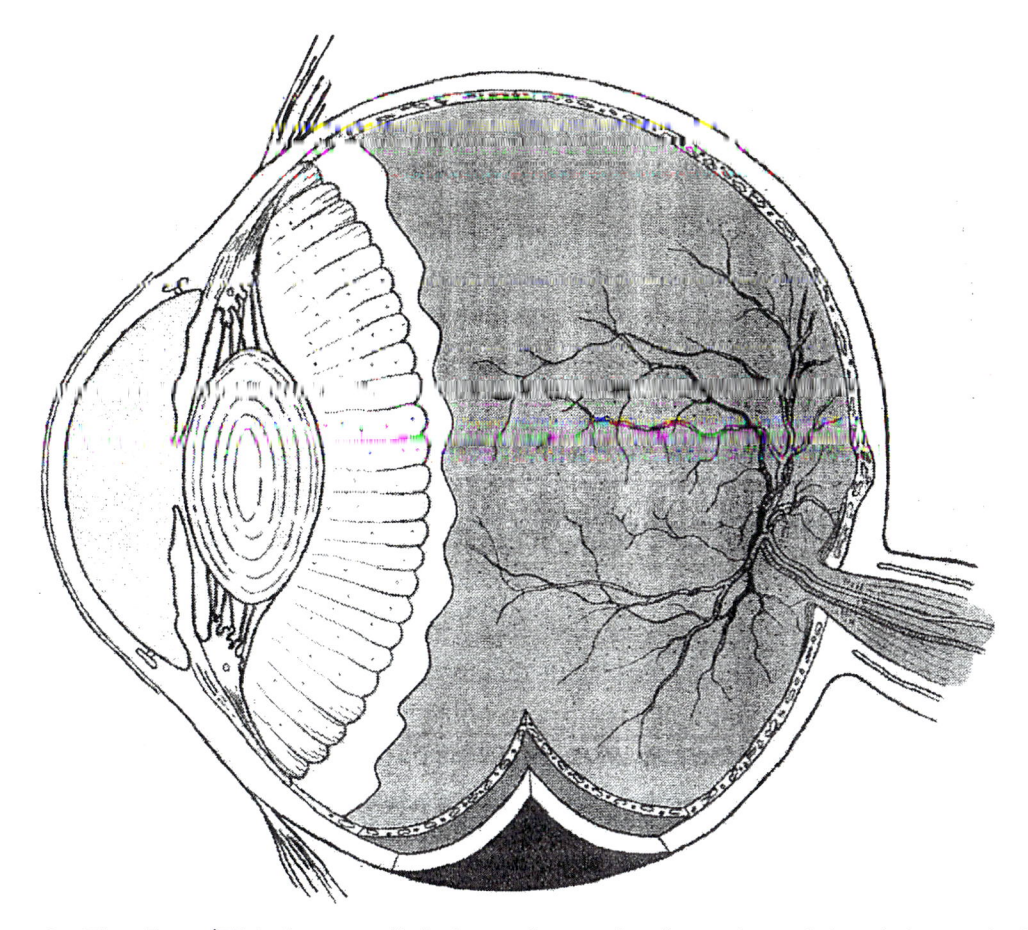

Figure 2. The Eye. (This is a medial view of a sagittal section of the right eyeball.)

Locate the following structures:

ANTERIOR STRUCTURES
- Conjunctiva
- Cornea
- Anterior cavity (with aqueous humor)
- Anterior chamber
- Posterior chamber
- Canals of Schlemm
- Pupil
- Iris
- Ciliary body
- Ciliary process
- Ciliary muscle
- Lens
- Suspensory ligament
- Medial rectus muscle
- Lateral rectus muscle

POSTERIOR STRUCTURES
- Ora serrata
- Sclera
- Choroid
- Retina
- Vitreous chamber (with vitreous humor)
- Central retinal artery
- Central retinal vein
- Optic disc (blind spot)
- Optic nerve (CN II)

INTEGUMENTARY SYSTEM

INTRODUCTION

BASIC LAYERS

- The **epidermis** is the superficial layer of the skin that is avascular and consists of epithelial cells.

- The **dermis** is the deep layer of the skin that lies beneath the epidermis that helps support the epidermis. This layer is thicker than the epidermis and consists of connective tissue, blood vessels, nerves, hair follicles, and glands.

- Beneath the two layers to the skin is the **hypodermis.** This layer is not part of the skin but it serves to anchor the skin to bone and muscle beneath as well as supplying the layers with blood vessels and nerves.

FUNCTIONS

- Protection
    - From trauma
    - From pathogens
    - From the environment
- Sensation

    The basic receptors mediating touch:

    - **Hair root plexuses:** free nerve endings that wrap around hair follicles and monitor movement of the hairs; located in the hairy skin
    - **Meissner's corpuscles:** oval-shaped clusters of dendrites surrounded by connective tissue capsules; found in the dermal papillae of hairless skin
    - **Merkel's discs:** flattened, dish-shaped free nerve endings which are in contact with the Merkel cells of the stratum basale of the epidermis
    - **Ruffini's corpuscles:** elongated receptors situated deep in the dermis and in tendons and ligaments
- Thermoregulation
- Excretion
- Vitamin D Synthesis

PART 4: SPECIAL SENSES

EXERCISE

SKIN MODEL

Find the structure listed on a skin model.

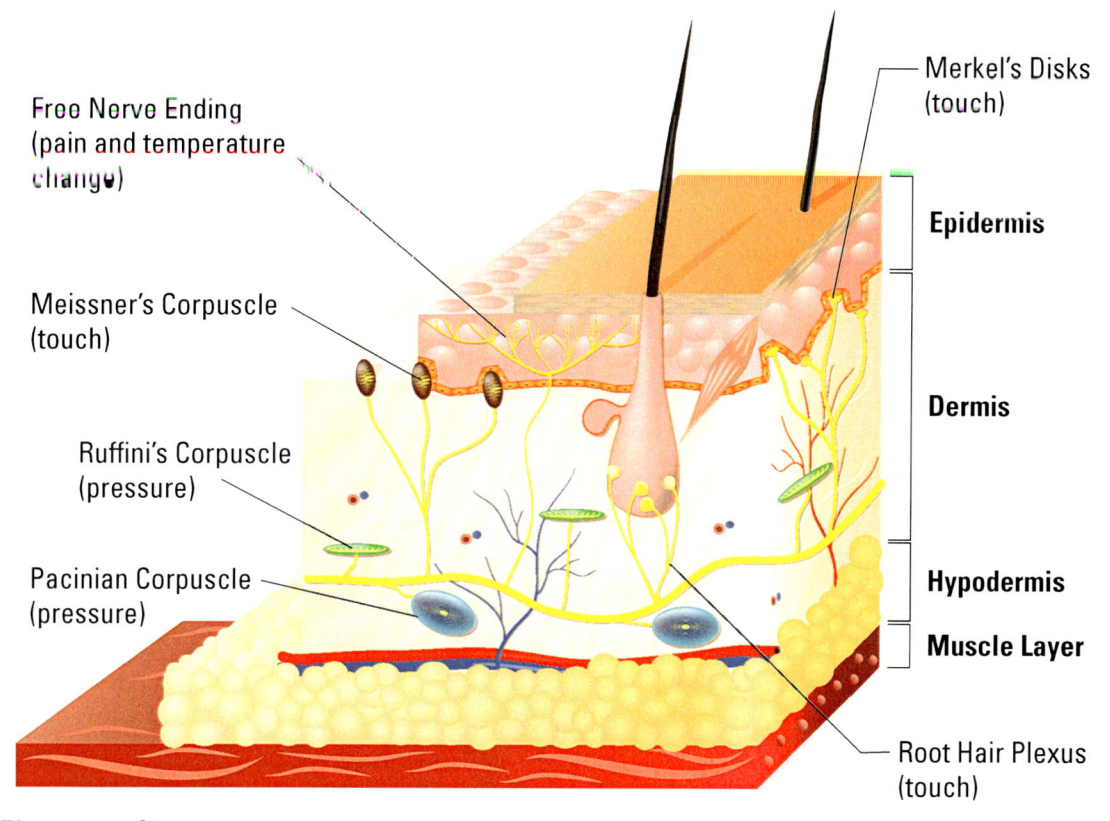

Figure 3. Skin.

SENSORY TESTS

SIGHT

VISUAL ACUITY TEST

Visual acuity is the sharpness of vision or resolving power of the eye. A sensitivity test of vision sharpness, clearness and distinction using a Snellen Eye Chart indicated by a relative distance comparison (i.e., vision 20/20, etc.).

The purpose of the following exercises is to evaluate the function of the eye. Go through the tests and record your results on the charts at the end of the exercise.

MATERIALS

- Snellen chart mounted at eye level on the wall
- 20-foot mark on the floor

PROCEDURE (WORK IN PAIRS)

One person is the test subject and is positioned at the 20-foot mark. The other person is positioned at the Snellen chart and will conduct the test.

1. Remove any corrective eyewear prior to conducting this test. The test subject standing at the 20-foot mark covers the right eye with a cupped hand and reads the letters on the Snellen chart starting at the top and working down the chart. Continue reading letters, line by line, until the observer detects errors. Record the value from the left hand column of the smallest line that was read without errors on Table A for the left eye. For example, line three on the right column would be recorded as a visual acuity of 20/70.

2. Repeat the procedure by covering the left eye and reading the chart with the right eye.

3. Repeat the procedure using both eyes.

4. If the test subject has corrective eyewear, repeat the above test wearing the corrective lenses.

5. Students should now switch positions and repeat Steps 1–4.

6. Record results in Table 1.

INTERPRETATION

If a subject accurately reads line three, that person's visual acuity is 20/70, and that person has 20/70 vision. A person with 20/70 vision can read at 20 feet what a person with normal 20/20 vision can read at 70 feet. The lower the bottom number is in the ratio, the better that person's vision.

Table 1. Visual Acuity Test Results

	Acuity (without corrective eyewear)	Acuity (with corrective eyewear)
Left Eye		20/15
Right Eye		20/40
Both Eyes		20/20

ASTIGMATISM TEST

Astigmatism is an uneven curvature of the lens surface and/or the corneal surface. The astigmatism test is conducted using an astigmatism chart. Astigmatometry is the measurement of the abnormal, unequal curvatures along different meridians in one or more of the refractive surfaces (cornea, lens) of the eye. Blurred vision results from the light rays not focusing at a single point on the retina.

MATERIALS

- Astigmatism chart mounted at eye level with a 20-foot mark on the floor

or

- A smaller astigmatism chart held one foot from the eye

PROCEDURE

1. Remove any corrective eyewear prior to conducting this test.
2. The test subject is positioned 20 feet from the wall-mounted chart or positions a smaller chart one foot away from the eye.
3. Test each eye using a cupped hand as above.
4. Look at the white circle in the center of the chart. If all the black lines appear equally black and equally sharp, then there is no astigmatism. If there is any blurriness or inconsistency of darkness, there is astigmatism.
5. If the test subject has corrective eyewear, repeat the procedure wearing the corrective lenses.
6. Results for astigmatism are recorded on Table 2.

Table 2. Astigmatism Test Results.

	Present without Corrective Eyewear	Absent without Corrective Eyewear	Present with Corrective Eyewear	Absent with Corrective Eyewear
Left Eye				
Right Eye				

NEAR-POINT ACCOMMODATION TEST

This is the measurement of the near-point accommodation of the lens for close vision. At close vision, an increase in the curvature of the lens occurs in order to focus the light rays on the retina. **Accommodation** involves changes of curvature of the eye lens that occur when adjusting for vision at various distances. When focused on a near object, the lens has increased curvature to focus light rays on the retinal surface. When viewing a distant object, there is less curvature of the lens. The following test determines a person's near-point accommodation.

MATERIALS
- Index card with the typed word "TEST"
- Ruler

PROCEDURE (WORK IN PAIRS)

1. Remove any corrective eyewear prior to conducting this test.

2. Test each eye using a cupped hand.

3. Hold the index card at arms length from the eye. Slowly move the index card toward the eye until the image begins to blur. The observer measures the distance from the eye to the card.

4. Results are recorded on Table 4.

5. If the test subject has corrective eyewear, repeat the procedure wearing the corrective lenses.

Table 3. Normal Age-Related Near-Point Accommodation.

Age	Centimeters	Inches
10	7.5	2.95
20	9.0	3.54
30	11.5	4.53
40	17.2	6.77
50	52.5	20.7
60	83.3	32.8

Table 4. Near-Point Accommodation Test Results.

	Without Corrective Eyewear (in cm)	With Corrective Eyewear (in cm)
Left Eye	3.5	
Right Eye	3.5	

BLIND SPOT DETERMINATION

This is the confirmation of the existence of the **blind spot,** the point on the retinal surface where nerve fibers leave the eye to become the optic nerve. Photoreceptors are absent at this point. When light rays reach this point, no visual response is detected. The determination verifies that the blind spot exists.

MATERIALS
- Blind Spot Determination Card

PROCEDURE
1. Hold the Blind Spot Determination Card at arms length from the eye.
2. While closing the left eye, focus the right eye on the cross printed on the card.
3. Slowly bring the test card toward the eye until the circle disappears from the field of vision.
4. Repeat the determination with the right eye closed. This time the left eye is focused on the circle and the cross will disappear from the field of vision.
5. Results are recorded on Table 5.

Table 5. Blind Spot Determination Results.

Left eye blind spot found?	2
Right eye blind spot found?	3.5

PART 4: SPECIAL SENSES

COLOR BLINDNESS DETERMINATION

Color blindness is the inability to distinguish certain colors, and is a sex-linked hereditary condition resulting from the lack of one or more cone photoreceptor types. Color blindness affects about 8% of males and 0.5% of females.

MATERIALS
- Ishihara's Design Charts for Color Deficiency

PROCEDURE (WORK IN PAIRS)
1. Color plates are to be viewed at arm's length and under natural light if possible.
2. Working in pairs, view each of the plates and describe the colored pattern on each plate. If a colored pattern is not detected, the person is color blind for that color.
3. Results are recorded on Table 6.

Table 6. Color Blindness Determination Results.

How many of the cards were identified correctly?	14
Which colors, if any, were you unable to identify?	none

1. 12
2. 8
3. 5
4. 29
5. 74
6. 7
7. 45
8. 2
9. nothing
10. 16
11. squiggle
12. 35
13. 96
14. 100

PERIPHERAL VISION TEST

Peripheral vision involves retinal stimulation beyond the macula, which is the spot on the back of the retina. This test measures the ability to make visual discrimination of an object at the periphery (lateral edge) of vision.

MATERIALS

- Vision disk
- Set of 11 sight cards

PROCEDURE (WORK IN PAIRS)

1. While sitting, test subject holds the Vision Disk against the forehead using the fold-down handles. The test subject then looks straight ahead under the Vision Disk, focusing on the focus marker.

2. The partner, while standing behind the test subject, moves the arm on top of the disk to the left side to the 120° mark. A random sight card from the collection is placed in the slit on the arm.

3. The partner now slowly swings the arm with the inserted sight card toward the front of the test subject. While the test subject's eyes remain focused on the hole in the focus marker, the test subject announces when the card is first seen. Record this number on Table 7 as the limit of left side field of vision.

4. The partner continues to slowly move the arm toward the front of the test subject. The test subject identifies the letters aloud as soon as the letters can be read. Record this number on Table 7 as the limit of left side reading field of vision.

5. Repeat the test for the right side and record results on Table 7.

6. Calculate the Total Range of Field of Vision and Total Range of Reading Field of Vision by taking the sum of the left and rights sides for each field of vision.

Table 7. Peripheral Vision Test Results.

Limit of Left Side Field of Vision	80	Limit of Right Side Field of Vision	70
Limit of Left Side Reading Field of Vision	10	Limit of Right Side Reading Field of Vision	14
Total Range of Field of Vision		Total Range of Reading Field of Vision	

PUPILLARY DISTANCE REFLEX TEST

The **pupillary distance reflex** test is the indication of the relationship and accommodation between pupil size and viewing distance. Increased light (therefore wider pupil diameter) is necessary for viewing an object at a distance. Accommodation should occur when focusing at different distances.

MATERIALS
- Whiteboard
- Printed text page

PROCEDURE (WORK IN PAIRS)

1. Test subject focuses on a whiteboard across the room for 60 seconds. While closely observing the pupil size of the test subject, the partner places a printed text page about 6 inches from the test subject's eyes and asks the test subject to focus on the printed page. Note any changes in pupil size.

2. Results are recorded on Table 8.

Table 8. Pupillary Distance Test Results.

Pupil Diameter Change Observed	Constricted

HEARING

Receptors in the inner ear are responsible for the sense of hearing. **Conduction impairment,** leading to a hearing loss, results from damage to the middle ear. It often is due to infections involving the tympanic membrane or ear ossicles, although it can be also caused by simply an accumulation of earwax. Hearing aids are beneficial in treating this form of hearing loss, since they act to first amplify and then conduct sounds through the temporal bone to the cochlea, the site of the receptors for sound. Both of the following physiological tests (the **Rinne Test** and **Weber's Test**) are used to screen persons with suspected conduction deafness.

RINNE TEST

A vibrating tuning fork is held in contact with the skull (usually at the mastoid process) until the sound is lost. Fork prongs are then held close to the auditory orifice, when if hearing is normal, a faint sound will again be heard—air conduction is greater than bone conduction, indicative of normal sound conduction mechanism through the middle ear.

MATERIALS
- Tuning fork (256 Hz)

PROCEDURE (WORK IN PAIRS)

1. Strike a tuning fork on your palm.

2. Place the handle of the fork on the subject's mastoid process, with the fork's prongs pointing downward and behind the ear.

3. When the subject cannot hear the humming noise any longer, move the prongs so that they are close to, but not touching, the external auditory meatus.

4. If the subject hears a hum once again, normal hearing is indicated. If not, a conduction problem is suspected.

Table 9. Rinne Test Results.

Is there suspected conduction impairment in:	Yes or No
Right Ear	No
Left Ear	No

WEBER'S TEST

A vibrating tuning fork is held in contact with several points in the midline of the head or face to determine in which ear the sound is heard by bone conduction. The ear on that side has a lessened response due to sound conducting mechanism disorder.

MATERIALS
- Tuning fork (256 Hz)

PROCEDURE (WORK IN PAIRS)

1. Strike a tuning fork on your palm.

2. Place the handle on the midsagittal line of the subject's forehead.

3. Ask the subject whether the loudness of the sound seems to be equal on both sides, right and left. If so, normal hearing is indicated. However, if one side is noticeably louder than the other, a conduction impairment is suspected on that particular side.

Table 10. Weber's Test Results.

Is there suspected conduction impairment in:	Yes or No
Right Ear	No
Left Ear	No

SOUND LOCALIZATION TEST

Our hearing is stereophonic, and binaural hearing enables us to localize sounds. The ability to pinpoint the exact source of the sound depends on two factors: the difference in the loudness of the sound reaching the two ears and the difference in the arrival time of the sound at the two ears.

A hearing localization test of binaural hearing (relating to both ears); can measure sound intensity and sound arrival time.

MATERIALS
- Tuning fork (256 Hz)
- Cotton balls or earplugs

PROCEDURE (WORK IN PAIRS)

1. After the subject closes his eyes, strike a tuning fork on your palm.

2. Place the vibrating fork at various locations about 10 to 12 inches from the subject's head and ask him to indicate the position of the fork.

3. Now, plug one ear with cotton or earplugs and repeat the above procedure, noting any differences in his ability to correctly describe the location of the vibrating fork.

    - Is it easier to pinpoint the location of the vibrating tuning fork with or without one ear plugged? _____

HEARING ACUITY TEST

This is a sensitivity test of hearing sharpness, clearness, and distinction.

MATERIALS
- Ticking clock
- Tape measure

PROCEDURE (WORK IN PAIRS)

1. Ask subject to close his eyes.

2. Starting approximately 15 feet away from the subject's right side, slowly walk toward the subject while holding a ticking clock in front of you.

3. Subject is to indicate when he can first distinguish the ticking noise.

4. Repeat the above procedure from the subject's left side and note any differences between the two ears.

    a. Distance from right ear at which ticking clock can first be heard: 14

    b. Distance from left ear at which ticking clock can first be heard: 14

PART 4: SPECIAL SENSES

EQUILIBRIUM

Receptors in the inner ear are responsible for the two types of equilibrium, static and dynamic.

Static equilibrium deals with one's position, relative to gravity, when one is stationary. So, it enables a person to know whether he is right side up or upside down. **Dynamic equilibrium** is involved with changes in one's position during motion, such as sensory information regarding the direction and speed of movement, acceleration and deceleration.

Receptors for static equilibrium are found within the **utricle** and **saccule** of the inner ear. The walls of both of these structures feature a thickened area known as the **macula**, which contains hair cells covered by a gelatinous layer called the **otolithic membrane**. A layer of **otoliths**, dense calcium carbonate crystals, extends over the otolithic membrane's surface. When the head is tilted, the otolithic membrane and otoliths are pulled by gravity and move downward, in the direction of the tilt, bending the hairs. This initiates the nervous impulse.

The following exercises illustrate a subject's ability to use sensory information supplied by the utricle and saccule alone, without any help from the sense of vision.

ROMBERG TEST

With feet apart, subject stands with eyes open then closed. If closing the eyes increases the unsteadiness, a loss of proprioceptive control is indicated and the sign is positive.

PROCEDURE (WORK IN PAIRS)

1. Have the subject stand, with feet together and eyes open, for two minutes. Note whether or not the subject sways from side to side or forward and backward, using the following rating system to record the results:

    - 0 = no sway
    - 1 = slight sway
    - 2 = moderate sway
    - 3 = excessive sway

2. Repeat this procedure, but now have the subject close his eyes. Again record the amount of sway demonstrated. Excessive sway indicates possible equilibrium problem.

    - Amount of sway with eyes open: 0
    - Amount of sway with eyes closed: 0

POINTING ACTIVITY

With feet apart, subject stands with eyes open and points to various body parts with either hand; then repeats with eyes closed. If closing the eyes decreases coordination, a loss of proprioceptive control is indicated.

PROCEDURE (WORK IN PAIRS)

1. Have the subject stand, with eyes open, and point with the right hand to various body structures, such as the tip of the nose, middle of the forehead, and ear on the opposite side of the head.

2. Repeat this procedure, still with the eyes open, but this time using the left hand.

3. Now, repeat the entire above procedure (with first the right hand and then the left hand), but this time ask the subject to close his eyes. Was the subject more accurate at pointing to the requested body structures when the eyes were open or when they were closed?

   - Eyes open: _same_
   - Eyes closed: _same_

TASTE (GUSTATION)

Taste is considered to be a chemical sense, since the stimulating molecules must be dissolved in solution in order for them to be effective. The receptors for taste sensations are located in taste buds, which in turn are found in elevations called **papillae** on the tongue's surface.

There are three types of papillae containing taste buds:

1. **Fungiform papillae:** mushroom-shaped structures covering the tongue's entire surface.

2. **Vallate** or **circumvallate papillae:** large elevations arranged in an inverted formation at the back of the tongue.

3. **Foliate papillae:** found on the lateral edges of the tongue; during childhood, most of these taste buds degenerate.

Each individual taste bud contains three kinds of epithelial cells:

1. **Gustatory receptor cells:** with a gustatory hair protruding from each cell through the taste pore to the external surface.

2. **Supporting cells:** which surround the receptor cells.

3. **Basal cells:** located at the outer edge of the taste buds. The basal cells produce supporting cells, which then develop into the gustatory receptor cells.

There are considered to be five basic taste sensations:

1. Sweet
2. Salty
3. Sour
4. Bitter
5. Umami (savory)

Each is perceived by different taste buds found in specific regions of the tongue. Measuring the sense of taste; locating areas of the tongue that are sensitive to basic taste categories (sweet, salty, sour, bitter) to determine the distribution of various gustatory receptors.

MATERIALS

- Sterile swabs
- Paper towels
- Paper cups or medicine cups
- 5% sucrose solution (sweet)
- 10% NaCl solution (salty)
- 1% acetic acid (sour)
- 0.1% quinine sulfate (bitter)

PROCEDURE (WORK IN PAIRS)

1. Using a paper towel, dry the tongue.
2. Apply a few drops of a 5% sucrose solution (found in the dropper bottle) to the swab.

3. Rub the swab across the tip, sides and back of the tongue, noting where the sugar solution can be tasted.

4. Repeat this procedure using each of the other three solutions. Be sure to rinse the mouth with water and then to dry the tongue once again between applications. Use a new sterile swab each time.

5. Draw a simple diagram of the tongue in the space provided and map the location(s) where each solution can be tasted.

    Use this key:
    - st = sweet
    - sy = salty
    - sr = sour
    - b = bitter

CUTANEOUS SENSATIONS

In general, somatic sensations result from the stimulation of sensory receptors found in the skin and subcutaneous layer, mucous membranes, muscles and tendons. These receptors are not evenly distributed over the body. Some body regions contain a high concentration of them while other areas have only a few.

The **cutaneous** sensations are those produced specifically through the stimulation of receptors found in the skin's surface. They include the following four types: **tactile, thermal, pain,** and **proprioceptive.** Different receptors are responsible for the perception of each of these various sensations.

This laboratory activity deals with the tactile sensation of touch. Crude touch allows one to know that something has made contact with the skin, although the exact location, texture, size and shape cannot be perceived. Fine touch enables one to pinpoint the exact site of contact as well as to discriminate the size, shape, and texture of the object.

Distribution of receptors varies greatly over the body. For instance, the **Meissner's corpuscles** are plentiful in such places as the hands, soles of the feet, tip of the tongue and lips. **Merkel's disks** are abundant in the hands, fingertips, lips, and external genitalia. Found primarily in the hands and soles of the feet, **Ruffini's corpuscles** are sensitive to the stretching that takes place when the extremities are moved.

TWO-POINT DISCRIMINATION

Measurement of the ability to detect cutaneous stimuli relating to sensitivity differences in various regions of the body. Reporting the distance threshold between two distinct points.

MATERIALS

- Aesthesiometer (calipers)

PROCEDURE (WORK IN PAIRS)

1. Ask the subject to close his eyes and place his arm, palm up, on a table.

2. Adjust the aesthesiometer so that the two points are touching each other.

3. Place the points on the tip of the subject's index finger and ask whether he feels one or two points of contact.

4. Gradually move the points farther apart (by 1 millimeter increments) until the subject first reports feeling two distinct points of contact. Record the distance between aesthesiometer points at this time. This is known as the **two-point threshold.** This is the minimum distance at which two points of contact can be discriminated.

5. Repeat the procedure for the palm of the hand, dorsal forearm and posterior neck.

6. Record the two-point threshold results (in millimeters) on Table 11.

Table 11. Two-Point Discrimination Results.

Area	Distance (in millimeters)
Tip of Index Finger	5
Palm of Hand	7
Dorsal Forearm	3
Posterior Neck	8

PART 5
REPRODUCTIVE DIVISION

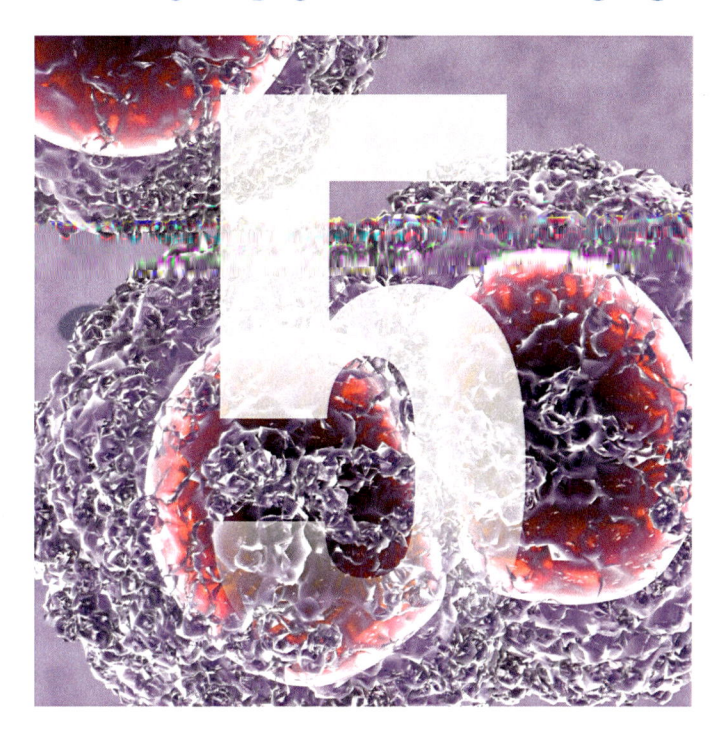

MITOSIS AND MEIOSIS

MITOSIS

Mitosis is a portion of cell cycle that allows somatic cells to grow and replicate. Every cell is at some point in the cell cycle, which begins with the formation of a new cell (interphase) and ends with the formation of two new cells after cytokinesis. Interphase is divided into three different periods: gap 1 phase (G1), synthesis (S), and gap 2 phase (G2). In gap 1, growth processes occur as well as the synthesis of new compounds other than DNA. S-phase indicates the time in which each chromosome inside the cell's nucleus synthesizes new genetic material. At the end of S-phase, each chromosome contains an identical pair of chromosomal DNA called sister chromatids that are attached at the centromere. During gap-2, cell prepares for division by mitosis and cytokinesis.

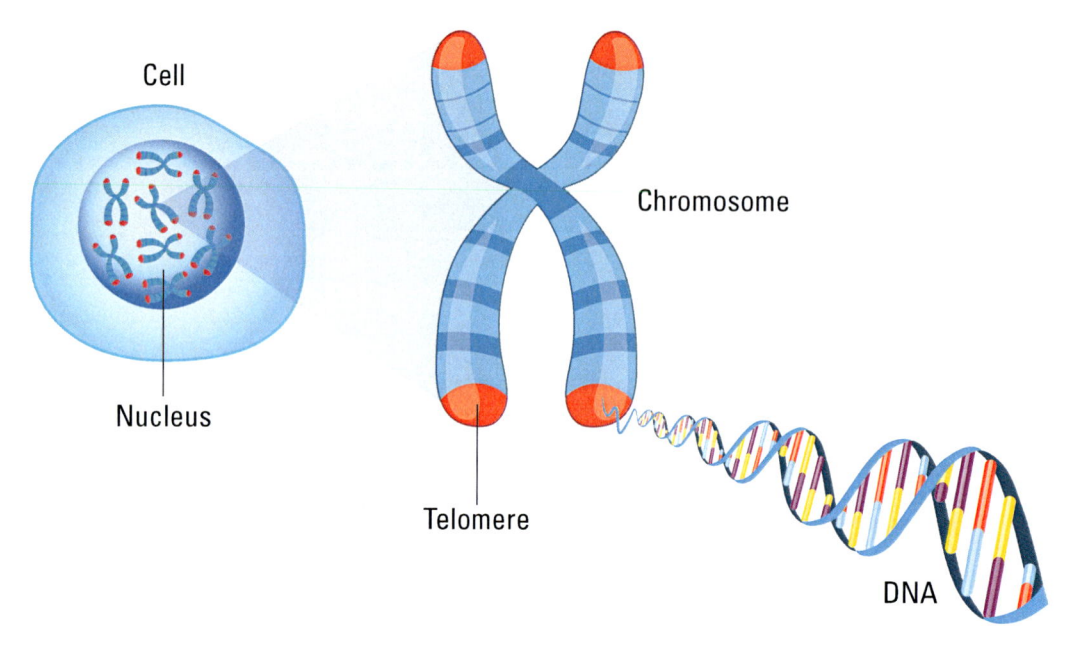

Figure 1. Cell, Chromosome, and DNA.

The stages of mitosis are as follows:

- **Prophase:** Nucleoli disappear, nuclear envelope fragments, and each duplicated chromosome appears as two sister chromatids joined by their centromeres. Mitotic spindle begins to form polar and kinetochore spindle fibers. Centrosomes move away from each other.

- **Metaphase:** Centrosomes are now located at the opposite poles of the cell. Chromosomes move toward the middle or equator of the cell. Each chromosome has kinetochore fibers attached to them at the centromere as they prepare to separate the sister chromatids.

- **Anaphase:** Two sister chromatids begin to separate from each other as kinetochore fibers pull them toward opposite poles of the cell.

- **Telophase:** Two daughter nuclei form inside the cell and chromosomes become less condensed. The mitotic apparatus disassembles. Mitosis is complete after Telophase and cytokinesis.

- **Cytokinesis:** This is the division of the cytoplasm to form two new daughter cells. Cytokinesis begins with the formation of a cleavage furrow during telophase. Each daughter cell has a complete set of chromosomes and now enters the G1 phase of interphase.

Interphase   Prophase   Prometaphase   Metaphase

Anaphase   Telophase   Mitosis Completed

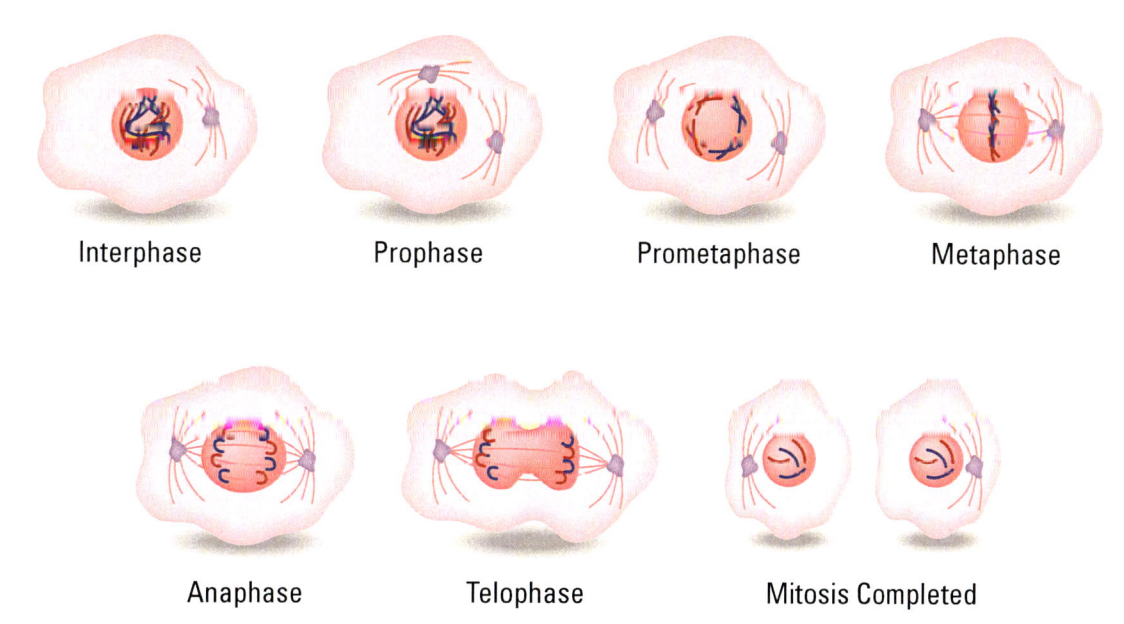

Figure 2. Mitosis.

MEIOSIS

Meiosis is the process which produces gametes (sperm and ovum). During meiosis the chromosomes are copied once and divided twice, reducing the number of chromosomes by half, which is referred to as a reduction division. In sexual reproduction, haploid (1*n* or 1 set of chromosomes) gametes (egg and sperm) fuse to form a diploid (2*n* or 2 sets of chromosomes) zygote. Genetic material is also shuffled during meiosis so that each haploid cell carries a new and unique set of genes.

The stages of meiosis are as follows:

- **Interphase before meiosis:** DNA is replicated (similar to mitosis).

- **Prophase I:** Homologous chromosomes condense and pair. **Crossing over** occurs, lined up sister chromatids exchange genetic material.

- **Metaphase I:** Microtubule spindle apparatus attaches to chromosomes.

- **Anaphase I:** Homologous pairs of chromosomes separate.

- **Telophase I:** One set of paired chromosomes arrive at each pole. After cytokinesis, there are two daughter cells each receiving one of the pair of homologous chromosomes. At this point in meiosis, the daughter cells are considered haploid.

- **Prophase II:** DNA does not replicate between meiosis I and meiosis II. Spindle fibers form between centrioles in the two daughter cells created by meiosis I. There is no **crossing over** in prophase II.

- **Metaphase II:** Chromosomes align along the equator of the cell.

- **Anaphase II:** Sister chromatids separate.

- **Telophase II:** Chromatids arrive at each pole. After cytokinesis, meiosis is complete. There are now four daughter cells that are haploid, each having half the original number of chromosomes than the parent cells before meiosis began.

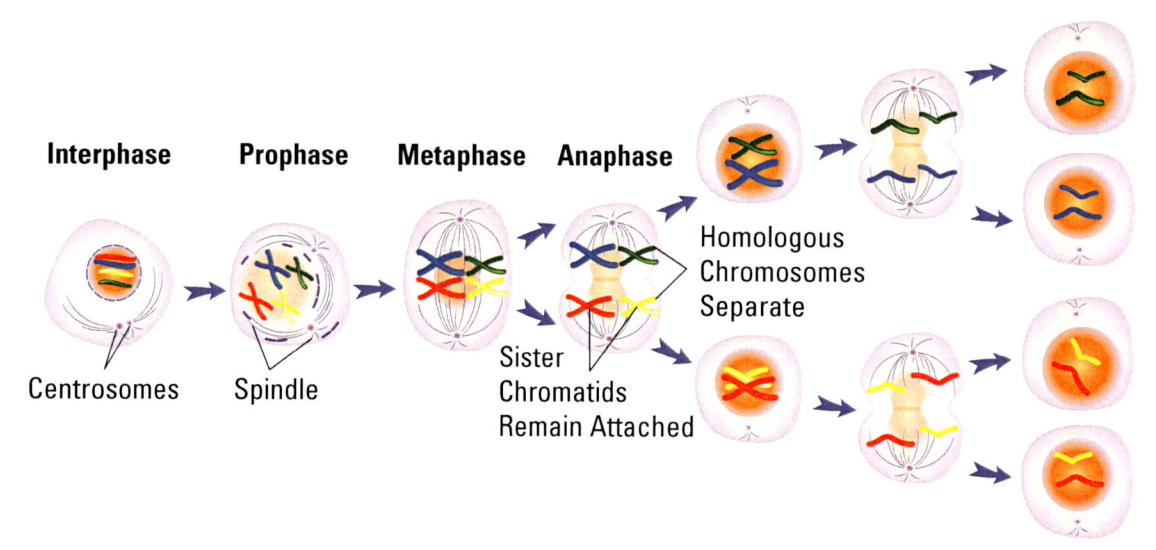

Figure 3. Cell Division (meiosis).

COMPARING MITOSIS AND MEIOSIS

- Mitosis occurs in somatic cells and results in two daughter cells that are diploid ($2n$).

- Meiosis occurs in certain cells within the ovaries and testes and results in four haploid ($1n$) daughter cells due to the two rounds of cell division.

- In Meiosis, crossing over occurs in prophase I, allowing for genetic material to be exchanged between homologous chromosomes.

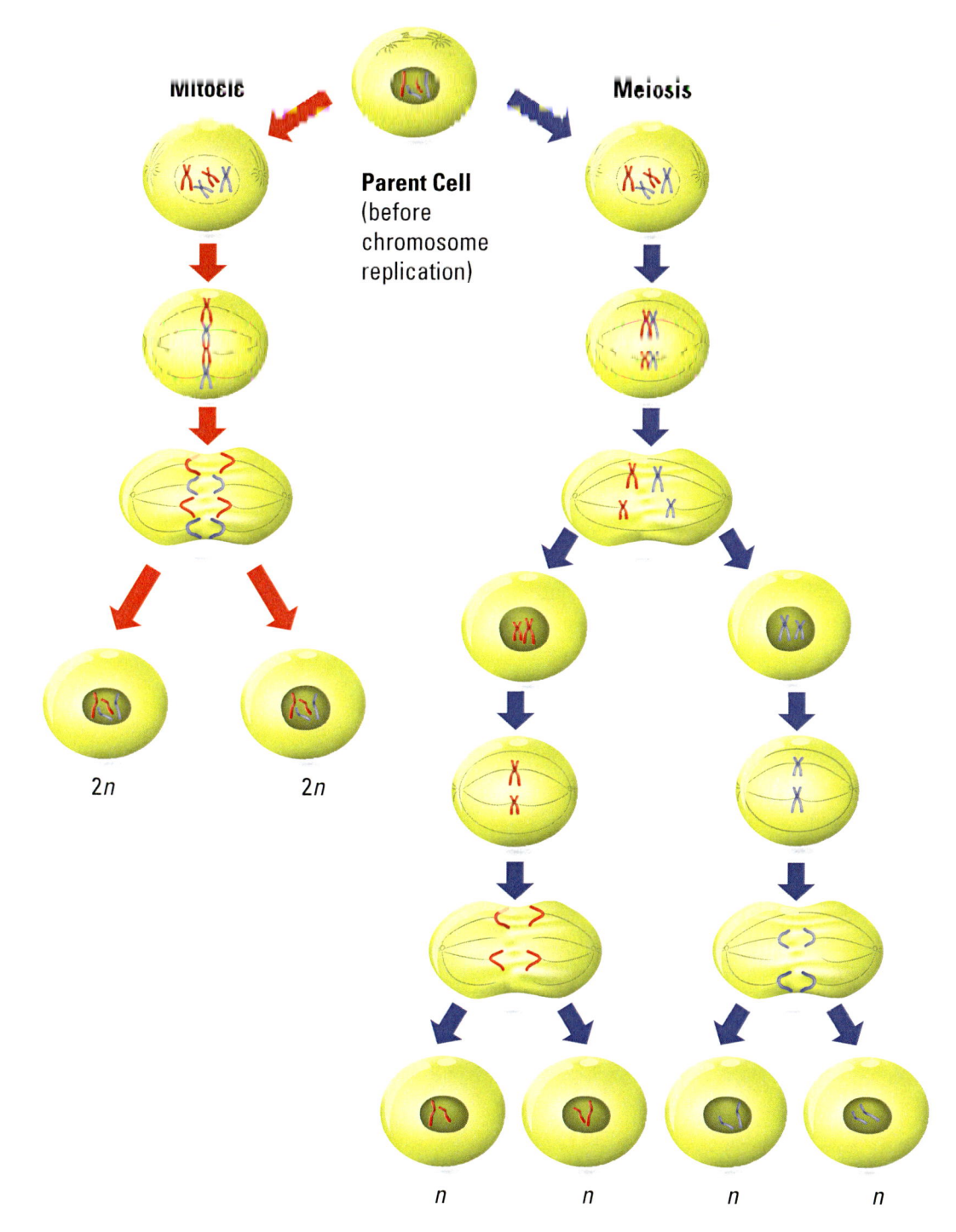

Figure 4. Mitosis versus Meiosis.

MALE REPRODUCTIVE SYSTEM

THE TESTIS

INTRODUCTION

The testes are paired glands which produce the male gametes called sperm. They are covered with tough, white connective tissue. The outer layer is the **tunica vaginalis,** the inner layer is the **tunica albuginea.** The testes are divided by **septa** into **lobules** into which are packed hundreds of tightly-coiled **seminiferous tubules.** Inside the seminiferous tubules, spermatogenesis occurs forming sperm. Once formed, the sperm cells mature outside of the testes in the epididymis.

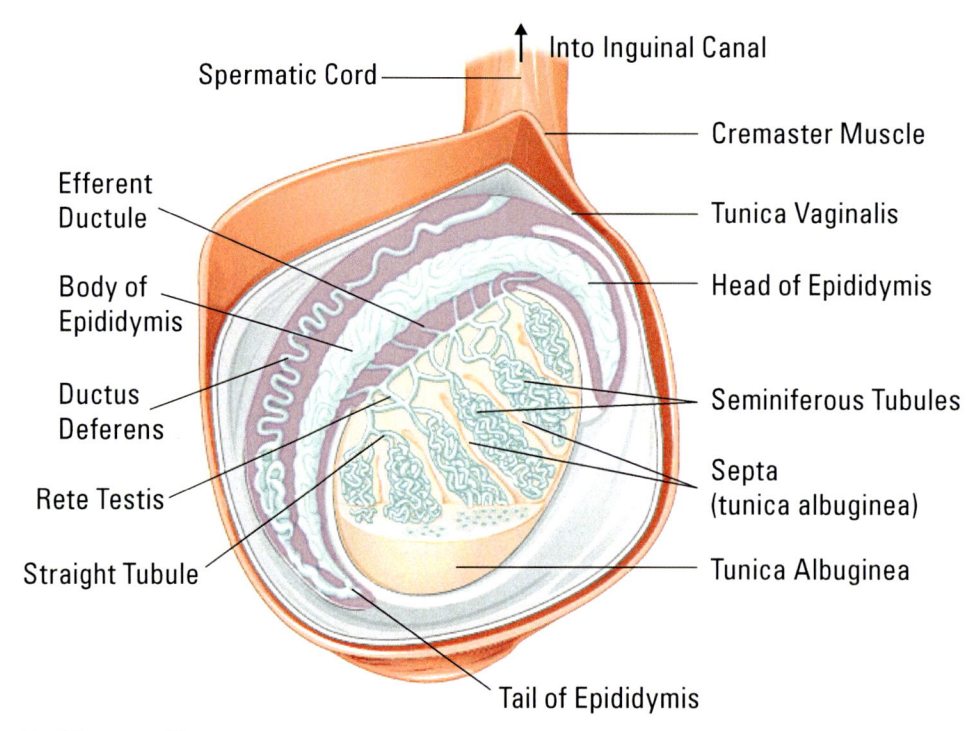

Figure 5. Human Testes. By Figure 28 01 03.JPG: OpenStax College (Original file: Anatomy & Physiology, Connexions Web site. http://cnx.org/content/col11496/1.6/, Jun 19, 2013.) derivative work:Miguelferig (This file was derived from Figure 28 01 03.JPG:) [CC BY 3.0 (http://creativecommons.org/licenses/by/3.0)], via Wikimedia Commons from Wikimedia Commons. https://commons.wikimedia.org/wiki/File%3AFigure_28_01_03_gl.jpg

EXERCISE

Examine both the external and internal aspects of the sheep testis. Locate the following structures:

- Tunica vaginalis
- Tunica albuginea
- Septa
- Lobules
- Seminiferous tubules
- Epididymis

SPERMATOGENESIS

Spermatogenesis is the formation of the male gamete, sperm. Obtain a microscope slide of a testicular lobule and locate each of the following developmental stages:

- Spermatogonium
- Primary spermatocyte
- Secondary spermatocyte
- Spermatid
- Spermatozoan

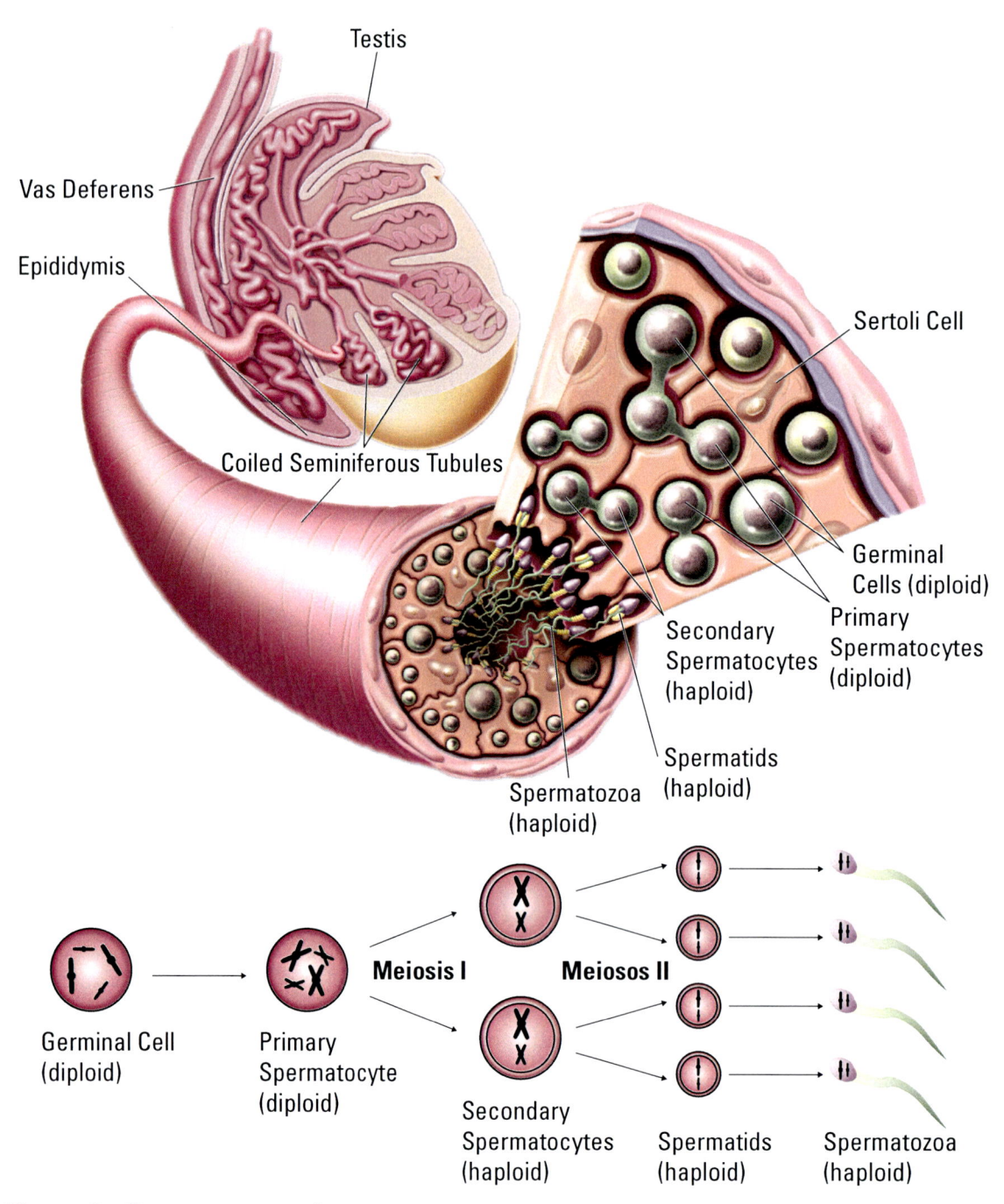

Figure 6. Spermatogenesis.

PART 5: REPRODUCTIVE DIVISION

EXERCISE

Draw sketches of the male gametes in the various stages of spermatogenesis. Pay particular attention to cell morphology and location of the cells within lobules of the seminiferous tubules.

Testicular lobule 100×

Spermatogonium 400×

Primary spermatocyte 400×

Secondary spermatocyte 400×

Spermatid 400×

Spermatozoan 400×

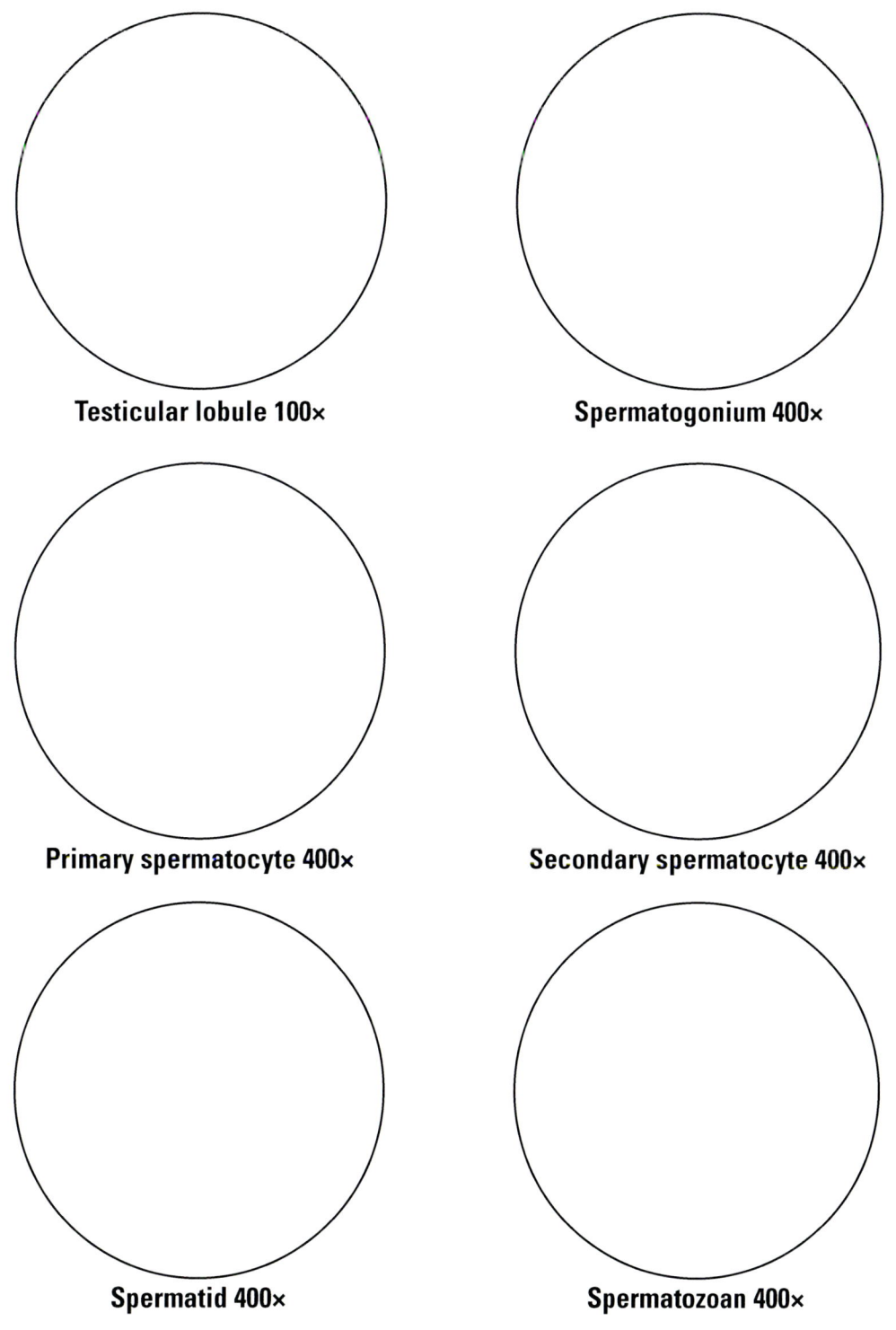

Figure 7. Human Testis—Spermatogenesis.

FEMALE REPRODUCTIVE SYSTEM

OOGENESIS

THE OVARY

INTRODUCTION

The ovaries, like the testes, are paired glands. The ovary and the testis are homologous structures. The ovaries, however, are in the pelvic cavity and held in place by ligaments.

The exterior of the ovary is composed of a single cell layer, the **germinal epithelium.** The interior of the ovary is called the **stroma** and is divided into a dense, outer layer called the **cortex** and a loose, inner area called the **medulla.** The developing follicles in oogenesis are located in the cortex.

PART 5: REPRODUCTIVE DIVISION

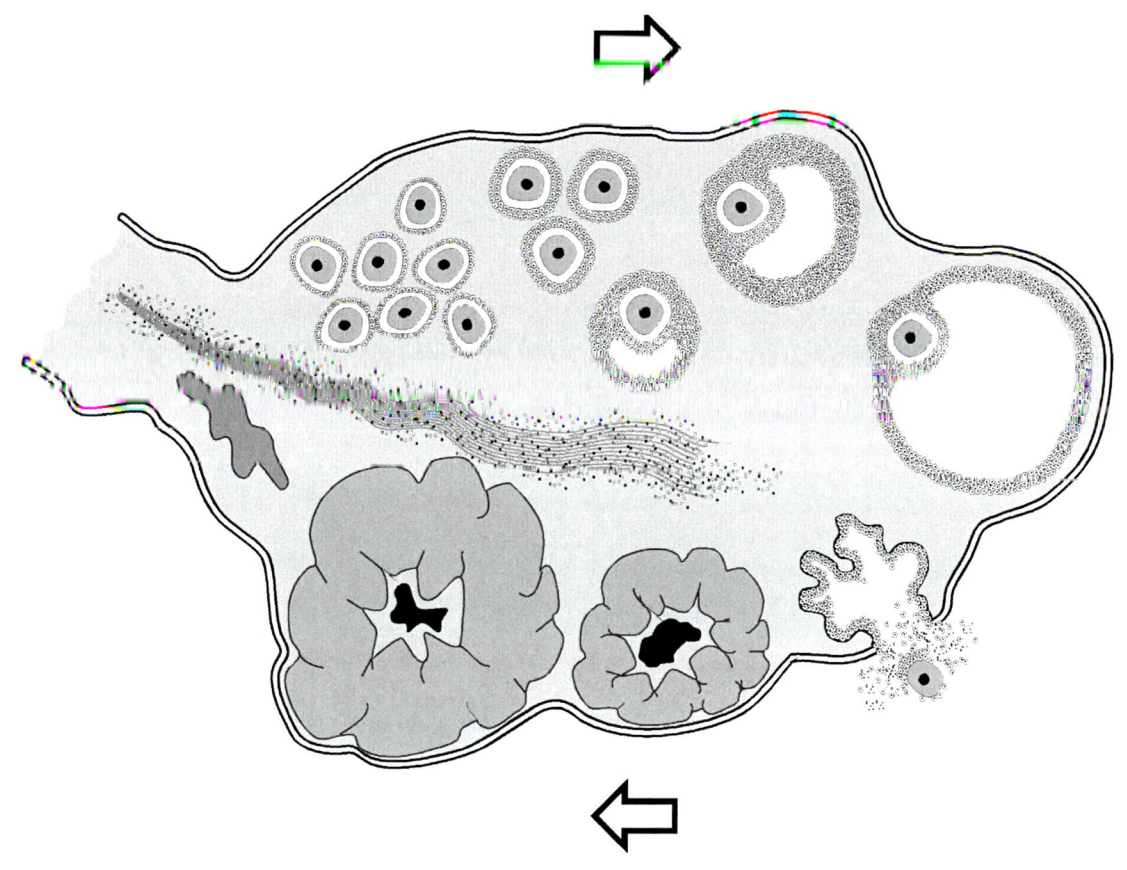

Figure 8. Human Ovary.

Locate the following structures:

- Germinal epithelium
- Tunica albuginea
- Ovarian cortex
- Ovarian medulla
- Primordial follicle
- Primary follicle
- Primary oocyte
- Secondary follicle
- Secondary oocyte
- Mature Graafian follicle
- Corpus hemorrhagicum
- Ovulation
- Early corpus luteum
- Mature corpus luteum
- Corpus albicans

147

EXERCISE

Examine a pig ovary. Note the outer surface. Cut the ovary open. Locate the following structures:

- Germinal epithelium
- Stroma
- Cortex
- Medulla
- Corpora lutea

Identify different stages of follicular development. Especially note the multiple yellow-orange **corpora lutea.** These structures occur due to multiple ovulation and birth in the pig.

OOGENESIS

Oogenesis is the formation of the female gamete (sex cell). Obtain a microscope slide of an ovary and locate each of the following developmental stages:

- Growing follicle
- Secondary follicle
- Graafian follicle
- Corpus luteum
- Corpus albicans

EXERCISE

On the following page, draw sketches of the female gametes and follicles in the various stages of oogenesis. Pay particular attention to cell morphology and location within the cortex of the ovary.

PART 5: REPRODUCTIVE DIVISION

Primary follicle 400×

Secondary follicle 400×

Graafian follicle 400×

Corpus luteum 400×

Corpus albicans 400×

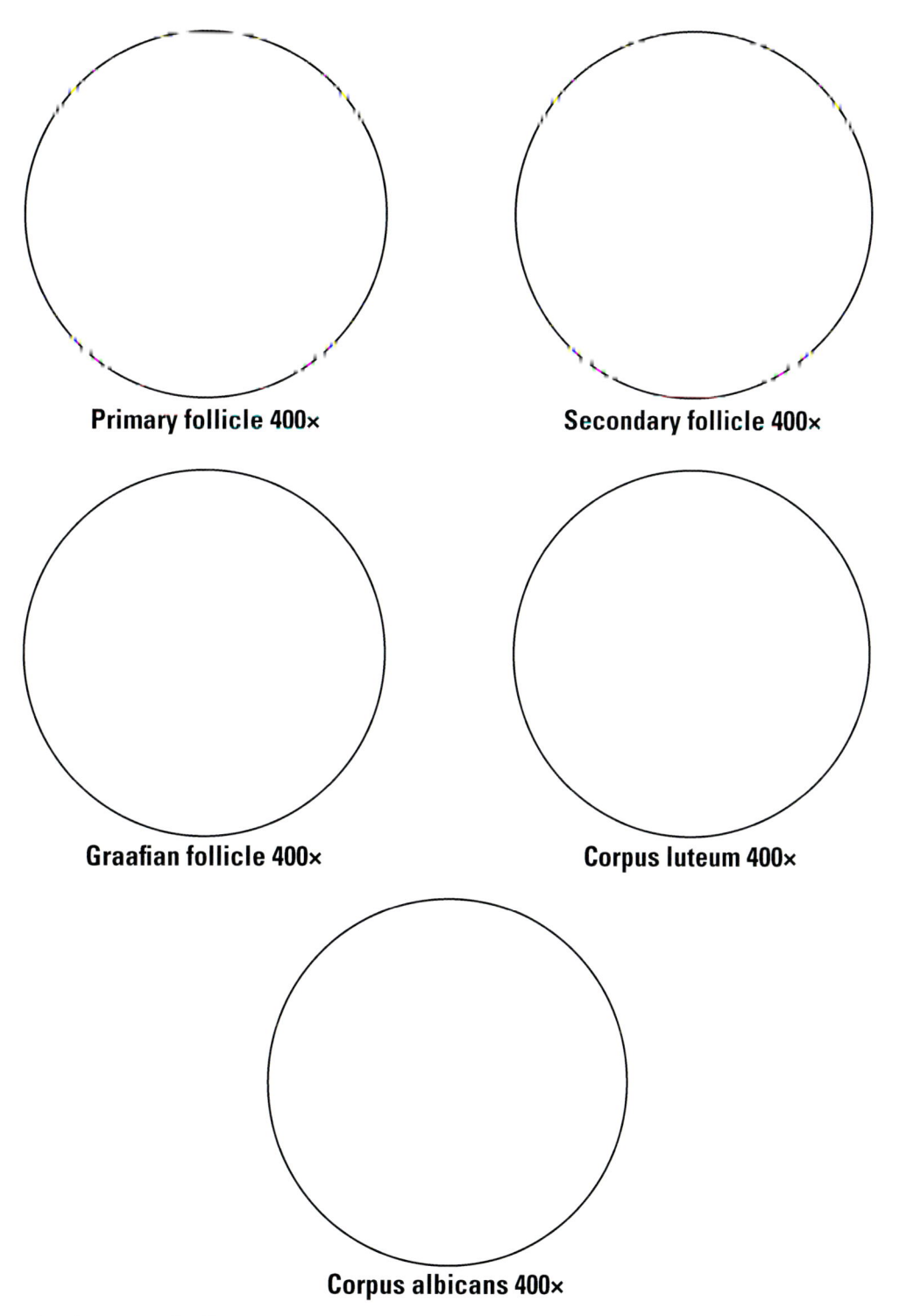

Figure 9. Oogenesis Stages.

THE MENSTRUAL CYCLE

The length of the menstrual cycle ranges from 24 to 35 days, with an average length being 28 days. The cycle can be divided into four phases; "menstrual phase," "preovulatory phase," "ovulation," and "postovulatory phase." The following chart is a summary of the hormones involved in each phase and the events triggered by these various hormones.

Table 1. Menstrual Cycle Phases.

Phase	Day of Cycle*	Hormone	Source	Action
Menstrual Phase	Day 1–Day 5	FSH (Follicle-stimulating hormone)	Anterior Pituitary Gland	Stimulates development of ovarian follicles
Preovulatory Phase	Day 6–Day 13	FSH	Anterior Pituitary Gland	Stimulates development of graafian follicles and stimulates ovarian follicles to secrete estrogens
		Estrogens	Ovarian Follicles (especially graafian follicle)	Stimulates repair and build-up of uterine endometrial lining
Ovulation	Day 14	LH (Luteinizing hormone) (surge at about days 12 and 13)	Anterior Pituitary Gland	Causes ovulation and development of corpus luteum
Postovulatory Phase	Day 15–Day 28	Progesterone (and estrogens)	Corpus Luteum	Finishes preparation of endometrium for possible implantation

*Based on 28-day cycle

If fertilization and implantation do **not** take place during the postovulatory phase, the high blood levels of progesterone and estrogens from the corpus luteum inhibit LH secretion from the anterior pituitary gland.

Consequently, the corpus luteum degenerates, forming the corpus albicans. This in turn results in decreased blood levels of progesterone and estrogens. These decreased hormone levels initiate another menstrual cycle (menstruation), since the endometrial lining is no longer being hormonally maintained.

SPERMATOGENESIS VERSUS OOGENESIS

Spermatogenesis begins at puberty and continues throughout life. In spermatogenesis, the four haploid daughter cells from meiosis become four viable sperm after further development through a process called **spermiogenesis**. In Oogenesis, stem cells or oogonia complete their mitotic divisions and begin their first meiotic division before birth and are arrested at prophase I until puberty. After puberty, primary oocytes are stimulated to continue oogenesis. Division of the daughter cells is uneven, the smaller cells are called **polar bodies** and degenerate. The larger cell produced from the first meiotic division, or the secondary oocyte, does not complete its final meiotic division until after fertilization.

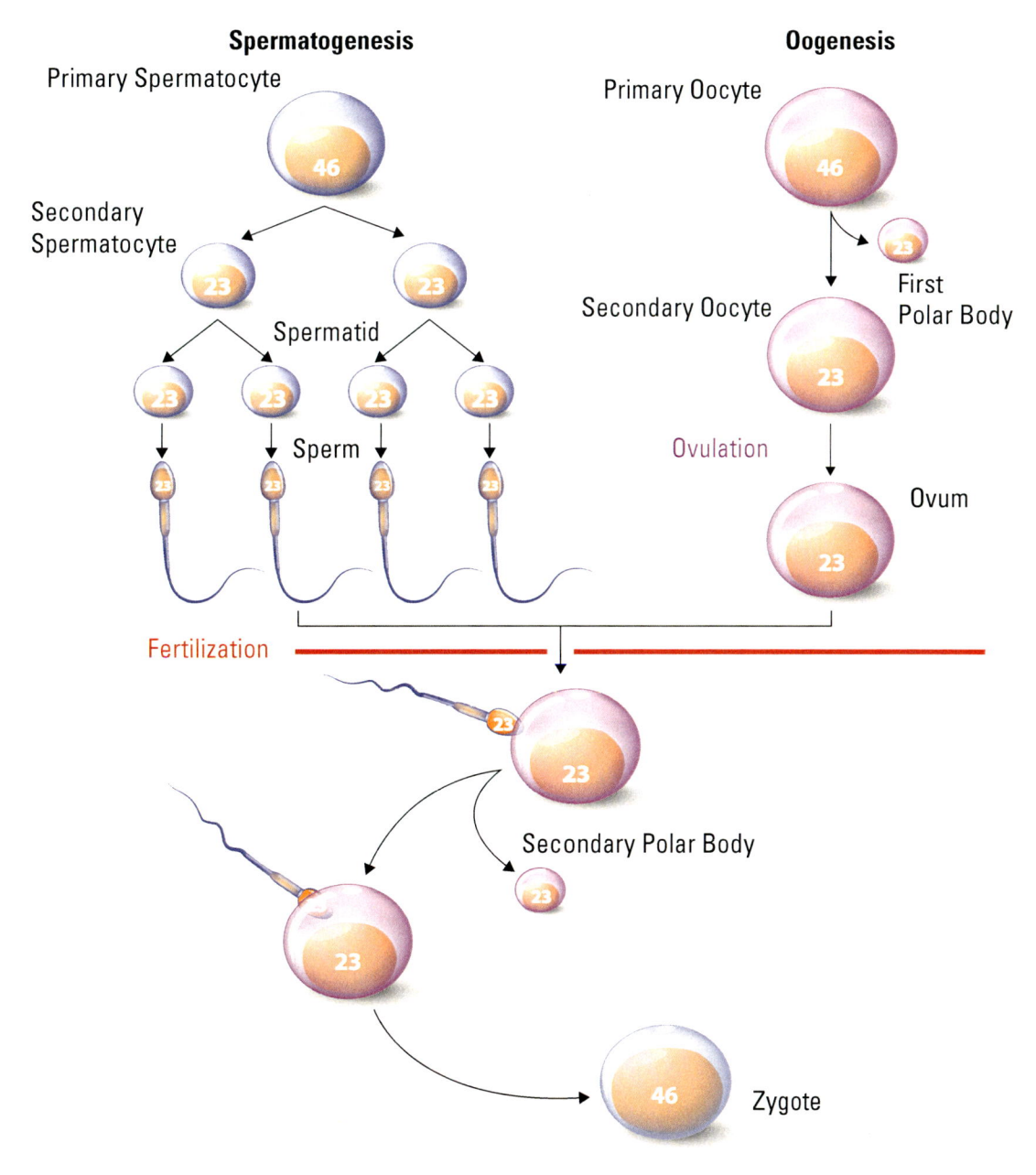

Figure 10. Spermatogenesis versus Oogenesis.

EMBRYOLOGY DEVELOPMENT

HUMAN EMBRYO DEVELOPMENT

In Figure 11, label the illustrations showing structures of development at the indicated stages.

FERTILIZED EGG
- Zona pellucida

TWO CELL STAGE
- Blastomere
- Cleavage furrow

FOUR CELL STAGE
- Blastomere
- Cleavage furrow

EIGHT CELL STAGE
- Blastomere
- Cleavage furrow

16 CELL STAGE
- Morula

BLASTOCYST
- Blastocele
- Trophoblast

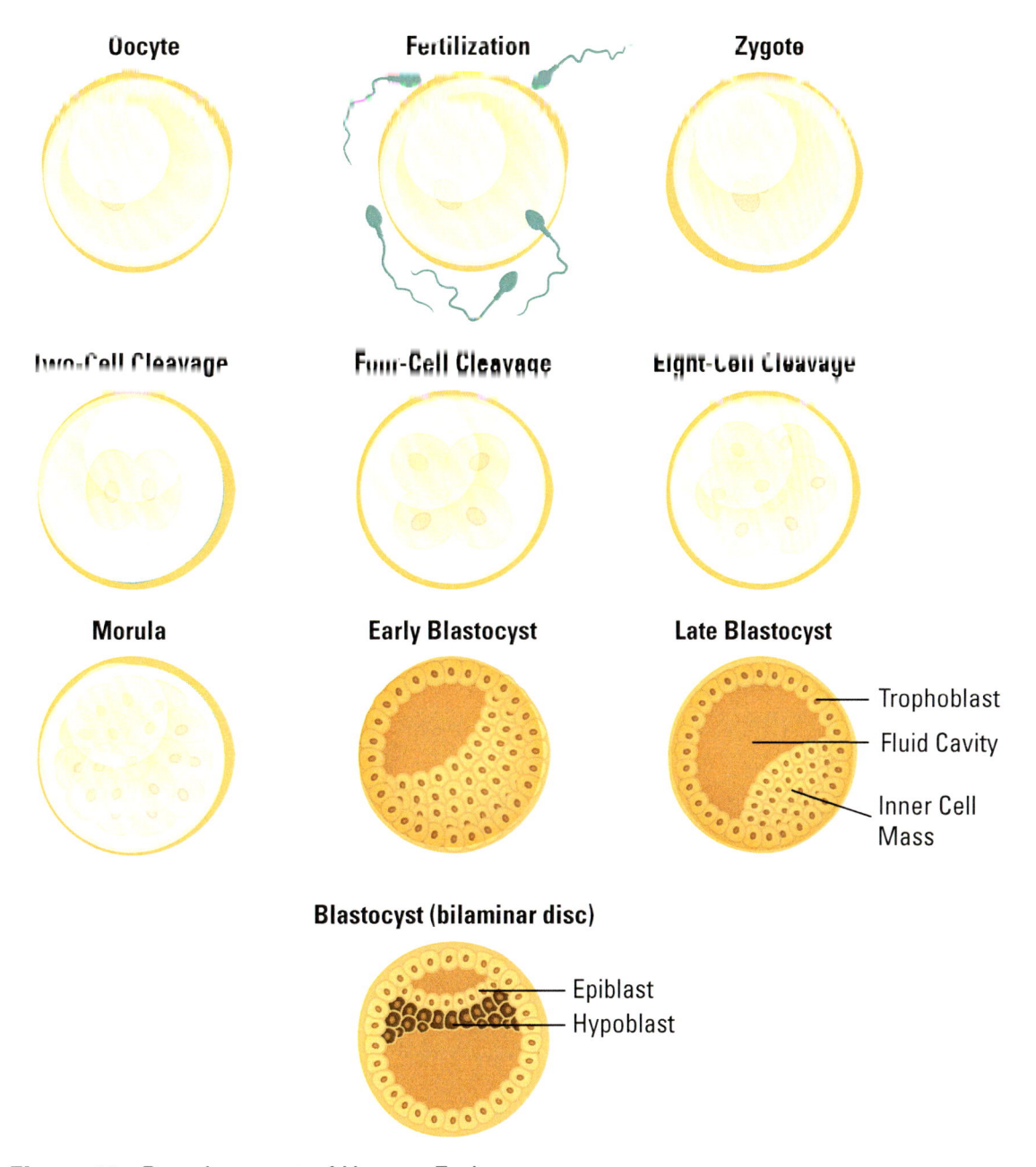

Figure 11. Development of Human Embryo.

CHICK DEVELOPMENT

On the following page, sketch each of the chick embryo serial microscope slides listed below and label the structures indicated.

18-HOUR SERIAL SLIDE
- Primitive streak

24-HOUR SERIAL SLIDE
- Primitive streak
- Hensen's node
- Head folds

33-HOUR SERIAL SLIDE
- Heart
- Forebrain
- Midbrain
- Hindbrain
- Somites

48-HOUR SERIAL SLIDE
- Forebrain
- Midbrain
- Hindbrain
- Somites
- Flexion
- Torsion

60–72-HOUR SERIAL SLIDE
- Forebrain
- Midbrain
- Hindbrain
- Eye
- Auditory vesicle

96-HOUR SERIAL SLIDE
- Forebrain
- Midbrain
- Hindbrain
- Eye
- Allantois

PART 5: REPRODUCTIVE DIVISION

18-Hour Serial Slide
© Biophoto Associates/Science Source

24-Hour Serial Slide
© Biophoto Associates/Science Source

33-Hour Serial Slide
© Biophoto Associates/Science Source

48-Hour Serial Slide
© Biophoto Associates/Science Source

60–72-Hour Serial Slide
© Biophoto Associates/Science Source

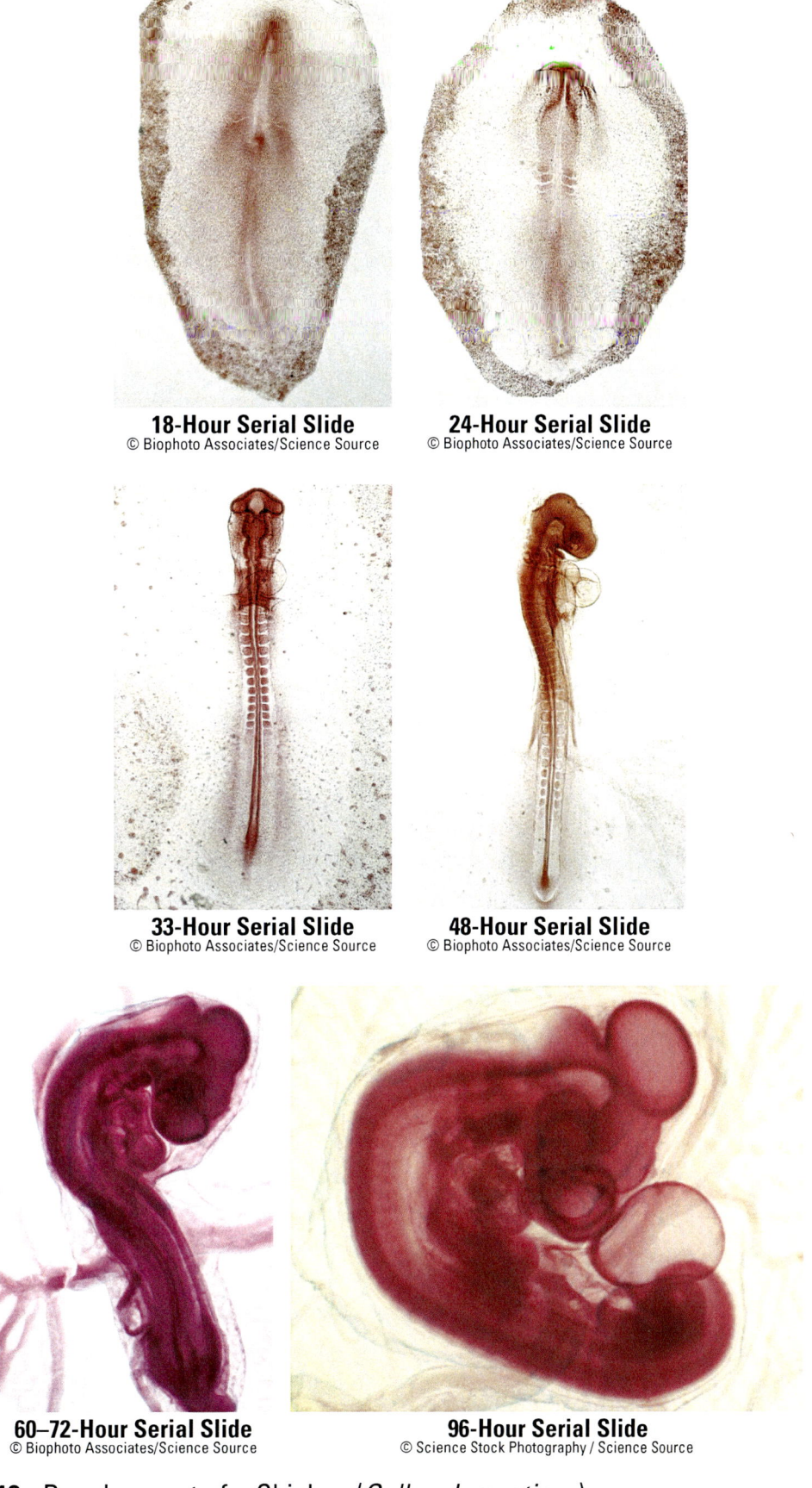

96-Hour Serial Slide
© Science Stock Photography / Science Source

Figure 12. Development of a Chicken (*Gallus domesticus*).

155

PART 5: REPRODUCTIVE DIVISION

18-hour developmental stage

24-hour developmental stage

33-hour developmental stage

48-hour developmental stage

60–72-hour developmental stage

96-hour developmental stage

Figure 13. Development of a Chicken.

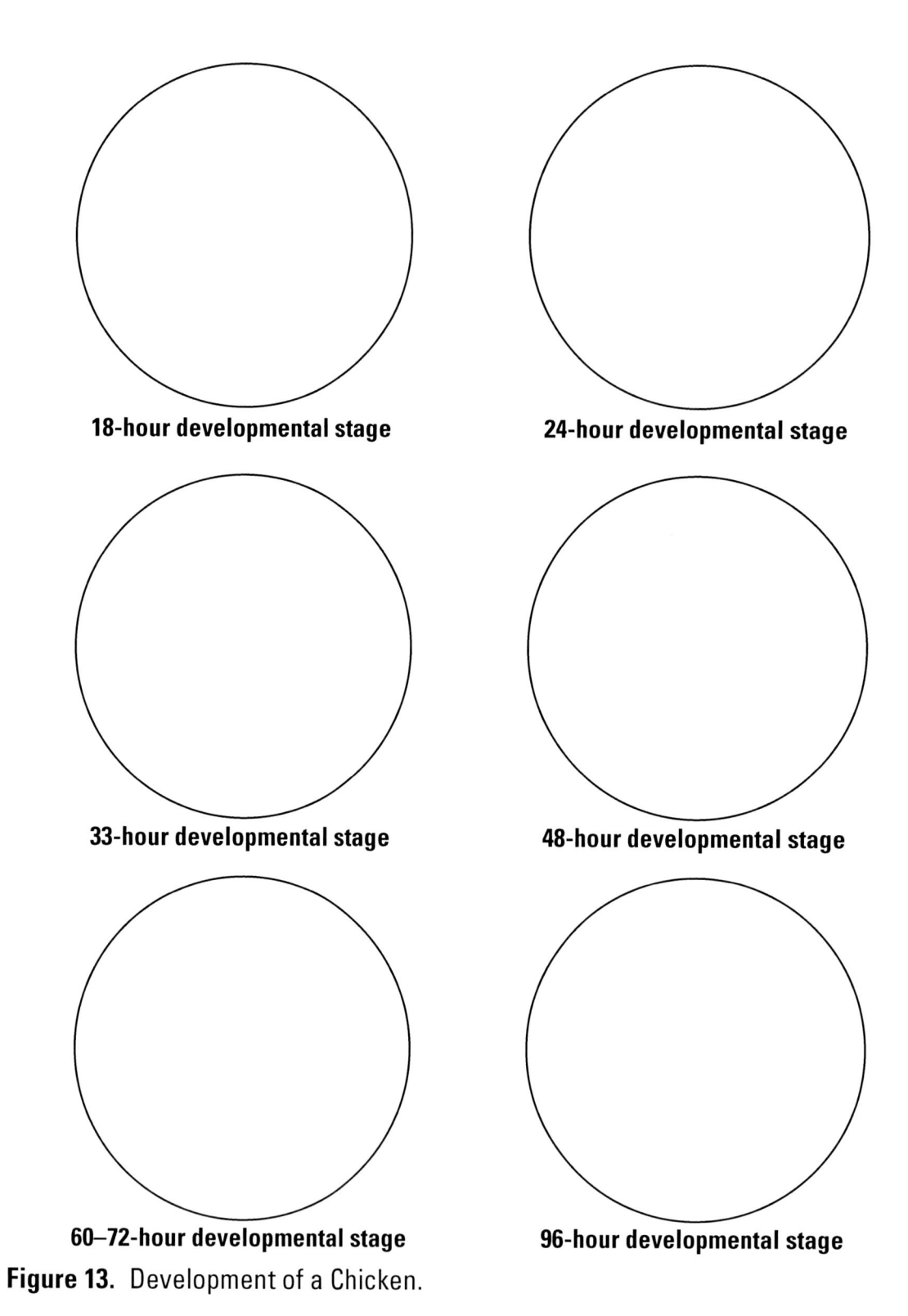

MAMMALIAN MATERNAL AND FETAL STRUCTURES

There are a number of different types of mammalian placentas, varying by species and structure:

1. **Discoidal placenta:** in primates (including humans); villous chorion in one area of the placenta

2. **Cotyledinary placenta:** in ruminants (cows and sheep); clusters of villous chorion throughout the endometrium

3. **Zonary placenta:** in cats and dogs, villous chorion in bands throughout the endometrium

4. **Diffuse placenta:** in pigs and horses; villous chorion in diffuse random tufts

FETAL MEMBRANES

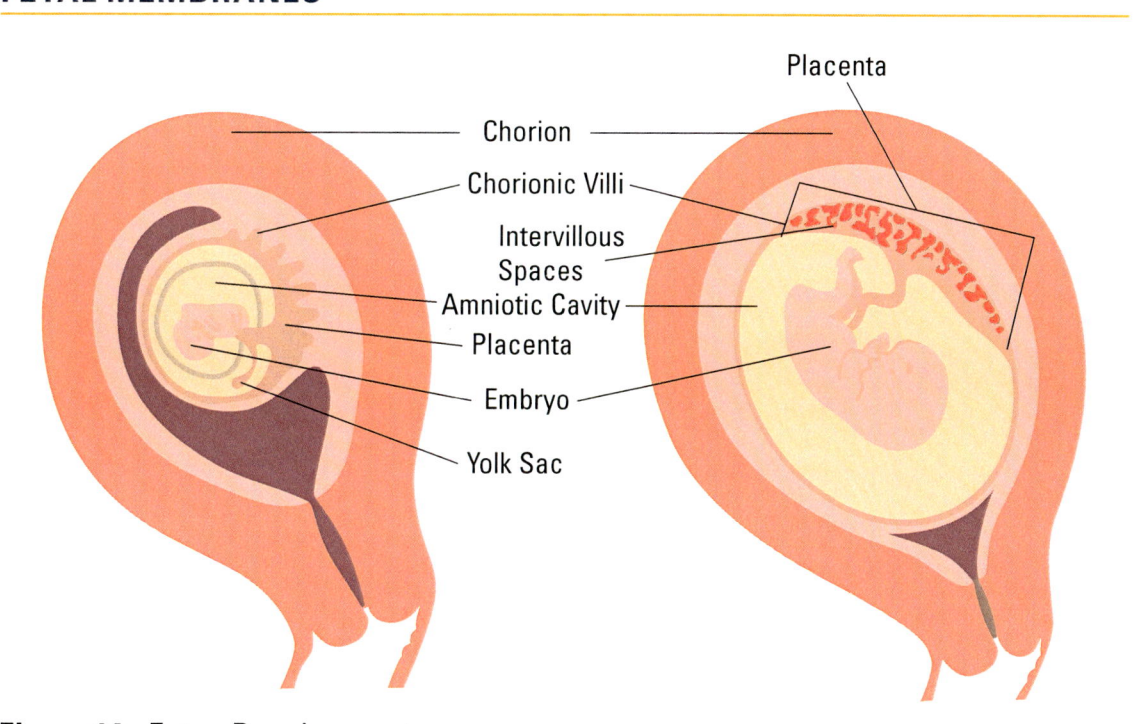

Figure 14. Fetus Development.

Figure 15. Fetal Membranes.

Locate the following structures:

- Amnion
- Amniotic cavity
- Smooth chorion
- Villous chorion
- Decidua basalis
- Decidua capsularis
- Decidua parietalis
- Umbilical cord

EMBRYOLOGY DEVELOPMENT SUMMARY

SLIDESHOW PRESENTATION

1. *Comparative embryology*

2. The purpose of this presentation is to gain an understanding of the developmental processes. It includes a study of **mitosis** and **meiosis, fertilization, and early embryonic development.** Many processes of development in various organisms are similar. We will view some of these processes and relate them to human development.

3. We will begin by viewing **mitosis.**

4. This photo shows an onion bulb with roots, projecting downward, that can be sectioned to study **mitosis.** The growing portion of these roots is at their tips and thus this is the region where the equal cell division, **mitosis** will take place.

5. This is a medial longitudinal section of an entire root tip containing many cells undergoing **mitosis** toward the tip at the right. The next series of photographs are a series of high power photomicrographs of individual cells showing great detail of the **mitotic division.**

6. The cell spends most of its time preparing for cell division in a stage of mitosis called **interphase.** At this stage the chromosomes are not clearly discernible. They appear as a dark smudge within the cell. This is the stage in which the chromosomes are replicated to form **chromatids.**

7. In **early prophase,** the **chromosomes** having replicated now begin to become visible.

8. In **late prophase,** the replicated chromosomes are completely distinguishable. They are scattered throughout the cell, not taking any particular orientation.

9. The cell now prepares to undergo the cellular division. In **early metaphase** the replicated chromosomes migrate to the center of the cell.

10. In **late metaphase** the replicated chromosomes are completely aligned at the center of the cell. We can view the **spindle fibers,** which are processes that radiate from opposite ends of the cell and connect to the **chromatids.** They will be responsible for the separation of the **chromatids** and their migration.

11. In **early anaphase** the **spindle fibers** begin to pull the **chromatids** apart. The chromatids move to opposite ends of the dividing cell.

PART 5: REPRODUCTIVE DIVISION

12. In **late anaphase** the **chromatids** are now once again called **chromosomes** since they have separated. They have almost completely migrated to the opposite poles of the cell.

13. The cytoplasm of the cell will now begin to divide in **early telophase.**

14. New nuclear membranes, or in the case of the onion, cell walls, will form enclosing each new set of chromosomes.

15. This final frame shows the two daughter cells whose nuclei are just entering **interphase,** thus completing the cycle.

16. It is now necessary to gain an understanding of the developmental sequence from **fertilization** to **cleavage.** To do this, we will study the **Ascaris** round worm. Photomicrographs show sections of the **Ascaris** uterus depicting **sperm entrance, maturation of the egg,** and **cleavage of the egg.**

17. The first slide shows the entrance of a characteristically shaped **spermatozoan** into an **oocyte.** This is **fertilization.** The **spermatozoan** is the triangular-shaped structure located at 5 o'clock within the egg.

18. In the human, the **spermatozoan** enters the egg before the egg completes its meiotic division. This is also true of **Ascaris.** In the human, the **spermatozoan** enters the **secondary oocyte** which must undergo a second meitoic division. On some slides we will see the extrusion of a **polar body.**

19. Once the **spermatozoan** enters the egg, the **spermatozoan** begins to undergo a change in shape. In this photo, the **spermatozoan** is on the left and the egg nucleus is on the right.

20. Notice that the sperm has become circular at the right. The egg nucleus in this stage is in **metaphase** since it is completing its **meiotic division.**

21. The **spermatozoan** nucleus is now not very distinct. Note the **metaphase spindle fibers** of the egg nucleus.

22. The visible egg nucleus undergoes **anaphase.**

23. The **spermatozoan** nucleus in the center in this slide is visible. At the left a **polar body** is being extruded.

24. *No narration* or *slide.*

25. The egg has completed its meiotic division, and the **spermatozoan** and the egg nucleus are in the process of **fusing.**

26. In this photo, one cannot distinguish the **spermatozoan** from the egg nucleus. They are termed **pronuclei** before they fuse.

PART 5: REPRODUCTIVE DIVISION

27. The mature fertilized egg will undergo a series of mitotic divisions called **cleavage**. The first cleavage division is illustrated by a series of seven slides (no slide).

28. This cell is in the **early prophase** stage.

29. Here is a photo showing **late prophase**.

30. The cell undergoes **metaphase**. The **chromosomes** are aligned at the center of the cell. In an animal or human cell the **spindle fibers** radiate from cell organelles called **centrioles**, the circular dark areas at each pole of the cell. Note at 3 o'clock a **polar body** is still clinging to the egg during first cleavage division.

31. This slide shows **early anaphase**.

32. This slide shows **late anaphase**

33. In the animal or human cell, **telophase** occurs by a pinching in at the top and bottom of the cytoplasm, with the cell masses finally splitting.

34. The **first mitotic cleavage division** is now complete.

35. Several cleavage divisions will now take place in succession: two cells form four, four cells form eight, etc. (no slide).

36. This illustrates **second cleavage** to show a **four-cell stage**.

37. **Third cleavage** produces an **eight-cell stage**.

38. In human development, this photo shows a fertilized egg called a **zygote**. The **zona pellucida** is evident surrounding the **zygote** and is now helping to prevent a second **spermatozoan** from entering the egg. Within are the **pronuclei** from the male and female.

39. **Cleavage** will take place. Remember, this is the series of **mitotic divisions**: one cell forming two, two cells forming four, four cells forming eight, eight cells forming sixteen, etc. the cells resulting from successive cleavages are called **blastomeres**. This photo illustrates the second **cleavage** producing the **four-cell stage** containing four **blastomeres.**

40. Once the **fourth cleavage** has produced a **16-cell stage,** it is called a morula. This is now a solid ball of cells. The **morula** continues to divide forming the **32-cell stage** as shown in the photo.

41. The cells begin to move, the solid ball begins to hollow out forming the **blastocyst**. Within the **blastocyst,** cells will cluster forming the inner cell mass. This photo shows the **inner cell mass** in the upper right area of the **blastocyst.**

PART 5: REPRODUCTIVE DIVISION

42. The cells of the **inner cell mass** of the **blastocyst** will differentiate to form a **bilaminar disc** or **embryonic disc**. This disc will differentiate into the **hypoblast** and **epiblast**. The photo illustrates a **blastocyst** with the cells starting to differentiate to form the **bilaminar disc**.

43. At the **blastula stage** rather than having a round hollow ball of cells we have a disc called a **bilaminar disc** or **embryonic disc** composed a two plates of cells, the **hypoblast** and **epiblast**. Some differentiation will take place to form **ectoderm** from the **epiblast** and the **endoderm** from the **hypoblast**. Again migration of cells will occur. Cells will migrate across the upper surface of the ectoderm plate, down through a groove, and come to rest between the ectoderm and endoderm plates forming a third layer of cells called the **mesoderm**. These three types of cells; **ectoderm, mesoderm,** and **endoderm** are called the primary germ layers. We will view chick development slides since the chick develops in the form of a disc as does the human.

44. This slide is a view looking down on the upper surface of the ectoderm plate. The endoderm is below, but is not visible. The chick is about 16 hours old and clearly shows the **primitive streak** which is the groove where migration of the cells will take place to form the mesoderm. The primitive streak is **homologous** (or similar in structure) to the dorsal lip of the blastopore in the frog. Thus, this stage could be called a gastrula when the cells begin to migrate. The head will develop at the top of this streak.

45. In this slide the cells have started to migrate forming the mesoderm. They migrate from the anterior end of the primitive streak at first in a region called **Hensen's Node.** This node moves posteriorly down the primitive streak as the embryo continues to develop. We can clearly see the **head folds** which have formed anterior to Hensen's Node. The chick is 18 hours old.

46. This is a 20–22-hour whole mount. Hensen's Node has moved posteriorly. It is in the region about ¾ of the way down the primitive streak where the streak becomes blurred. Just above Hensen's Node are structures called **somites** that are beginning to form. The somites will become the vertebrae and some muscles. Keep an eye on the somites in the following photos.

47. The 24-hour chick displays developed somites and a well developed head process. The primitive streak has about disappeared at this stage.

48. The 27–29-hour whole mount clearly shows the development of the head and somites.

49. At 33 hours in the chick (or 21 days in the human), the **heart** becomes visible. The darker regions illustrate the formation of the lobes of the **brain**. The lighter sac, just above the somites is the heart.

50. At 38–43 hours, the embryo begins to bend its head. This process is called **flexion**. In the spinal region, the embryo also begins to twist. This is called **torsion**.

51. At 48 hours, we can see definite flexion and torsion. Two new structures are now clearly visible. Above the heart are the cup-shaped **eyes**. To the left of the heart is the **otocyst** or the **auditory vesicle**. The large blood vessels are the **vitelline veins** that connect to the yolk for means of nutrition in the chick.

52. These features are also seen in the 56 hour whole mount.

53. During 60–70 hours, the **limb buds** begin to form. The instructor will point these out to you (no slide).

54. At 72 hours, the chick has completely folded over. Note at the tail region, there is a small sac called the **allantois**.

55. In the 96-hour slide, the allantois is seen as a large clear sac. It is an outpocketing or evagination from the hind-gut that serves as a storage reservoir for waste products formed by the embryo. It will degenerate during later development. We have seen many different organisms develop. I have been careful to choose only those stages and sequences that occur during the human development.

56. The human embryo becomes a fetus at the eighth week in development. All of the organs have been formed that are to be formed, they now must grow and further organize. The following series of slides will show the human embryo and fetus undergoing the process of **ossification** or bone formation.

57. This is a five-week, 9-mm, human embryo. The sac that is visible is not the allantois, but is the yolk sac. **Yes,** we do have a yolk sac, but is does not contain yolk as in the chick. It later degenerates.

58. This slide shows a lateral view of an eight-week, 22-mm fetus. The fetus has been stained with a red stain to show the developing ossification centers.

59. This is a ventral view of the same fetus.

60. This slide shows a 10-week, 54-mm lateral view of the fetus.

61. A ventral view …

62. … and a dorsal view of the same fetus are shown.

63. This slide shows an 18-week, 125-mm, lateral left view of the fetus.

64. Here is a lateral right view of the same fetus.

65. This shows an enlargement of the lateral left view of the same fetus. Can you identify the bones of the skull?

PART 6
GENETICS

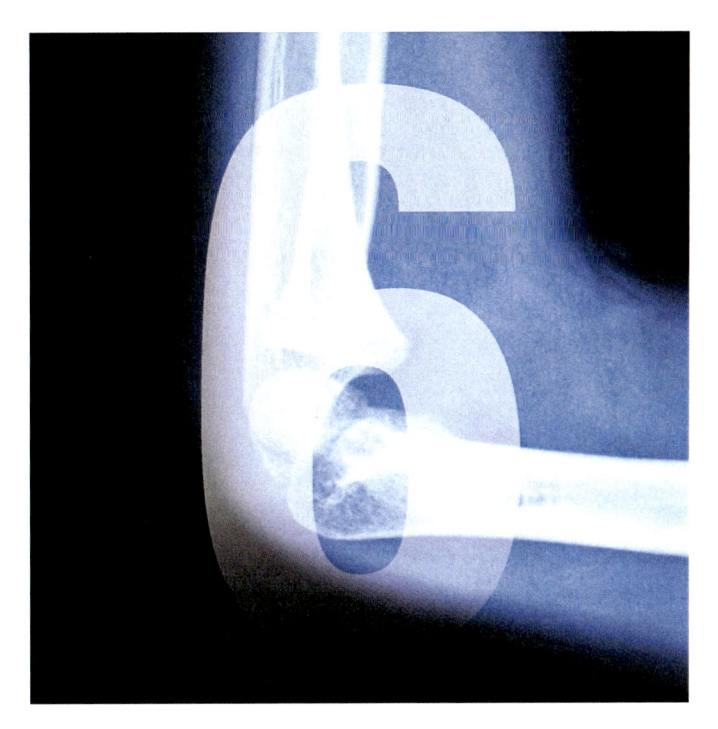

GENETICS TERMINOLOGY

- **Gene:** The unit of heredity transmitted in the chromosome; through the interaction with other genes and gene products, controls the development of hereditary characteristics.

- **Allele:** A particular form of a gene at a recognized site on a chromosome.

- **Genotype:** Actual genetic composition of an organism; the sum total of genetic information of the organism.

- **Phenotype:** An expressed or detectable physical or chemical trait of an organism.

- **Dominant:** Trait *expressed* even in the presence of an alternate form of the gene; the phenotypic expression of only one of two gene forms in an organism.

- **Recessive:** Trait that is *inhibited* in the presence of an alternate form of the gene.

- **Homozygous:** Having *identical* alleles at a given location in both chromosomes of the homologous pair.

- **Heterozygous:** Having two *non-identical* alleles at a given location in both chromosomes of a homologous pair.

- **Sex-linked trait:** A trait expressed by a gene form carried on the X chromosome.

- **Incomplete dominance:** A situation in which neither gene form is expressed completely; the hybrid offspring has a phenotype intermediate to the parents.

- **Codominance:** The individual expression of both gene forms, expressed equally in the organism.

- **Lethal allele:** An allele that, when homozygous, causes death of an organism, yet has no effect when carried in a heterozygote. (i.e., homozygous recessive).

- **Monohybrid cross:** A cross involving parents that differ only by a single trait, or a cross in which only a single trait is followed.

- **Dihybrid cross:** A cross involving parents that differ by only two traits, or a cross in which two separate traits are followed.

- **Punnett square:** A method used to determine the proportion of various genotypes possible from the cross of two parents (male indicated down left side of the square, female indicated across the top of the square).

GENETICS PROBLEMS

1. A homozygous tall pea plant is crossed with a short pea plant.

   a. What are the genotype(s) of the offspring? + percent frequency of each

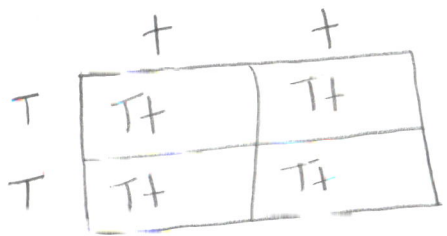

	t	t
T	Tt	Tt
T	Tt	Tt

   TT = 0%
   Tt = 100%
   tt = 0%

   b. What are the phenotype(s) of the offspring? + percent frequency of each

   Tall = 100%
   Short = 0%

2. Cross two of the F₁ offspring from the problem above.

   a. What are the genotypes of the offspring? + percent frequency

	T	t
T	TT	Tt
t	Tt	tt

   homozygous dominant TT = 25%
   heterozygous Tt = 50%
   homozygous recessive tt = 25%

   b. What are the phenotypes of the offspring? + percent frequency

   Tall - 75%
   Short - 25%

3. Phenylketonuria (PKU) is a recessive genetic disorder in which an individual with the disease cannot manufacture the enzyme phenylalanine hydroxylase. As a result, phenylalanine cannot be metabolized. Phenylalanine builds up in the blood and causes brain damage leading to mental retardation.

   a. If both of the parents are carriers for PKU (Pp), what is the chance of an offspring being a *sufferer* of PKU?

	P	p
P	PP	Pp
p	Pp	pp

   25% chance PKU

   b. If one parent is a carrier and the other parent does not carry the recessive allele, what is the chance of an offspring being a *sufferer* of PKU?

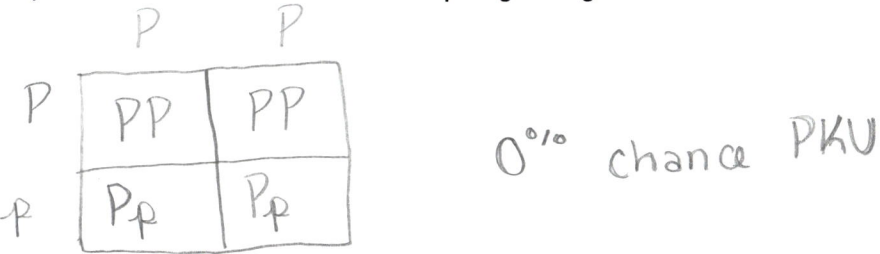

	P	P
P	PP	PP
p	Pp	Pp

   0% chance PKU

4. Mr. Smith has blue eyes and both of his parents have brown eyes. Mrs. Smith has a blue-eyed mother and a brown-eyed father and her eyes are brown. Mrs. Smith has 20 brothers and sisters, all with brown eyes.

   a. What are the genotypes for the following individuals?
   - Mr. Smith: __bb__   Mrs. Smith: __Bb__
   - Mr. Smith's father: __BB, Bb__   Mrs. Smith's father: __BB__
   - Mr. Smith's mother: __BB, Bb__   Mrs. Smith's mother: __bb__

   b. What color eyes will Mr. and Mrs. Smith's children have? + percent frequency

	B	b
b	Bb	bb
b	Bb	bb

   Bb - 50% — Brown
   bb - 50% — Blue

PART 6: GENETICS

5. In four o'clock flowers, the red (R) bloom color is incompletely dominant to the white (r) bloom color. The heterozygote (Rr) results in a pink bloom.

   a. Cross a red four o'clock and a white four o'clock. What will be the genotype(s) and the phenotype(s) of the offspring?

   percent frequency

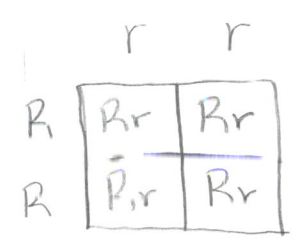

	r	r
R	Rr	Rr
R	Rr	Rr

   Rr – 100% – pink

   b. Cross two flowers of the F_1 from above. What will be the genotype(s) and phenotype(s) of the F_2?

   percent frequency

	R	r
R	RR	Rr
r	Rr	rr

   RR – 25% – red
   rr – 25% – white
   Rr – 50% – pink

6. Some alleles do not have a dominant-recessive relationship. Sometimes both alleles are expressed simultaneously. This is called codominance. ABO blood types are an example of this relationship. One allele, A (or I^A) produces the A antigen. Another different allele, B (or I^B) produces the B antigen. A third allele, O (or i) produces either antigen. A and B are dominant to O. A and B are codominant to each other. An individual who receives both alleles will have type AB blood.

a. A mother and father both have type A blood. What are the possible blood types of their children?

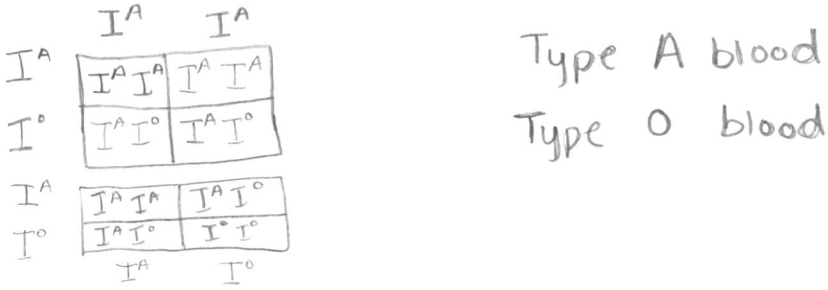

	I^A	I^A
I^A	$I^A I^A$	$I^A I^A$
I^O	$I^A I^O$	$I^A I^O$

	I^A	I^O
I^A	$I^A I^A$	$I^A I^O$
I^O	$I^A I^O$	$I^O I^O$

Type A blood
Type O blood

b. A mother and father both have type AB blood. What are the possible blood types of their children?

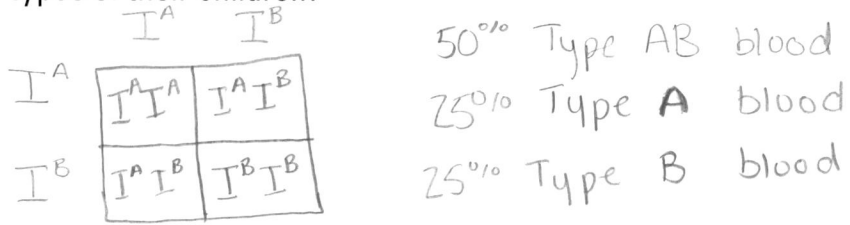

	I^A	I^B
I^A	$I^A I^A$	$I^A I^B$
I^B	$I^A I^B$	$I^B I^B$

50% Type AB blood
25% Type A blood
25% Type B blood

c. If the mother is type B and the child is type O, who would be the more probable father; one male who is type A, or another male who is type AB?

Type A blood

d. If the mother is type B and the child is type AB, who would be the more probable father; one who is type B, or another who is type A?

Type A blood

7. Hemophilia is a recessive, sex-linked trait. The allele for normal clotting (H) is carried on the X chromosome as is the allele for abnormal clotting (h).

   a. If a normal male (X^HY) and a female who carries the allele for hemophilia have a child, what is the chance of their offspring being a *sufferer* of hemophilia?

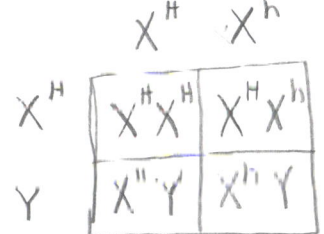

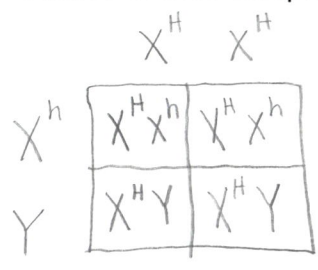

	X^H	X^h
X^H	X^HX^H	X^HX^h
Y	X^HY	X^hY

   25% chance hemophilia

   b. If a male sufferer of hemophilia and a normal female have a child, what is the chance of their offspring being a *sufferer* of hemophilia?

	X^H	X^H
X^h	X^HX^h	X^HX^h
Y	X^HY	X^HY

   0% chance hemophilia

8. Colorblindness is also a recessive, sex-linked trait.

   a. If a colorblind male (X^cY) and a female who carries the allele for colorblindness have a child, what is the chance of their offspring being a *sufferer* of colorblindness?

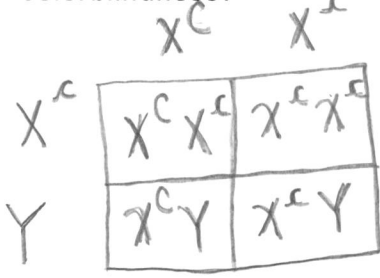

	X^C	X^c
X^c	X^CX^c	X^cX^c
Y	X^CY	X^cY

   50% chance colorblindness

PART 6: GENETICS

HUMAN KARYOTYPING

INTRODUCTION

A **karyotype** is a set of chromosomes, which have been arranged in a particular grouping by using shape, size, and **centromere** position as identifying characteristics.

A normal human karyotype has 23 pairs of chromosomes:

- 22 matching pairs of chromosomes called **autosomes** ← all traits but sex
- One pair of **sex chromosomes**
    - XX—both X chromosomes determines a female
    - XY—(1) X chromosome and (1) Y chromosome, determines a male

Karyotyping can be performed if a chromosomal abnormality is suspected as the cause of a disease or developmental problem.

Karyotyping is performed by taking a photograph of chromosomes extracted from a cell. The chromosomes are then cut out and arranged in a standardized format. Extra chromosomes, missing chromosomes or abnormal chromosomes can be identified through this procedure.

EXERCISE

1. Examine a normal male karyotype.

2. Obtain a photograph of the chromosomes of an unknown individual. Complete the karyotype to identify these characteristics:

    a. Number of chromosomes

    b. Sex of individual

    c. Any possible genetic disorders

    Possible genetic conditions are:

    - Down Syndrome (Trisomy21)—47, XX, +21
    - Klinefelter Syndrome—47, XXY
    - Turner Syndrome—45, X
    - Male 46 XY
    - Female 46 XX